THE MEDIUM IS STILL THE MESSAGE

THE MEDIUM IS STILL THE MESSAGE

Marshall McLuhan for Our Time

Grant N. Havers

NORTHERN ILLINOIS UNIVERSITY PRESS
an imprint of
CORNELL UNIVERSITY PRESS
Ithaca and London

Copyright © 2025 by Cornell University

All rights reserved. Except for brief quotations in a review, this book, or parts thereof, must not be reproduced in any form without permission in writing from the publisher. For information, address Cornell University Press, Sage House, 512 East State Street, Ithaca, New York 14850. Visit our website at cornellpress.cornell.edu.

First published 2025 by Cornell University Press

Library of Congress Cataloging-in-Publication Data
Names: Havers, Grant N., 1965– author.
Title: The medium is still the message : Marshall McLuhan for our time / Grant N. Havers.
Description: Ithaca [New York] : Northern Illinois University Press, an imprint of Cornell University Press, 2025. | Includes bibliographical references and index.
Identifiers: LCCN 2024048431 (print) | LCCN 2024048432 (ebook) | ISBN 9781501783661 (hardcover) | ISBN 9781501782930 (paperback) | ISBN 9781501782947 (epub) | ISBN 9781501782954 (pdf)
Subjects: LCSH: McLuhan, Marshall, 1911–1980. | Mass media—Philosophy. | Mass media—Social aspects.
Classification: LCC P92.5.M3 H38 2025 (print) | LCC P92.5.M3 (ebook) | DDC 302.23092—dc23/eng/20241217
LC record available at https://lccn.loc.gov/2024048431
LC ebook record available at https://lccn.loc.gov/2024048432

For Charles, Lucia, and Maximilian, who already have an inkling of what this book is all about

There is no inevitability where there is a willingness to pay attention.

—Marshall McLuhan

Contents

Acknowledgments ix

Introduction 1
1. A Biography 11
2. Understanding and Misunderstanding Media 23
3. Making History through Media 36
4. Rear-View Mirror Politics 49
5. Mother Goose and Peter Pan Executives 64
6. New Media Are Nature 82
7. The Divided Global Village 95
8. The Retrieval of the Book 110
9. The Electric Cave 126
10. Surviving the Apocalypse 145
Conclusion 161

Notes 163
Bibliography 185
Index 199

Acknowledgments

I have been reading and studying the ideas of Marshall McLuhan for thirty years. Throughout this exploration I have drawn inspiration from dialogues with Joshua Wettergreen, Christopher Morrissey, Justin Bonanno, and Dwight Friesen, all experienced readers of McLuhan. Thoughtful exchanges with Daniel Gackle, Marcus Wang, and Richard Marcy on a variety of topics have also been instructive. The two anonymous readers of this work offered incisive suggestions to make it more relevant to the everchanging realm of media in the present age. I thank them all.

Without the encouragement of my editor, Amy Farranto, I would not have written this book in the first place. After reading an article on McLuhan that I wrote for *Chronicles* in 2022, she suggested that it could be a template for a book. Amy's wise and diligent editing of the resultant book has been invaluable. The expert oversight of my production editor, Karen Hwa, as well as the meticulous revisions suggested by Eric Levy during the copyediting process, greatly helped to make this book intelligible to a wide readership. My wife, Therese, also deserves my gratitude for her tough-minded reading of the manuscript in its early stages, offering critical analysis when it was needed.

I dedicate this book to my young children, Charles, Lucia, and Maximilian, who are already making sense of the digital cave that surrounds us all. Their gentle spirit, curiosity, and wisdom give me reason to hope that the media can once again become our servants, not remain our masters.

INTRODUCTION

The most famous philosopher of media in the twentieth century was once suspected of drug possession. Marshall McLuhan recounted this story in a 1969 interview with *Playboy* magazine. He had just received an honorary doctor of laws from the University of British Columbia in Vancouver, and on the flight back home to Toronto, he told a colleague that he had gone to Vancouver to pick up his "LL.D." He noticed one of the passengers on the flight looking at him "with a strange expression." When he arrived in Toronto, two customs officials ushered him into a room where they interrogated him and searched through his luggage. He was asked if he knew Timothy Leary, the famous figure of the 1960s counterculture, to which he responded in the affirmative. One of the guards demanded to know where he had hidden his stash. "Where's the stuff? We know you told somebody you'd gone to Vancouver to pick up some LL.D." McLuhan finally managed to convince him that an LL.D. is not the same as lysergic acid diethylamide, the notoriously potent hallucinogen. Unlike LSD, he explained, an LL.D. "has nothing to do with consciousness expansion—just the opposite, in fact—and I was released."

As McLuhan joked to his *Playboy* interviewer, "In light of the present educational crisis, I'm not sure there isn't something to be said for making possession of an LL.D. a felony." Despite his use of humor in this anecdote, the message that he is drawing is deadly serious. In the same interview, he refers to the explosion of drug usage in the 1960s, which was "intimately related to the impact of the electric media." The implication of this analogy is that the users of new media are no more aware of its effects than the users of drugs are conscious of a narcotic's effects. In McLuhan's words, the new "penetrating" electric environment "in itself is a drugless inner trip."

McLuhan's key insight that media are not just tools that enable communication between human beings has enduring relevance. To be sure, the traditional meaning of "media" suggests this. A medium, which comes from the Latin word *medius* (middle), is the means by which two or more persons communicate with each other. Yet media also have unintended effects, which go well beyond the task of communication. The most important of these effects is the creation of an environment that encompasses every aspect of human existence. Put simply, the environment is the world in which we live. Everything within this environment, including politics, the economy, culture, identity, and religion, is transformed by the media. (The Greek word for environment is *perivallon*, which means "what surrounds us.") McLuhan summarized this truth in his most famous saying: *The medium is the message.*

In simple terms, a medium is so powerful that it determines the message (or content) of everything that involves human beings. There is nothing necessarily complex or mysterious about this concept. The *way* that we communicate with each other can become the primary message. For example, a politician who has a charismatic speaking style will probably garner more votes than a dull politician who struggles to communicate his ideas. McLuhan never denies that the content of their ideas has some importance. This content, however, is always "subordinate" to the medium.

There is more to "the medium is the message" than the simple truth that the style of communication often trumps substance. According to McLuhan, the reach of the media is so extensive that they can determine the content of any environment. As he explained in a 1965 interview with the British literary critic Frank Kermode, the best way to understand the meaning of "the medium is the message" is to appreciate how each medium "tends to create a completely new human environment," which "as such tends to have a kind of invisible character about it." This "invisible character" of a media environment is McLuhan's way of stressing how the effects of media are both unintelligible and saturating at the same time. As he explains in his interview with *Playboy*, "Precisely at the point where a new media-induced environment becomes all-pervasive and transmogrifies our sensory balance, it also becomes invisible." For example, the "drugless inner trip" that, McLuhan believes, is an effect of electric media such as television and computers is, put simply, the result of electric media's powerful tendency to involve every dimension of human existence all at once. Because these media can bombard our entire central nervous system, they make it hard to step back and think critically about the environment that they are creating. In accord with "the medium is the message," the technology in question has the same effect, regardless of the content. For example, a social media post on the Civil War has the same impact on the five senses as a post on the latest fashions in Paris.

McLuhan was the first prominent thinker to warn about the recurrent failure of human beings to understand the effects of media throughout history. His warning has not been heeded. The paradox to which he relentlessly points is that media enable communication and obscure understanding. Communication does not guarantee an understanding of the ways that the media alter human existence. As McLuhan puts it, media are "make happen" agents but not "make aware" agents. If there is any recurrent theme that appears in his vast oeuvre, it is the message that human beings do not grasp media's effects until it is too late to reverse them. None of this should suggest that we are helpless before the juggernaut of media-induced change. In the 1960s, the heyday in which he enjoyed great fame as a media celebrity, McLuhan used his popularity as an opportunity to provide guidance on how people can educate themselves on the nature of media. With enough of this guidance, they can control and even anticipate the effects of media. Since the death of McLuhan in 1980, however, it is far from obvious that there has been a degree of education sufficient to meet the task of fully comprehending new media-induced environments. The media "work us over," as McLuhan puts it, in ways that are unbeknownst to us, even to the creators of media. Making media is not the same as understanding their effects. Just because we create media does not mean that we are fully conscious of the environment that ensues from these devices. Indeed, the extensive usage of these machines does not guarantee critical insight either. Immersion in an environment is never the same as understanding it. McLuhan liked to quip that "we don't know who discovered water, but we're pretty sure it wasn't a fish."

At first glance, McLuhan's contention that human beings generally fail to understand the effects of media seems far-fetched. Surely the transformational power of media is abundantly evident in the third millennium. Every aspect of society has been visibly shaped by the impact of technological change. In the realm of politics, leaders must learn to carefully monitor their image and speech so that they avoid offending the masses of viewers who watch their every step on the internet or on television. Millions of lonely individuals turn to social media in search of an identity that they hope to find through the endless exchange of random or inane observations. Educators worry about the stark decline of literacy among the young, who not only have lost interest in the printed word but also seek out software that will write their papers for them. Governments grow anxious about their inability to control information and "misinformation" in an age when ideas move around the world at the speed of light. In short, are we not aware of the massive environmental changes that media have wrought?

Despite these instances of awareness, McLuhan would probably stick with his contention that most human beings have not grasped that the medium is *still* the message. Although he never denies that human beings become aware of media's effects, this awareness typically arises long after these technologies have taken root. For example, politicians and educators have expressed their misgivings about the addictive properties of smartphones and social media after they have become fixtures of our culture. Why do human beings fail to understand the effects of the media at their inception?

McLuhan, we shall see, offers different answers to this pivotal question. It is no accident, in his view, that the word "narcotic" comes from the Greek word *narcosis*, which means numbness or "blocking of perception." In brief, we fail to perceive the most important effects of technology, especially new media, until these machines are deeply embedded in our society. The more exposed we are to these media, the more numbness we experience. Worst of all, our drug-like addiction to the novelty of new media further blocks perception of their effects. Our intense familiarity with online media, instantaneous information, and involvement with every happening throughout the world has not automatically led to mass enlightenment.

Does it matter whether we develop enough awareness and knowledge of new media to anticipate and counter their effects before they happen? McLuhan's answer to this question amounts to a plea for greater control of media that can threaten every aspect of human existence. If we do not make a substantive effort to predict the effects of media, the consequences will be grave. A lack of understanding discourages or suppresses our ability to prepare for the unintended impacts of these media. Given the fact that many of these impacts threaten the survival of humanity, this lack of preparation poses an existential threat to life on this planet. The ongoing acceleration of innovation in the artificial intelligence (AI) industry has provoked understandable anxieties over the belated attempts by governments to regulate and control their products, which have the potential to replace human decision-making with the algorithms guiding them.

One of McLuhan's purposes that drives his analysis of media is to understand and anticipate the effects of media so that human beings can preserve the best features of civilization. This book builds on my previous scholarship on McLuhan, which focuses on understanding his *conservative* motivation to save humanity from technologies of its own making. This fact should not suggest that he favored or condemned media based on their impact on traditions that he valued. In his mature work, McLuhan is reluctant to judge media on moral grounds, an attitude that he thought discouraged an accurate understanding of technological change. At the very least, comprehension of media's effects should precede such judgment. That said, McLuhan believed that proper understanding of the media can help us resist changes that threaten civilization's gifts. As I show throughout this book, one of these blessings that he greatly favored is literacy. In his view, civilization began and ended with literacy and its attendant values of privacy, individuality, and self-reflection. The transition from a literate civilization to a postliterate one is not a development that McLuhan welcomed. Yet he was determined to understand the role that electric media play in effecting this transformation.

As McLuhan remarked in a 1966 interview with the journalist Robert Fulford, "I am resolutely opposed to all innovation, all change, but I am determined to understand what's happening because I don't choose just to sit and let the juggernaut roll over me." McLuhan then took aim at the popular image of him as a celebrant of new media (e.g., TV, computers) transforming the 1960s: "Many people seem to think that if you talk about something recent, you're in favor of it. The exact opposite is true in my case. Anything I talk about is almost certainly to be something I'm resolutely against, and it seems to me the best way of opposing it is to understand it, and then you know where to turn off the button." In sharp contrast to the fatalistic determinism of Sam Altman of OpenAI, who has warned that there is no "magic red button" to stop AI, McLuhan firmly rejects the impossibility of reversing technological change.

McLuhan's explanations for the persistent lack of awareness about media continue to be relevant to those of us who want to "turn off the button." This claim should not suggest that he thought that all his explanations withstood the test of time. The last thing that he wanted from his interpreters was the impression that his study of media amounted to a "fixed" (unchanging) point of view that was intolerant of revision. McLuhan was prepared to "junk" any statement that he made if events proved him wrong. Yet he never abandoned his contention that the medium is the message. Media will always create invisible environments that defy human understanding until it is too late to reverse them.

There is reason to hope if one makes the effort to study media with the care that they deserve. According to McLuhan, it is always possible to recognize patterns in the history of media. These patterns help us understand not only the past and present but also the future of technological change. Toward the end of his life, McLuhan demonstrated that these patterns were "laws," which exhibit tendencies and effects that all new media exhibit. Armed with this knowledge, human beings can become reasonably educated about the direction of media and their effects.

The problem is that people have generally not made this effort: this pattern of deliberate ignorance is one that McLuhan repeatedly identifies in his study of history. In making this warning, he is not taking on the posture of an elitist snob in academia who looks down on the woeful ignorance of the great unwashed. This ignorance does not leave anyone untouched, including the highly educated.

McLuhan sometimes made this point in a humorous vein. In 1977, the filmmaker Woody Allen asked him to appear in a cameo in *Annie Hall*. McLuhan played himself, chastising at a movie theater a pretentious professor of media and culture who, much to Allen's chagrin, was loudly claiming to be an expert on McLuhan's scholarship. McLuhan offered this pithy denunciation of the academic: "You know nothing of my work. You mean my whole fallacy is wrong." In short, even seasoned academics did not necessarily have any superior insight into the media, which often defied tidy or systematic definition. An appreciation for the illogical (fallacious) effects of media is both rare and essential, McLuhan contends.

The failure to understand media is nothing new: it is a pattern throughout history. McLuhan takes seriously the Italian philosopher Giambattista Vico's warning about the "conceit" of nations and scholars—namely, their tendency to assume that what they know counts as universal truths that are impervious to change. History has also revealed how the inventors of new media predict the effects of their creations about as poorly as anybody else. The ability of new media to create new environments that affect everything we do is lost on those who help to create these technologies. The unwillingness to understand that the medium is the message persists to this day.

It is not the purpose of McLuhan to assign blame for this ignorance to any human interest or institution. The rapidity of technological change in the last century has been so great that it has often left everyone blindsided. (The dramatic development of AI technology is, once again, a case in point.) Yet he also does not tolerate any attempt to evade responsibility for technologies that are, after all, the creations of human beings. To understand the media environments that we forge, an "ecology of media" is needed. By this he means a rigorous study of media as the cause of new environments that transform every institution within civilization.

After a biographical profile in chapter 1, the next five chapters provide an interpretation of McLuhan's diagnosis of the myriad ways in which human beings fail to comprehend that the medium is the message.

Chapter 2 explains McLuhan's most famous attempts to show why human beings struggle with understanding the "invisible" effects and environments that media usher into being. Instead of making this effort, we embrace attitudes that impede an accurate understanding. Throughout history, human beings have indulged in rear-view mirror thinking, which understands a medium only after it has become dominant. Plato's warning about the effects of writing is an early example of this tendency. Relying on our senses and moral indignation to help us understand media is pointless at this stage. We are also inclined to focus on the content of the medium, not the medium itself and its inherent tendencies or biases. Although it is easy to grasp that different media extend different senses, McLuhan's idea that some media can extend our entire personality in a narcissistic fashion unbeknownst to its users is a more crucial insight. McLuhan also warns of the danger in the temptation to believe that we can study media from a detached vantage point. Because the media have become our environment, there is little possibility of pure detachment. But this does not mean that greater involvement with media leads to insight. As the "fish in the water" metaphor suggests, immersion does not equal understanding.

Chapter 3 analyzes McLuhan's history of media by showing that there has never been a period of history in which societies have sufficiently understood the relation between media and their environments. A careful study of this history shows how different civilizations from antiquity to modernity create media without grasping how these technologies determine the way that we think about nature and history. Most civilizations have struggled to understand that we make history: it is not some natural force independent of our agency or understanding. Unless we also grasp that we make history through media, McLuhan contends, we will not understand the full effect of media throughout history. The paradox is that media make us as much as we make the media. History does not simply belong to the past. In accord with his concept of simultaneity, McLuhan contends that the past always coexists with the present. The ancient practices of orality and tribalism never completely vanished with the rise of writing and print. Indeed, they reemerged in the electric and digital ages. The good news that McLuhan announces, through his use of the Aristotelian idea of formal causality, is that we can now predict the future before it happens. We are not hapless victims of the history that media generate.

Chapter 4 focuses on how McLuhan helps us understand the differences between politics in the literate and postliterate periods of history. I devote particular attention to rear-view mirror thinking in the political realm, particularly as it applies to American conservatives who fail to understand that their most cherished traditions have been rendered obsolete. I specifically focus on the United States because, as McLuhan argues, it is the first nation in history that was founded on literacy and its attendant values such as privacy, individualism, freedom, and conformity to bourgeois order. Ever since the electric age ushered into being a new tribalism that rejects these values, Americans who want to preserve these values find it hard to comprehend why so many of their fellow citizens, including their leaders, repudiate these practices. Without an accurate understanding of how electric and digital media feed postliterate tribalism among ruler and ruled, any attempt to restore the literate culture of the American founding will just repeat the aporetic pattern of rear-view mirror thinking.

Chapter 5 interprets McLuhan's approach to how the media have shaped the history of capitalism from the age of print to the rise of electric media. Even the corporate owners of media usually fail to understand the changes that these technologies bring into being. Bourgeois values such as individual freedom, privacy, and the preservation of history or time would be impossible without print media and literacy. The postliterate capitalism of the electric and digital ages repudiates these values. Whereas the bourgeois industrialist cared little for his image in mass culture, the postbourgeois tycoon must cultivate an image that is likable and popular in an age of participatory media. The consequence of this shift is evident in the behavior of capitalists who seek out information about their consumers' most personal desires and preferences. Unlike their bourgeois predecessors, they are willing to work with the big state to surveil, cancel, and censor dissident voices. Rushing products to market for the sake of profit and popularity, without understanding their effects in a timely manner, illustrates the postbourgeois adherence to the bias of space at the expense of time. It is far from obvious that capitalism can survive amid the enormous pressures to erase the distinction between the private and public realms.

Chapter 6 focuses on how electric media potentially threaten to reinvent the biggest environment of all: nature and human nature. This phenomenon is particularly important to understand in the postliterate age, in which people seek a stable identity that they otherwise lack amid the flux of media-induced change. Electric and digital media even hold out the promise that the very identity of humanity can be replaced by technology. What McLuhan describes as the ancient gnostic desire to replace an imperfect material reality with a perfect spiritual one is making a comeback. Nevertheless, the media's *magical* attempts to transform human nature may prove to be illusory. The natural tribalist instincts that McLuhan calls "first nature" do not yield to the technological creations that he associates with "second nature." Attempts to escape this first nature through the creation of "discarnate identity," an existence in which human beings seemingly have no need of their natural bodies as they navigate the digital age, fosters the gnostic illusion of God-like spiritual power over nature. The lasting irony is that the violence of our first nature will only intensify within discarnate space.

Chapter 7 analyzes life in the "global village," a term that McLuhan popularized. This village is not necessarily a place of peace and unity, according to McLuhan. Rather, the world environment is full of tribalist violence and disorder, patterns that the electric media encourage. The attempts by powerful nations to impose their own will or identity on this village only inflame these divisions. Nations whose identities are rooted in individualism (e.g., the United States) struggle to understand tribalist adversaries. Additionally, the more involved that nations become in the affairs of the world, the more likely they will mimetically take on the features of their enemies. Greater interaction through media does not bring about peace so much as awareness of an enemy's ability to use electric media to control and dominate its own citizenry. McLuhan's reflections on the United States' intervention in Vietnam as well as its ongoing relationship with China shed light on this pattern. His thoughts on Canada's relative success in resisting and avoiding imposed patterns and identities provide some reason for hope within this fractious village.

The last three chapters discuss various ways that human beings can survive and overcome the most destructive effects that new media environments have constructed. In chapter 8, I explore McLuhan's cautious hopes for the retrieval of literacy through the rediscovery of the book. In his view, the reading of books is still the best means for the task of comprehending and countering the effects of the electric-digital environment. McLuhan even sympathized with "great books" programs dedicated to teaching the young how to read the magisterial works of philosophy, theology, and literature, as long as this reading helps us understand the postliterate age and its effects. Some books fulfill this task better than others. McLuhan is very critical of Plato's hostility to poetry as an expression of making, which the Greek philosopher sees as inferior to the quest for what is eternal and permanent. This attitude has encouraged a disdain for what human beings create—a mentality that hardly encourages the study of media. To break down the dualistic opposition between what is eternal and what is created, McLuhan urges an intellectual exploration of the bicameral mind. This consists of a left hemisphere, which favors objective rationality, and a right hemisphere, which encourages intuitive creativity. The ideal civilization, McLuhan believes, would avoid this false opposition altogether. Finally, I examine McLuhan's interpretation of the Genesis narrative. We are not just "second Adams" who possess the God-like knowledge of creation. We must also act as if we are "first Adams," humbly recognizing that we live in an order that we did not create. God blesses us with many powers, except the power to become gods ourselves.

Chapter 9 reveals how McLuhan, despite his animus toward Plato, takes a pivotal lesson from his philosophy. He draws an analogy between the electric-digital environment and Plato's parable of the cave, a place in which human beings are woefully unaware of the darkness that surrounds them. Given the ignorance that holds sway over the "electric cave," McLuhan doubts whether rational self-interest in the Machiavellian sense can liberate us from this darkness. Although McLuhan is dubious about the prospect of democracy emancipating the multitude from the cave, he cautiously appeals to the populist myth of a vigilant citizenry that has the wisdom to anticipate and control the effects of new media.

The final chapter discusses McLuhan's reflections on how electric and digital media may bring about the apocalypse, which could be either a great awakening or the final conflict between good and evil. The God-like power over nature and creation that these media seem to enable make the possibility of an "Anti-Christ" very real. The paradox of Christianity, as McLuhan understands it, is that God-like knowledge gives us the freedom and power to incarnate both good and evil. One of the most obvious examples of this paradox is the desire to live as a discarnate identity, free of one's natural body. This way of living threatens to further erode any human attachment to a natural order (the Book of Nature) that once checked the human desire to aspire to a God-like authority over creation. Discarnate identity also threatens human survival by encouraging a dangerous dependence on technologies that do not require human agency. McLuhan's answer to this danger lies in the retrieval of the natural law tradition, which rejects the dualistic opposition between nature (the body) and divinity (the soul).

The conclusion offers a brief discussion of McLuhan's meditations about how a literate civilization, for all its flaws, has the best chance of understanding both the natural and unnatural effects of media. The media are in our hands. Without this understanding, we will continue to be slaves to what we create.

1

A BIOGRAPHY

Herbert Marshall McLuhan was born in Edmonton, Alberta, on July 21, 1911, to Herbert McLuhan, a real estate agent and insurance salesman, and Elsie (*née* Hall), an actress, elocutionist, and teacher. Despite his parents' often strained and unhappy marriage, his father's congenial personality and his mother's love of poetry and rhetoric had a lasting impression on his character. In 1913, his only sibling, Maurice, was born. Two years later, the family moved to Winnipeg, Manitoba, which was enjoying an economic boom resulting from the demand for raw materials that the Canadian military needed to fight World War I. While his brother would go on to be ordained by the United Church of Canada, Marshall would become the twentieth century's preeminent philosopher of media.

McLuhan took his lifelong love of literature to the University of Manitoba, obtaining his bachelor of arts in English in 1933 and his master of arts in 1934. Even in these early years of his intellectual journey, according to one biographer, he intuited that "all of life—mental, spiritual, and physical—was governed by laws that are still largely unknown to human beings." This search for eternal laws or patterns coincided with a tough-minded evaluation of the political and economic turmoil of the 1930s. His master's thesis on the Victorian novelist and poet George Meredith reflected McLuhan's burgeoning sympathy for modern authors critical of the social ills perpetrated by the Industrial Revolution. As a graduate student, McLuhan wrote several articles for the student newspaper, *The Manitoban*; these pieces revealed his misgivings about the crudity of the modern world, especially the capitalist system that was on the brink of collapse during these years of economic depression. McLuhan never forgot the intensity of the agrarian protests in the prairie hinterland against the financial interests of eastern Canada, which dominated the economic fortunes of yeoman farmers struggling to eke out a living. In *Counterblast* (1954), McLuhan chided western Canada "for its meekness in filling the coffers of Bay Street." In an interview with the Canadian journalist Peter C. Newman in the 1970s, he reiterated these populist sentiments, noting that all the decisions about Canada's diverse regions are made in Toronto. The "miseries" of these regions, he observed, originate there as well. McLuhan's interest in studying how centers try to dominate margins in Canada, the United States, and all over the global village became a lifelong preoccupation (see chapter 7).

Studies in England

Before he set off to England in 1934 for further study at Cambridge University, McLuhan was already showing an interest in Catholic writers such as G. K. Chesterton, whose celebration of Christian civilization and opposition to rapacious capitalism strongly resonated with the young scholar. McLuhan also credited Chesterton with inspiring the idea of "percepts," the playful use of clichés that sharply contrasted with the strict usage of "concepts." Whereas concepts focus on studying causes that lead to effects, percepts encourage the paradoxical anticipation of effects before causes bring these into being. This distinction is central to McLuhan's mature studies of technological change (see chapter 3).

In 1936, McLuhan completed a second bachelor of arts in English at Cambridge, a degree that he considered far superior to both of the degrees he had obtained at the University of Manitoba. During his studies in England, McLuhan further cultivated his deep interest in Catholic writers such as Chesterton, Gerard Manley Hopkins, Hilaire Belloc, and James Joyce. He became particularly enamored with Chesterton's and Belloc's philosophy of distributism, which called for a society of small businesses and farms that would operate independently of big business and the big state. This program, which offered an alternative to both capitalism and communism, inspired McLuhan to join the Distributist League. Although he eventually abandoned his adherence to distributism, McLuhan retained his skepticism about the willingness of big capitalists to defend their most cherished traditions (e.g., private property) in the face of technological change and statist intervention (see chapter 5).

Other influences at Cambridge shaped his interests and directions. The "New Criticism" of Professor I. A. Richards revolutionized the study of English language and literature, replacing the traditional focus on philology with one on critical analysis. Richards insisted on studying the meaning of words in poetry and their multiple effects on readers, who could then comprehend how the study of English is identical to the study of communication itself. Richards's student and colleague F. R. Leavis applied this method not only to literature but to the social environment by studying the effects of advertising and popular culture on the collective mind. Besides his preoccupation with these effects, Leavis's lamenting of the loss of a premodern organic community during the Industrial Revolution resonated with McLuhan's support for distributism. McLuhan credited T. S. Eliot along with Leavis for discovering how to "train, simultaneously, esthetic and moral perceptions in acts of unified awareness and judgment." This holistic approach, which demonstrated how the study of language can enable an interconnected understanding of one's entire environment and its effects, had a lasting effect on McLuhan. He was not, however, advocating a one-way determinism in which the participants were mere pawns of their contexts. As McLuhan and his son Eric later observed in *Laws of Media: The New Science*, the "audience, as ground, shapes and controls the work of art."

The Young Teacher Returns to North America

McLuhan discovered that his deep interest in the English literary tradition was not necessarily shared by a younger generation increasingly shaped by the rise of popular culture. He left Cambridge in 1936 to take up a position as a teaching assistant at the University of Wisconsin. In his tutorials, McLuhan used ads, newspapers, and pulp fiction to stimulate the interest of students baffled by the classical works of English literature. His interest in the Catholic tradition intensified, and in 1937 he was received into the church. Although his mother, who had raised her sons in a loosely Protestant tradition, worried that her firstborn's newfound faith would make it hard for him to find a suitable academic job in a majority-Protestant country, he managed to secure employment in a few Catholic schools in North America.

In 1937, McLuhan accepted a teaching position in the Department of English at St. Louis University, a Catholic institution where he taught until 1944 (except for 1939–40, when he returned to Cambridge). During this period, he came to admire the Southern literary tradition; the agrarian sympathies and anticapitalist biases of Southern writers such as Donald Davidson, Allen Tate, and John Crowe Ransom particularly appealed to him. While visiting his mother, who was teaching drama at the Pasadena Playhouse in California, McLuhan met a young Texan actress named Corinne Keller Lewis, whom he married in 1939.

At St. Louis, McLuhan deepened his understanding of Catholic scholasticism, including the philosophy of St. Thomas Aquinas. Although McLuhan admitted in an interview in the late 1960s that he lacked "a background in scholastic thought, never having been raised in any Catholic institution," the influence of his faith had a decisive effect on his studies of mass media. McLuhan's meticulous study of language, theology, and philosophy culminated in his Cambridge doctoral dissertation, "The Classical Trivium: The Place of Thomas Nashe in the Learning of His Time," which was supervised by the Shakespearean scholar Muriel C. Bradbrook. This thesis, which McLuhan defended *in absentia* in 1943 due to wartime conditions, celebrated the medieval "trivium" of grammar, rhetoric, and logic. McLuhan especially emphasized how the logical (or dialectical) mind, which has dominated Western philosophy, requires the tempering force of rhetoric and grammar. These disciplines are invaluable precisely because they study the paradoxical (or nonlogical) meaning of language. Paradox, the coexistence of opposing forces, is a recurrent theme throughout McLuhan's oeuvre.

In his last year at St. Louis University (1943–44), McLuhan struck up a friendship with the famous English painter, novelist, and essayist Percy Wyndham Lewis. His mother informed him that Lewis was teaching at another Catholic institution, Assumption College Ontario, where she had attended one of his lectures. Soon after this revelation, McLuhan took the train to Windsor to meet Lewis. Throughout the 1930s, McLuhan had already read with admiration many of Lewis's writings on the role of the artist and the effects of mass culture. He also deeply respected Lewis's paintings, which represented the styles of vorticism (which Lewis originated) and cubism. Lewis's artistic talent lay in his ability to create exaggerated geometric forms that enabled one to view his paintings from multiple vantage points. While teaching in St. Louis, he and his colleague Felix Giovanelli arranged lectures and portrait commissions for Lewis. Although McLuhan later distanced himself from Lewis's "moralistic" judgments of mass culture, he always retained respect for the paradoxical method with which Lewis approached his subjects. When McLuhan was hired as head of the English Department at Assumption in 1944, he looked forward to collaborating with Lewis on publishing a new periodical. Lewis's return to England in 1945 put an end to this joint project.

Life in Postwar Toronto

In 1946, McLuhan and his growing family settled in Toronto, where he took up a professorship in English literature at St. Michael's College, a Catholic affiliate of the University of Toronto. He held this position until his death in 1980. Although St. Michael's had a conservative Catholic reputation, McLuhan's unconventional usage of popular media in his classes was tolerated, albeit uneasily, by his colleagues. As he had already done at other schools, McLuhan often showed slides of comic strips, advertisements, and clips from periodicals to expose the spiritual vacuity, crude materialism, and sensationalistic violence of mass culture. His driving assumption was that the real educators of students in the post–World War II era were mass media and that it was up to teachers to counter this influence by helping their students to understand these technologies. By 1952, McLuhan and his wife were raising four daughters and two sons. This reality encouraged McLuhan, who was unhappy with his modest salary as an associate professor, to engage in scholarship that could help support his large family.

For all these reasons, McLuhan looked forward to the publication of his first book, *The Mechanical Bride: Folklore of Industrial Man*, in 1951. His choice of title was inspired by his long-held perspective that the media of advertising, comics, and magazines had succeeded in reducing all aspects of life to a mechanistic automatism. Despite some positive reviews, the book had poor sales. McLuhan's disappointment led him to the sobering conclusion that his first book was made obsolete by the advent of television. By the end of the 1950s, he had also repudiated the "extremely moralistic approach" that underlay *The Mechanical Bride*. From this point on, McLuhan vowed to understand media as objectively as possible, without letting personal distaste get in the way of this study.

McLuhan amply demonstrated this new attitude in different ways. He was encouraged by the fact that his colleague Harold Adams Innis, a professor of economics at the University of Toronto, had included *The Mechanical Bride* on one of his course's reading lists. Although McLuhan's friendship with Innis was a brief one (Innis died in 1952), the influence of Innis's historical studies of media had a lasting impact. McLuhan praised Innis for being the first thinker in history to understand the hidden "biases" within media: these tendencies typically led to transformational effects that were not fully understood until it was too late to reverse them. McLuhan was so impressed with Innis that he described his 1962 work *The Gutenberg Galaxy: The Making of Typographic Man* as a mere "footnote of explanation" to Innis's studies.

In collaboration with the anthropologist Edmund Carpenter, McLuhan conducted a seminar on media and culture. Out of this pedagogical experience came a magazine entitled *Explorations*, which was funded by a grant from the Ford Foundation. This periodical, which was published between 1953 and 1959, featured articles on media composed by various scholars from a variety of fields, a fact that reflected McLuhan's unconventional (at the time) breaking down of barriers between disciplines. It also reflected his conviction that the adequate study of the media was a project that needed several "explorers," not just one magisterial guide. To this end, McLuhan invited diverse scholars such as the anthropologist

Dorothy Lee, the art historian Siegfried Giedion, and the urbanologist Jacqueline Tyrwhitt to write for the journal.

With a nod to the medieval trivium, the purpose of *Explorations* was to explore "the grammars of such languages as print, the newspaper format and television" to understand how old and new media modify "not only human relations but also sensibilities." Many of the ideas aired in *Explorations* reappeared in McLuhan's second book, *Counterblast*. Published in 1954, this work was loosely based on Wyndham Lewis's short-lived magazine *Blast*, which appeared near the start of World War I. Packed with provocative aphorisms and biting commentary on the history and nature of the media, *Counterblast* was meant to be an ironic response to the 1951 Massey Report, which offered several recommendations on how the Canadian federal government could develop a national policy on the arts and sciences. As was the case in his other works, McLuhan turned to satire and humor to demonstrate that human beings are generally ignorant of the effects of media.

By the end of the 1950s, McLuhan had built up a reputation for being a daring thinker, one that attracted several students to his camp. He was also unafraid of challenging the established wisdom held by most of his colleagues, who dismissed or ignored the impact of technological change. Although he often insisted that he opposed the process of this change, he was also determined to understand it in the hope that he could "kick them in the electrodes." McLuhan also understood, in the new age of television, that any realistic prospect for this understanding would happen only if he could reach a wide audience, far beyond the skeptical halls of academe. He gave a well-received speech as keynote speaker at the annual convention of the National Association of Educational Broadcasters (NAEB) in Omaha in 1958 on how the "processing and packaging of information," not the actual information itself, was the new force that was transforming business. Impressed with McLuhan's focus on the form, as opposed to the content, of media, the NAEB invited him to create a syllabus for the study of media that would be suited to eleventh-grade students. To test the validity of this document, which required students to dialogue about the effects of media, he succeeded in persuading some Toronto high schools to adopt the syllabus. This approach to pedagogy was the template for his last book, *City as Classroom: Understanding Language and Media* (1977), which he coauthored with his son Eric and Kathryn Hutchon.

Although McLuhan's *Report on Project in Understanding Media*, which he submitted to the NAEB in 1960, had little immediate impact, his findings anticipated many of the themes that he elaborated on in his later works. McLuhan was also receiving a steadily increasing number of speaking invitations from business executives in established firms. The lack of comprehension that these tycoons often expressed in response to his playful and cryptic sayings about media persuaded McLuhan that media can encourage a "somnambulistic state" in even the most powerful individuals who are immersed in the fields of emergent technology. He enjoyed telling the executives of General Electric, IBM, and Bell Telephone during invited speaking engagements that they were in the business of moving information, not making products.

McLuhan's intention was no more to insult his corporate audience than to offend the scholarly defenders of literate culture. Yet offend them he did with his thesis that print media and the written word, which privileged the visual sense, had often yielded negative effects on civilization, including mass conformity, nationalistic violence, and rapacious capitalism. McLuhan fully developed this analysis in *The Gutenberg Galaxy*, which won the Governor-General's Award for Non-fiction in 1962. As in earlier books of his, he employed an unconventional style, an antilinear mosaic of long quotations from various authors, followed by his own commentaries. Much to the chagrin of his growing number of critics in academe, McLuhan contended that television had already obsolesced the culture of literacy, carrying in its wake fateful consequences that had not yet received due attention.

Celebrity Status in the 1960s

The fame that came with the publication of *The Gutenberg Galaxy* spurred McLuhan on to continue his work. By this time, he was becoming better known as a theorist of communication than as a professor of English literature. Although Corinne urged her husband to accept one of the many lucrative offers that he was receiving from various universities in the United States, McLuhan decided to stay in Toronto after his university gave him the opportunity to create his own institution, officially named the Centre for Culture and Technology in 1963, dedicated to the study of "the psychic and social consequences of all technologies." McLuhan had full autonomy to run it as he saw fit, offering a seminar every Monday night that was open to everyone. This dialogue often drew visits from famous personalities, including Prime Minister Pierre Trudeau, the pianist Glenn Gould, and the journalist and author Malcolm Muggeridge.

The second half of the 1960s saw McLuhan evolve into a media phenomenon all his own. In addition to receiving high fees for numerous speaking engagements organized by corporations, McLuhan was becoming a household name throughout the world. (The French even coined a new word—*mcluhanisme*—in recognition of his influence.) The publication of *Understanding Media: The Extensions of Man* in 1964 was the chief catalyst for this fame and fortune. The most famous idea that McLuhan's book popularized was "The medium is the message." This phrase captured his long-held assumption that the medium itself, as opposed to the content that it communicates, has the greatest impact on human behavior.

Throughout the 1960s, McLuhan oscillated paradoxically between hopeful predictions and apocalyptic judgments of new electric media. Around this time, he popularized the idea of the world as a global village, a concept that he owed to the influences of Wyndham Lewis and the Catholic mystic Pierre Teilhard de Chardin. This entity was impossible without TV, which had the potential of either bringing the world together in the spirit of peace and harmony or reminding people of their tribalist differences, resulting in violence and instability. Predictably, those who worked in the media industries were drawn to a scholar who promised to make sense of the unnerving social and technological changes that were sweeping the planet during the 1960s. The San Francisco advertising executive Howard Gossage was so impressed with *Understanding Media* that he and his friend Gerald Feigen, a Bay Area doctor, put on a festival in honor of McLuhan in August 1965 in San Francisco. Gossage also introduced McLuhan to influential representatives of the press and the advertising industry in New York and California. In late 1965, *Harper's* and other magazines featured articles about McLuhan. The following year, 120 articles on McLuhan appeared in almost every major periodical in North America and Great Britain. Celebrities such as John Lennon and Abbie Hoffman were flocking to his door, and McLuhan was receiving attention in the least likely places. Goldie Hawn and Henry Gibson playfully inquired on the set of *Laugh-In*, "Marshall McLuhan, what are ya doin'?" All this dizzying fame led the journalist Tom Wolfe, writing a profile for *New York* magazine, to query, "Suppose he is what he sounds like, the most important thinker since Newton, Darwin, Freud, Einstein, and Pavlov . . . What if he is right?"

This fame came with costs as well as benefits. McLuhan's desire to reach as many people as possible to stimulate greater awareness of the effects of new media came from a noble intention. He increasingly saw his books as "probes" meant to explore as well as provoke thinking and participation, not to impose a fixed point of view that would turn off readers. McLuhan's application of the probe inspired a few of his most famous publications in the late 1960s. *The Medium Is the Massage: An Inventory of Effects* (1967) consisted of a collage of photos drawn from TV and magazines alongside McLuhan's aphorisms and commentary. Although the title was a publisher's misprint of his famous probe "the medium is the message," McLuhan thought the new title should be kept because it captured more vividly the power of the media to bombard our senses in subtle ways. It has sold almost one million copies worldwide. In 1968, *War and Peace in the Global Village* appeared; it followed the same style of visual images juxtaposed with McLuhan's reflections. In each book, the graphic designer Quentin Fiore provided the illustrations. These books were probes, designed to encourage the reader's awareness of what the media can do, at a time when the media's massaging of the public's consciousness was impeding this important task.

McLuhan clearly wanted to effect change while understanding it. His various attempts to encourage the participation of his readers through probes and his tendency to "put on" his audiences by offering catchphrases and puns for their amusement were meant to achieve these outcomes. To put on was the opposite of to "put off" by making a moralizing judgment that would likely cause the audience to lose interest. His apparent flippancy in the process irritated many. As he once remarked to a group of reporters, "People make a great mistake trying to read me as if I were saying something. I poke these sentences around to probe and feel my way around in our kind of world." McLuhan's embrace of popular media as the means by which to generate some enlightenment also provoked harsh assessments from many academic quarters, particularly scholars who thought that any engagement of the popular was vulgar. His willingness to write articles for popular magazines such as *TV Guide*, *Glamour*, *Playboy*, and *Vogue* did not help him improve his image among the literati. The historian Paul Johnson called McLuhan an "enemy of society" for producing a "pseudo-science" that lacked any empirical credibility. One of McLuhan's most savage critics was Carroll Quigley, a professor of history at Georgetown University. In 1968, Quigley penned an essay entitled "McLuhan as a Global Verbalizer" for the *Washington Star*. Accusing McLuhan of being unable to think or read, he added this obloquy: "McLuhan is not interested in communication either as transmitter or receiver. . . . McLuhan neither knows nor cares to know how electronic systems really operate. Instead he pounds away at these misconceptions. . . . McLuhan's ignorance is monumental, almost total. . . . How could a man like this win the fame and fortune our society provides to him?" Another critic complained that McLuhan was an "anti-intellectual" whose "noisy deification makes his ostentatious spurning of the intellectual process potentially harmful to all professions." With readers like these in mind, McLuhan wrote in a letter to Malcolm Muggeridge, "I felt like a person who had turned in a fire alarm only to be branded as an arsonist."

McLuhan's rise to fame came with other costs. The relentless media spotlight had adverse effects on his health. In 1960, McLuhan had the first of many strokes, in this case one so severe that a priest gave him the last rites. From the late 1950s onward, he had also experienced several blackouts, sometimes while he was giving a talk in public. Poor health often dogged him during his greatest triumphs. In March 1967, McLuhan delivered in two parts the prestigious Marfleet Lectures on the theme "Canada in the Electronic Age." The first part was titled "Canada in the Borderline Case," while the second part was "Towards an Inclusive

Consciousness." Around this time, on March 6, 1967, *Newsweek* ran a cover story titled "The Message of Marshall McLuhan."

Later that year, McLuhan was awarded the Albert Schweitzer Chair in the Humanities at Fordham University in New York City, a position that was generously funded for one year. He and his family enjoyed the academic and media attention that the Big Apple offered during this sabbatical leave. Tony Schwartz, an advertising executive, worked hard to arrange some public lectures for McLuhan during the 1967–68 year. Eugene Schwartz, a pioneer in the promotion and selling of self-help books, collaborated with McLuhan to create the *DEW-LINE* newsletter, which contained McLuhan's latest insights meant for executives eager to navigate the effects of media. The newsletter, which his son Eric edited, was inspired by the Distant Early Warning Line of Arctic radar stations that Canada and the United States operated on Inuit land between 1952 and 1957. The periodical later came with a "DEW deck," a deck of cards that performed a similar function as this radar system. Just as these stations were designed to warn of incoming Soviet missiles, the cards contained aphorisms and puns that were meant to warn of harmful technological effects. As Cait McKinney explains, "The cards functioned like a Magic 8 Ball: a user facing a decision could pull a card from the deck and read its aphorism as a through-line to pondering their problem." McLuhan believed that a playful product of this sort would raise awareness of the media's effects among consumers who no longer looked to conventional print media for insights. Put differently, the aphorisms would play the role of probes.

As 1967 came to a close, McLuhan continued to suffer even more severe blackouts. X-rays revealed the cause: McLuhan had a tumor the size of an apple lodged under his brain. Although it was benign and operable, without surgery it also had the potential to cause tremendous damage. While McLuhan feared the prospect of an operation, he agreed to what turned out to be a twenty-two-hour ordeal, the "longest neurological operation in the history of American medicine," according to a biographer. Although the tumor was removed, there were harmful effects that plagued McLuhan for the rest of his life—nervousness, hypersensitivity to noise, and some loss of memory.

After returning to Toronto in 1968, McLuhan was still in great demand as a commentator on the tumultuous events of his time: the Vietnam War, race riots, pollution of the environment. His accumulated wealth enabled him to purchase an Edwardian mansion for his large family in Wychwood Park, a private neighborhood enclave, replete with trees and ponds, that had once been an artist's colony in the nineteenth century. Perhaps grateful for his return to Canada, the University of Toronto gave McLuhan a coach house as the new location for his center. He was also busily working on new books that were meant to further demonstrate the enduring relevance of his insights into the media. In 1968,

McLuhan and Harley Parker published *Through the Vanishing Point: Space and Poetry in Painting*, a volume comprising reproductions of paintings as well as the authors' interpretations. In 1970, he and Wilfred Watson published *From Cliché to Archetype*, which analyzed the pattern of an ordinary saying or cliché becoming a universal truth or archetype through the magic of media. In the same year, *Culture Is Our Business* appeared, yet another book that consisted of advertisements placed alongside McLuhan's reflections. Two years later, McLuhan and his friend Barrington Nevitt came out with *Take Today: The Executive as Dropout*, a subtle analysis of the changing relation between media and corporate power. None of these books sold well. By the early 1970s, media interest in McLuhan was declining. He was also attracting fewer graduate students to his classes. McLuhan wondered whether his ideas had had any impact on the public at large. As he once admitted to a reporter in the mid-seventies, "All the publicity never helped in getting people to understand what I say."

Final Years of Activism and Engagement

In the early 1970s, McLuhan at times turned to activism as the means to change the world. His passionate interest in preserving traditional neighborhoods in Toronto prompted him to collaborate with the American activist Jane Jacobs in protests against the Spadina Expressway. This project threatened to increase traffic congestion as well as destroy homes and park lands in the city core. In public statements, McLuhan predicted that the city would commit "suicide" and repeat "the mistakes of American cities" if it were completed. He even produced a short film, with the help of the filmmaker David MacKay, entitled *A Burning Would* (inspired by a pun in *Finnegans Wake*: "A burning would has come to dance inane") that called for an end to the expressway's construction. Throughout the 1970s, McLuhan also became more involved in environmentalism, warning of the "garbage apocalypse." This unprecedented crisis was the result of a process where "ruins, junk, and garbage have become a new kind of environment."

As the debate over the legalization of abortion in Canada intensified during this time, McLuhan became a vigorous advocate for the pro-life camp. In a letter to Jim Davey, an adviser to Prime Minister Trudeau, McLuhan politely warned his correspondent that "the best-intentioned bureaucrats in all governments are busily engaged in creating bigger and blacker King Kongs every day of the week." McLuhan was also opposed to the reforms of Vatican II for embracing changes that would accelerate the "Protestantization" of the church, including the abandonment of the Latin Mass and traditional doctrine on purgatory and hellfire. Catholics who supported this reformation of the church were thoughtlessly demanding "a blossoming of liberal individualism" at a time when the global village was becoming more tribalist and traditionalist. True to form, he recognized in all these cases the unmistakable pattern of human beings remaining oblivious to the effects of their actions.

Despite being plagued by heart attacks and high blood pressure throughout the decade, McLuhan ambitiously entertained the completion of several projects, including a series of books that would discuss the history of theories of communication from Plato to Freud. After his brain tumor operation, he also became intensely interested in the functions of the "split" brain. Specifically, growing research into the difference between the logical bias of the left hemisphere and the intuitive bias of the right hemisphere vindicated his long-held contention that human beings had failed to prepare for the effects of new media because of an excessive reliance on logical categories. Most human beings focus on causes preceding effects (as logic dictates), not effects preceding causes (as intuition encourages). This interest in the split brain, as well as his formulation of the laws of media, inspired McLuhan to collaborate with his son Eric on articulating what a scientific study of these effects would look like in a media environment. The University of Toronto Press would posthumously publish the fruit of these labors, *The Laws of Media: The New Science*, in 1988. In this volume, the McLuhans developed a "tetrad," based on four laws of media, which could predict how a new medium or technology will transform the environment (see chapter 3).

Although McLuhan never recaptured the dizzying level of media attention that he had experienced in the 1960s, he regularly received invitations for talks and lectures around the world. These moments often contrasted sharply with his worries about the small number of students that were attending his seminars at his center as well as his suspicions that some of his colleagues wanted to shutter the place altogether.

In September 1979, McLuhan suffered a massive stroke, inflicting the cruelest of fates on a theorist of communication. He was unable to read or speak in the last year of his life. Although his wife and children tried to teach McLuhan to communicate again, these efforts were in vain. After the university heard of his failing health, the decision was made to close the center that had been his academic home since the early 1960s, despite the protestations of allies as diverse as Pierre Trudeau, Woody Allen, and Tom Wolfe. This decision devastated McLuhan, but he lived long enough to enjoy the moral support of friends who came to visit him. He also witnessed the fulfillment of one of his most famous predictions: the transformation of entertainment "into a form of politics," with the election of the Hollywood actor Ronald Reagan to the presidency in November 1980.

In the early morning hours of New Year's Eve 1980, McLuhan passed away in his sleep. He now belonged to eternity.

2
UNDERSTANDING AND MISUNDERSTANDING MEDIA

In his last taped lecture in 1979, McLuhan observed, "Man's technology is the most human thing about him." Although it is imprudent to summarize too easily the rich diversity of his ideas that evolved over the course of several decades, this statement comes as close to a summary as one can find. If there is a recurrent theme in McLuhan's vast oeuvre, it is this: what we create reveals who we are. Whenever human beings create technologies or tools, they express their thoughts, desires, and purposes. Therefore it is imperative to understand what exactly technology reveals about humanity. This chapter will explain why McLuhan believed that human beings have generally been unable or unwilling to understand the media that they create.

The Effects of Media

In the most basic sense, technologies are "extensions" of our physical bodies, as McLuhan explains throughout *Understanding Media*. Throughout history, they typically extend one part of the body in a manner that amplifies or strengthens the power of this body part. These tools allow our bodies to perform a task that we could not do on our own. In the process, they help us conserve our energy and increase our power over the rest of the world. For example, the stone ax extends the hand to touch things that are out of the hand's reach. The wheel extends the foot by allowing us to travel to places that are too far away for walking. The telescope and microscope extend the eye by allowing us to see objects that are not immediately visible to the visual sense. The computer extends the brain by storing in its memory vast amounts of information that the brain cannot hold on its own.

Media are technologies that enable communication between human beings. With this fact in mind, McLuhan once remarked that the word "medium" comes from the Latin word for "public." These tools typically extend at least one of the five senses, often at the expense of the others. Print media extend the eye, allowing us to see or read about phenomena that are otherwise inaccessible. Smartphones extend the eye and ear, permitting us to see and hear people who are too far away for in-person contact.

The idea of a medium as the extension of a sense is not hard to understand. With a nod to the laws of media, an extension is an enhancement of something that human beings already have. What is more challenging to understand is McLuhan's far more important insight that human beings generally fail to comprehend the extent to which the technologies they have forged throughout history shape and influence them. In a lecture given at Fordham University in 1967, McLuhan made the same point rather bluntly: "I can assure you that history reveals that people have never, in any age of the human past, ever known what they were doing, that is, what the effects would be of what they were doing." This idea is, at first glance, counterintuitive. How can human beings fall short of understanding the tools they deliberately create for their own purposes?

Throughout his academic life, McLuhan was determined to provide several answers to this question. First, it is important for human beings to recognize, based on the historical record, that the effects of technology are the key to understanding technologies. The problem is that these effects are usually unintended. As a result, they are almost never understood until they are deeply entrenched in human society. Henry Ford, for example, never anticipated that his invention of the automobile, which enabled the mass movement of populations from the countryside to the cities, would destroy the rural way of life that he cherished.

For McLuhan, the primary issue is not whether these unintended effects are good or bad. More than once he warns against the temptation to judge these effects on ethical grounds, given the fact that they are usually too entrenched to reverse their impact in any case. In *The Mechanical Bride*, he issues this warning: "The time for anger and protest is in the early stages of a new process." In a similar vein, McLuhan once compared the posture of "moral caution and alarm" to "the screech of a chicken whose neck has been laid on the chopping block."

An attitude of moral indignation also does not account for the fact that some effects are good while others are bad. On a positive note, McLuhan credits the car with improving racial relations between whites and Blacks in the South because it is "the great leveler of physical space and of social distance as well." The inventors of electric media never intended the disappearance of childhood. Yet the massive success of TV and other electric media in exposing children to an adult world even before they reach grade school, McLuhan and Wilfred Watson note in *From Cliché to Archetype*, has had the effect of "wiping out differences between child and adult, so far as experience is concerned." This insight inspired Neil Postman, a student of McLuhan's, to study this phenomenon in *The Disappearance of Childhood* (1982). Even the most powerful figures in the media industry still do not understand this profound consequence. When Facebook/Meta's Mark Zuckerberg promised politicians and parents at a congressional hearing on the harmful effects of online content that industry-leading efforts would remove toxic messages that have been linked to adolescent suicide, he was ignoring the larger problem of how social media are addictive, regardless of the "content moderation" being applied. This practice is meant to remove offensive or inappropriate content that violates the standards of a social media platform. As the social psychologist Jonathan Haidt argues, McLuhan would probably identify this focus on content as analogous to "the juicy piece of meat carried by the burglar to distract the watchdog of the mind." It is far more important to study the unintended effects of technology, which usually do not reflect the intentional use of content. With McLuhan's "juicy piece of meat" metaphor in mind, Haidt faults Zuckerberg for misunderstanding how the bias (to use Innis's term) of this medium is to prematurely introduce children to the adult world. In Haidt's words, "Let me be clear: there is no way to make social media safe for children by just making the content less toxic. It's the phone-based childhood that is harming them, regardless of what they watch."

Why is it so difficult for human beings to understand, predict, and address these effects? One sobering answer that McLuhan provides is that human beings are not naturally inclined to make the mental effort needed to analyze technologies, especially new ones. As he warns in his last taped lecture, "We cannot trust our instincts or our natural physical responses to new things. They will destroy us."

McLuhan never claims that this insight is original on his part. In his doctoral dissertation on the Elizabethan satirist Thomas Nashe, he notes that the ancient Greek philosopher Heraclitus also warned against undue trust in the senses as the pathway toward understanding reality. In *Laws of Media*, McLuhan and his son Eric favorably quote Vico on how the "human mind is naturally inclined by the senses to see itself externally in the body, and only with great difficulty does it come to understand itself by means of reflection." The human brain is not equipped to deal with rapid and unpredictable change of any kind. McLuhan was particularly interested in the science of cognition (especially after his brain tumor operation in 1967) because it reveals the stark limitations that nature imposes on human understanding. Human nature has never caught up with historical change, a pattern to which McLuhan constantly pointed. The structure of nerves and brain stem known as the diencephalon had completed its evolution before the discovery of fire or clothing. Thus, the brain, given its primal origins, cannot be expected to respond to the effects of new technologies and environments. In the electric age of "all-at-onceness" or instantaneous information, the limitations of the brain become more obvious. Unless the process of change slows down, it is unlikely that human cognition can keep up with the effects of this process. As McLuhan once put it, "The civilized world deals with one thing at a time."

It is no surprise that human beings prefer to slow down their own understanding of rapid change, even though this reaction discourages an accurate understanding of the media in question. McLuhan called this pattern of behavior "rear-view mirror" thinking. By judging the present in terms of the past, we are looking at reality through the rear-view mirror: "Man is only consciously aware of the environment that has *preceded* it." We understand an environment only after a new one has displaced it. In the process, the past becomes very intelligible. The downside is that the visibility of the past becomes clearer only when it has already become obsolete. A new medium that surpasses the power of an old one will highlight the importance of the latter. This pattern reveals how human beings cope, albeit inadequately, with the effects of a new medium. McLuhan explains: "Because we are benumbed by any new technology—which in turn creates a totally new environment—we tend to make the old environment more visible." McLuhan deliberately uses the term environment to underscore the fact that human beings are enmeshed within a context that they create: they are never detached from this environment. Nevertheless, we are not hapless pawns of what we create. As Kierkegaard put it, "Life can only be understood backwards, but it must be lived forward."

The reinvention and rediscovery of the past have often occurred on a mass scale. This "age-old human habit," McLuhan observes, constantly appears throughout history as a pattern, one that is "mostly involuntary." The Middle Ages saw ancient Rome in its rear-view mirror. The Renaissance saw the image of the Middle Ages in its mirror. The nineteenth century's Industrial Revolution saw the Renaissance. The twentieth century was focused on the preceding century. In short, whole societies do not "see the present, not very much of it." In general, humanity becomes aware of how technology has transformed the environment only after the fact. Current attempts to restore the predigital educational environment by banning cell phones and smartphones from school classrooms illustrate this pattern. Although several educators warned about the addictive effects of these devices years before they became fixtures in classrooms, school authorities are forbidding their usage long after children and adolescents have grown dependent on them.

McLuhan never denies that human beings have the freedom and cognitive ability to understand and address the effects of new media, provided that they make the effort to do so. He is neither a technological determinist nor a fatalist, as we have seen. Additionally, McLuhan never contests that a "strategy of evasion and survival" amid rapid technological change is possible. Even if we could do little to alter the evolutionary limits of our brains, we could still reassess the way that we think about technological change. To be sure, the pattern that recurs throughout history is that human beings do not make this effort until it is too late. The ignorance that human beings generally show toward media is "deeply willed." Yet the good news that McLuhan offers is that a proper study of these media is possible in an age of rapid technological change that otherwise threatens to saturate the minds and senses of humanity.

To illustrate the benefits of studying media's effects, McLuhan often refers to Edgar Allan Poe's short story "A Descent into the Maelstrom" (1841). In this story, a sailor and his two brothers, who are on a fishing expedition, are caught up in a maelstrom or whirlpool. Yet, unlike his brothers, the sailor narrowly escapes the fate of drowning by studying the movement of this storm. In the process, he observes how fragments of various things disappear while other things reappear. He attaches himself to a barrel and thereby saves himself before other sailors eventually rescue him. In short, the sailor engages in what McLuhan calls "pattern recognition," or the study of how processes repeat themselves in history. This story also illustrates a lesson that he learned from the style of art known as vorticism: one can understand an immense vortex of energy without being swept up in it. The failure to study the media's patterns will leave human beings in the grip of great technological storms that threaten the very survival of civilization itself. After all, every new technology operates like the "Midas touch," transforming every institution of a society.

How Media Create Hidden Environments

This rethinking of technological change, McLuhan always contends, is a gargantuan task. In addition to the natural limitations of the brain and the senses, human beings have to cope with the fact that new media have always altered and even created environments in invisible ways. McLuhan's lifelong study of art persuaded him to focus on the media as "forms." A form is a work of art whose meaning lies in the effect that it has on the observer. A form, McLuhan contends, "acts upon you. It invades your senses. It re-structures your outlook."

Media operate in the same way, as McLuhan demonstrates. New media act like forms by creating hidden environments with indiscernible effects on people. In short, the form is the message.

McLuhan further explains the idea of a hidden environment by drawing an analogy between works of fiction and new technologies. Just as the subplot of a story is the implicit and hidden one that is also the most important part of a story, a new technology's reshaping of the environment is similarly imperceptible and important. As McLuhan remarked in his address at the "Vision 65" conference on human communication in October 1965, "The really total and saturating environments are invisible. The ones we notice are quite fragmentary and insignificant compared to the ones we don't see."

McLuhan's distinction between "figure" and "ground" is central to explaining his focus on the ways that human beings struggle to understand the invisible effects of media. In simple terms, the figure of the medium is the immediate object of attention, one that is easily intelligible to the visual sense. The ground, in contrast, is the invisible environment that the medium changes or creates. To be sure, McLuhan never claims that technology is the only force that shapes and alters an environment. In a 1973 seminar on transportation and urban affairs in Toronto, he posed questions about the political ground that shaped the decisions of the city's mayor. Although the mayor was the figure who was visible to the citizenry, the less visible ground that influenced him might be public opinion or "his buddies." Nevertheless, McLuhan remained convinced that the most hidden environment is largely a creation or reflection of new media. Even though the figures of media are perceptible to their users, their immersion in the environment that the media contrived impedes their understanding of changes "happening all around them—things that are really destroying our society!—the hidden environment or 'ground.'"

Even the most educated people are oblivious to the effects of media. According to McLuhan, the history of science reveals a great deal of preoccupation with the figure, or what is physically measurable according to the five senses (especially the eye). Yet this habit ignores the far more important effects that the medium imposes on the environment, which are not easily measurable in a manner that accords with the visual sense. As long as scientists use the eye to measure phenomena, they not only miss out on these invisible effects but also fall into the mistaken temptation of assuming that they are detached observers who are utterly objective and unbiased in their treatment of the universe.

The reader may legitimately ask why this paradoxical observation is necessarily true, given the ever-increasing sophistication of scientific knowledge in the modern age. From a scientific perspective, can anything truly be invisible or beyond human understanding? Although McLuhan values the findings of science, given his deep interest in human cognition, even science is not exempted from his cautionary note that every scholarly discipline has a tendency to see what it wants to see, not what is actually there. Like the fish unaware of its environment, human beings mistakenly assume that they observe phenomena from a vantage point that is separate from the phenomena in question. In *Laws of Media*, the McLuhans draw a careful distinction between the fallacious premises of traditional science and the "new science" that they hope their study of media will develop or inspire. Whereas "Western Old Science" studies media as "detached figures," the McLuhans explain, the "New Science" approaches media with a focus on "the ground of users and of environmental media effects."

The posture of pure detachment is oblivious to two facts that McLuhan always emphasizes. First, it implies a vantage point that is unaffected by the phenomena that the scientist studies. Put differently, one can assume one's objectivity or neutrality only if one is certain of having escaped from the ground or environment in which one exists. Then it is easy to assume that one's vantage point or theory is "fixed," or invulnerable to change. Given McLuhan's focus on the history of media as the story of endless change, it is unsurprising that he dismisses this posture of detachment as impossible. Neither total detachment nor a fixed perspective is possible amid a process of change. As long as scientists ignore the environment that is so often invisible or immeasurable, they, like everyone else, will become the prisoners of its effects. The flux of media is unintelligible to anyone who clings to an illusory fixed point of view. Those of us who continue to embrace this illusion, according to McLuhan and son, "will have no more control of this technology and environment than we have of the wind and the tides."

Second, detachment ignores the fact that people, whether they know it or not, participate in their environments; they do not simply stand back and observe them in a detached manner. In the electric age, there are only processes that engage people, not isolated things that they study. As McLuhan and Barrington Nevitt wrote in a 1973 essay, "There are no more spectators in lab or life, only participants in the Global Electric Theatre." To recall McLuhan's analogy between the subplot in a story and the hidden environment, what they both have in common is the involvement of an "audience." This focus on participation helps to explain why McLuhan thought of artists and psychologists as more suited than anyone else to the task of understanding the effects of media. The distinction between figure and ground is pivotal to the artist, who never feels detached from reality. The artist understands better than anyone that we participate in an environment precisely because we alter the environment with technologies. For this reason, the artist is determined to understand the effects of a new environment before they are visible or measurable to the scientific eye. "The artist in any field," state McLuhan and Nevitt, "is the person who anticipates the effects in his own times, both of new knowledge and of his own actions." McLuhan also praises Gestalt psychology for understanding the figure/ground distinction: "The *figure*, the gestalt, is visible while the *ground* remains invisible. Human perception encourages us to pay attention to the *figure* (a painting) and to ignore the *ground* (its frame, the wall, etc.)."

Artists and psychologists alike understand the fact that every figure or object of attention is inseparable from a larger context or environment, even though the latter may not be perceptible at a given time. According to the McLuhans, artists abolish the "merely outside world." The failure to recognize the necessity of this task leads to the danger of ignoring human responsibility for *both* figure and ground and how our technological creations reshape both. "Nothing has its meaning alone," write McLuhan and Nevitt in their book *Take Today*. "Every figure must have its ground or environment. A single word, divorced from its linguistic ground, would be useless. A note in isolation is not music."

Even though we are immersed in an environment of our own making, we are rarely aware of the extent to which we make this environment. It is McLuhan's purpose to help us understand the environment that we make, the effects of which are never independent of our existence or thought.

How the Medium Is the Message in the Electric Age

One of McLuhan's most famous attempts to illustrate the phenomenon of participation pertains to his analysis of television's impact. He not only rejects the conventional image of TV as a medium that encourages passivity in the audience; he also insists that TV encourages considerable involvement or participation from its viewers. TV is not a visual medium that one simply watches from a detached vantage point. In describing TV as "audile-tactile," McLuhan is explaining how this medium extends several senses at once, unlike print media, which extend only one sense (the visual). Whereas phonetic writing fragments the senses in favor of the eye, TV encourages "maximal interplay of all the senses."

Involvement with an environment, once again, is not the same as understanding it. Like any medium, TV creates a hidden environment that is not readily intelligible until its effects are well established. As McLuhan observes, "Everybody experiences far more than he understands." His distinction between "hot" and "cool" media cuts to the heart of understanding how TV operates in different environments, which it fundamentally alters. Whereas hot media (e.g., print, radio) encourage a low level of participation, cool media (e.g., speech, TV) encourage a high level of involvement. (This distinction reversed the traditional way of understanding "hot" as exciting and "cool" as forbidding.) Hot media are high definition, while cool media are low definition. These parallel distinctions are based on the amount of information that a medium provides. While hot media provide a high degree of information, cool media do not. Radio is a hot medium because it provides a great deal of content and information, which encourages passivity in its listeners. The more information that is provided, the less participation that is needed. For example, speech is a cool medium because the listener has to "fill in" or become more involved in the dialogue precisely because the latter does not one-sidedly provide all the information required. This process can be exhausting precisely because it demands so much participation. For this reason, the literate person will resent the time that a phone conversation consumes.

The invisible effects of TV are tremendously relevant to the realms of politics and journalism, as McLuhan was the first to point out. The fact that TV as a cool medium provides little content or information has transformed the nature of politics. In McLuhan's analysis of the Kennedy-Nixon debate of 1960, which was the first televised presidential debate in US history, Kennedy masterfully demonstrated that he was the first presidential candidate suited to TV because his "cool" image suited the nature of the medium. The fact that Kennedy had low-definition qualities allowed "the viewer to fill in the gaps with his own personal identification." There was no need for him to provide a great deal of information about what his policies would be if he were elected president. Kennedy had charisma, or what McLuhan describes as the ability to look "like a lot of other people." Unsurprisingly, those who watched the debate on TV saw him as the winner. Kennedy's ability to appear as several likeable persons compensated for the lack of precise answers that he gave during the debate. In sharp contrast, Nixon on TV had a hot image that was easily classifiable and uncharismatic precisely because Nixon looked only like himself. Yet those who listened to the debate on radio, McLuhan notes, "received an overwhelming idea of Nixon's superiority," given the fact that he provided the heavy amount of content and information that fits well with the low participation that this medium encourages.

One popular misconception that McLuhan seeks to debunk is the idea that the actual use of a medium determines its value, meaning, or influence. This idea suggests that the way in which human beings consciously use a technology determines its effects. What this assumption ignores is that every medium has a nature or form of its own. McLuhan learned from the pioneering studies of Harold Innis that each medium has a "bias," or inherent tendency toward fostering certain effects. Print media are biased in favor of preserving history or tradition: they are "time-oriented." Electric media, which enable the instantaneous dissemination of information across vast distances, are "space-oriented." The problem is that an inherent quality within a medium is usually invisible to most of its users. As McLuhan once polemically remarked, the denial of this truth about the nature of each medium is tantamount to asserting that "the smallpox virus is in itself neither good nor bad; it is the way it is used that determines its value." Even if it is conceivable that this virus can serve a good purpose, it is far more probable that it will be weaponized for a bad purpose, given its potential tendency toward this end. (This last point anticipates McLuhan's usage of Aristotle's idea of formal causality, which I discuss in the next chapter.)

The power of the medium to alter or obscure the intended content without the user understanding this process is so great that McLuhan alternately employed "the medium is the message" and "the medium is the massage." TV's massage or bombardment of our senses and cognition is usually so subtle that we lose interest in the content that TV is promoting. For example, the advertisement for a product on TV is far more important than information about the product itself. In fact, the ad *is* the information, selling an image that is associated with the product. A car commercial does not typically list the basic technical facts about the vehicle; it presents an identity that is incidental to the car. Thus, "the ad," McLuhan explains, "will become a substitute for the product, and all the satisfactions will be derived informationally from the ad, and the product will be merely a number in some file somewhere." In other words, these "satisfactions" reflect the effect of the medium on the user, not the technical details of the product. The product is the figure, while these effects represent the ground.

The real content of the medium turns out to be its user. The data that social media firms extract from their consumers is just the latest example of this pattern. (See chapters 5 and 7.) Throughout his scholarly career, McLuhan contended that it is far more important to study how a medium transforms the user unconsciously than to understand what the medium is selling. Once again, he targeted the temptation to treat a medium as an object whose effects merely reflect the consciously contrived purposes of the user. After all, a human being does not simply use a medium: he wears it like clothing. McLuhan praises the French symbolist painters for understanding that the creation of a poem or a work of art requires knowledge of the subliminal effect that it would have on the reader or observer before this effect actually materializes.

McLuhan does not favor or welcome any of these effects. The fact that TV, as he put it, subjects its audience to an "X-ray" that exposes the human yearning for involvement and connection is not necessarily a good thing. To be sure, the appeal of this involvement is understandable. The popularity of quiz shows such as *Jeopardy!* reveals what this medium does best: it involves the audience, which readily participates in the question-and-answer format as it happens. This involvement can sometimes have dramatic effects. When Jack Ruby shot Lee

Harvey Oswald live on TV days after the assassination of JFK in 1963, viewers felt naturally involved. Had the radio been the only medium to broadcast this event, the reaction would have been different. In this case, McLuhan averred, involvement encouraged "coolness and calm" among grieving TV viewers.

The calmness that TV sometimes instills with endless coverage does not always bode well for democracy. Viewers are so easily numbed by the cool image of a politician that they can ignore or disregard the lies that charismatic politicians openly state. A cool image compensates for deception. Kennedy's successor, Lyndon B, Johnson, learned this lesson to his cost. As McLuhan remarked in his interview with *Playboy* in 1969, "The people wouldn't have cared if John Kennedy lied to them on TV, but they couldn't stomach L.B.J. even when he told the truth." Citizens of a democracy can conflate the lies of a politician with facts if they hear them repeatedly. In fact, politicians who "flip-flop" on important issues may not lose any popular support from their electoral base so long as they deliver drama and theater on a regular basis. Most tellingly, the media focus far more on the private lives and the attendant deceptions of politicians than on the far greater existential danger posed by, say, the US national debt ($36 trillion at the time of writing). Political theater trumps economic reality.

Taking Control of Our Fate

The tendency of human beings to deceive themselves quite willingly is a paradox that explains McLuhan's recurrent interest in drawing connections between mythology, literature, and depth psychology. To understand how the unconscious is the hidden ground or environment of consciousness, one must understand how literature and myth often communicate the most important insights of psychology. For this reason, McLuhan was a great admirer of the Irish novelist James Joyce, whose final work, *Finnegans Wake* (1939), revealed what McLuhan and Watson called the "night-world." Joyce's novel, according to this interpretation, indulged in a combination of experimental language, puns, and metaphors in order to articulate the language of the unconscious or a dream world. The very title of Joyce's work is a play on words that also presents a fateful choice. In the context of the electric age, should human beings fixate on the past, as at an Irish wake, or should they also awake to the effects of a new age? McLuhan celebrated Joyce as one of the few authors in history who understood that we live "simultaneously" in the past, present, and future all at once, recognizing that history is not simply a linear process that ends in progress and enlightenment. Instead, history adheres to a "Finn cycle" by reversing direction, leading human beings back in time to a more primitive past. The fact that most human beings are unaware of the extent to which media can move history forward and backward reveals to McLuhan the power of the unconscious and its fateful relation to new technologies.

For this reason, McLuhan warns against a "somnambulistic" (dreaming awake) attitude toward new media. The appropriate response to this state of being is to understand it before one reawakens the person suffering from it. "Every man feels he has a right to defend his own ignorance even when it mucks up millions of lives," McLuhan writes. "My hope is to snap somnambulists out of their highly motivated and destructive trances." For this purpose, McLuhan often looks to myth, which comes from the Greek word *mythos*, meaning "story." Myth or narrative is one of the oldest forms of communication as well as an invaluable medium for disseminating timeless truths. The earliest hunter-gatherer civilizations, McLuhan explains, "had none of the literate means of classification of information. So they formed their information and their traditions into myths for the sake of retrieval, for the sake of restoring insights." This need for myth did not vanish with the rise of literacy. The story of King Cadmus, the founder of the ancient Greek city-state of Thebes, illustrates the subtle purpose of myth. Cadmus not only introduced the Phoenician alphabet to Greece but, according to legend, also sowed into the ground the teeth of a dragon that he had slain. These seeds generated armed men. It is no accident, according to McLuhan's interpretation, that the same hero who propagated the alphabet also created armies and empires. The message of this myth is that the rise of the alphabet and literacy enabled the creation of a vast military apparatus.

The Greek myth of Narcissus is very relevant to understanding the way that technological extensions of human beings actually work. It is no accident that the name Narcissus comes from the Greek word *narcosis*, which, we have seen, means numbness. Narcissus unknowingly fell in love with his own reflection in the water; he thought it was someone else. Users of new media similarly fall for a medium that they fail to understand as an extension of themselves. Vico, in his discussion of the poetic wisdom that underlay Greek thought, also refers to this pattern: "For when man understands he extends his mind and takes in the things, but when he does not understand he makes the things out of himself and becomes them by transforming himself into them." The users of media imagine themselves to be detached or separate from these objects without comprehending that these machines are the mirror images of themselves. People who search for an identity on social media do not realize that they are looking for themselves or at least for recognition of their existence. Creators of AI who conflate intelligence with the technics of information processing are unconsciously falling in love with their own intellects. They are unconsciously manifesting what

McLuhan calls "the true Narcissus style of one hypnotized by the amputation and extension of his own being in a new technical form."

Fortunately, human beings are not quite as trapped as Narcissus was by his own reflection. Zeus, after all, condemned him to this fate. As McLuhan once quipped, Zeus said to Narcissus, "Watch yourself." The fatalism that McLuhan associates with ancient Greek myth is not a malady that inevitably ails modern human beings. If there is any meaning to "fate" at all in the present age, it is a destiny that humanity has already imposed on itself with its own creations. The hidden media environment, not the technology, ultimately "changes people," McLuhan observes. The good news to which McLuhan cautiously points centers on the distinction between "feedback" and "feedforward." While the first focuses on the study of patterns in history, the second focuses on patterns in the present day before their full effects become entrenched. This anticipation of effects can help us "program" a fate that is of our own making.

Understanding these effects through education, McLuhan said, also "constitutes a civil defense against media fallout." Notwithstanding this cautious hope, he warns that the level of education needed to enlighten a society about the hidden effects of new media would not be easy to attain. The proper study of history—past, present, and future—requires a radical rethinking of human cognition as well as technology. The obstacles to this project have been strong. These impediments, which are usually institutional and intellectual, exist in the realms of politics, business, academia, and, of course, the media. As the following chapters will show, the collective tendency to ignore McLuhan's most important ideas endures to this day. Yet the failure to heed these ideas will result only in the perpetuation and intensification of electric (and digital) media's worst effects.

To comprehend the effects of media before they happen is not the only paradox to which McLuhan alludes. If human beings want to avoid the dreadful paradox of becoming servants to objects of their own making, McLuhan argued, they must cultivate a posture of "detached involvement" by studying the media without pretending to escape from their influence or effects. The good news is that this task is possible in an age of rapid technological change, which renders these effects visible. The bad news is that human beings have rarely made an effort to predict these effects, leaving future generations to live with the consequences of their lack of interest. This history is the subject of the next chapter.

3
MAKING HISTORY THROUGH MEDIA

McLuhan, as we have seen, contends that human beings generally misunderstand the effects of the media that they create. This ignorance stems from a profound failure to understand the sheer power of humanity to create new realities through technology. Instead we typically prefer to see reality as something "out there," independent of our existence or agency. In a 1967 interview with Gerald Emanuel Stearn, McLuhan claimed that most human beings understand "the idea of communication as something matching between what is said and what is understood." This assumption of "matching" suggests that communication bridges the gap between us and the external world or reality that we are trying to understand. Yet this posture ignores the fact that there is no reality outside of communication: through communication, we create the world. As McLuhan further explained, "Communication is *making*. The person who sees or heeds or hears is engaged in making a response to a situation which is mostly of his own fictional invention." Yet the reality that we transform also, paradoxically, transforms us. Although we are conscious of what we are making, we are, according to McLuhan and Barrington Nevitt, usually unaware of "how the world remakes us physically, psychically, and socially." In short, history is the greatest environment that we make through media.

For this reason, McLuhan associates the illusion of detachment with the premise that drives the activity of matching the human mind with external reality. Matching, or what philosophers call the correspondence theory of truth, presupposes detachment because it assumes that one must step back from reality to match the inner reality of the mind with the outer reality of the universe. The failure to find the right match or correspondence of these two realities, write McLuhan and Harley Parker presumably means that a person "is either hallucinating or living in a world of self-deception." Matching is, however, incompatible with participation, which breaks down the distinction between observer and observed. "Truth is not matching," McLuhan and Nevitt explain in *Take Today*. "It is neither a label nor a 'mental reflection.' It is something we make in the encounter with a world that is making us."

McLuhan consistently sees overwhelming evidence of human beings' capacity to create history without understanding the history that they are making. The history that we make in turn makes us. In short, history is the greatest environment that we can make, however unwittingly, through media.

Making History Simultaneously

Just as the world "remakes" us, the history of the world has an identical effect on humanity. Once again, the language of paradox is useful here. McLuhan credits the art form of cubism for revealing the paradox of studying something "simultaneously from different directions" to grasp multiple effects. Although McLuhan was a critic of Marxism, he would have agreed with Marx's oft-quoted paradox, "Men make their own history, but they do not make it just as they please; they do not make it under circumstances chosen by themselves, but under circumstances directly found, given and transmitted from the past." Put differently, we make history and history makes us. History is not something that exists independently of human existence. Rather, it is a human creation that also creates us, even though we are not aware of this paradoxical truth.

One of McLuhan's favorite ways to explain this two-way process in history is the idea of "simultaneity," which suggests that the past, the present, and the future always coexist, even though human beings are not always aware of this paradox. That is to say, human beings exist within all three periods of history even though they fail to understand that the past, present, and future are shaping them as well. McLuhan hoped that the speed with which information moves in the electric age would finally demonstrate that the media exist "simultaneous in time," intermingling prehistory with present history and future history. The electric media that we have made ideally help us understand how simultaneous history also makes us. In the electric age, users of media can think of history as a "mythic" narrative by merging the past, present, and future into an "electric nowness."

"Language alone," McLuhan writes in *The Book of Probes*, "includes all the senses in interplay at all times." In McLuhan's argot, the ideal sense ratio (balancing of the senses) understands how the past, present, and future interface with each other. Predictably, scholars who study history emphasize one sense at the expense of the others. In the process, they study the past as if it is something that no longer exists, thus ignoring William Faulkner's famous quip that "the past is never dead. It's not even past." As McLuhan puts it, "We shall discover in our social life as in our private life that there is no past that is dead." Simultaneity is particularly counterintuitive to intellects who are used to dividing up history according to carefully defined periods and eras. The idea of information assailing us "from all directions simultaneously" is hard to understand if one thinks in terms of what McLuhan calls "the static, continuous, connected spaces of the visual, civilized man of the past 2,500 years."

From a typically modern perspective, history is linear, or forward moving. As a result, one can understand how one period leads to another in sequential terms. The past precedes the present, which the future follows. Consistent with this perspective, it is tempting to conclude that history is a rational or logical process. The paradox that the present coexists with the past and future does not fit into this historiography. In fact, paradox, or what McLuhan calls "the technique for seizing the conflicting aspects of any problem," does not fit into a linear version of history. For this reason, McLuhan prefers to understand the effects of a new medium occurring at the same time in the electric age. The four laws of media, as illustrated by the tetrad, are simultaneous. Each medium (1) obsolesces an old pattern, (2) retrieves an older one, (3) enhances or extends an existing one, and (4) reverses this enhanced feature into its opposite. For example, the strict standards of the written word obsolesced vulgarity and slang, retrieved elitism within a democratic age, enhanced private authorship, and reversed the latter into a corporate reading public. The law of retrieval, or the pattern of retrieving a past medium or artifact that only seemingly disappeared from history, strikingly illustrates the pattern of simultaneity.

McLuhan is not categorically opposed to classifying history according to distinct stages. His own account of history, after all, begins with orality and ends with the electric age. Yet McLuhan warns against the temptation of rigidly relying on this methodology at the expense of understanding simultaneity. Although we live in the electric (or now digital) age, this fact should not suggest that older media have vanished altogether. While McLuhan often claims that each new medium replaces or obsolesces an old one, this does not mean that the older medium becomes irrelevant. This artifact can be retrieved as a work of art, becoming the content of the new medium. Just as the past can endure within the present, the future is perceptible at the same time. If we study changes that occur at the speed of light in the electric age, we can predict the effects of new media before they actually happen. (This is the meaning of "formal causality," which I discuss at the end of this chapter.)

Unfortunately, even distinguished scholars fall into the trap of looking backward or forward without paying due attention to the simultaneous present. The Romanian historian of religion Mircea Eliade (1907–86) is a case in point. Although McLuhan learned a great deal from Eliade's numerous studies of religious symbolism throughout history, he criticized Eliade's famous distinction between the "sacred" and the "profane" as simplistic and misleading. According to Eliade, a deep sense of the sacred characterized the mindset of "archaic" human beings who found and worshipped manifestations of the divine in the universe all around them. While McLuhan appreciates this portrait as an accurate description of life within preliterate cultures, he disputes Eliade's assumption that this understanding of the sacred eventually yielded to the modern and secular valorization of the profane, in which science reduces the universe to mere raw material for human usage. According to McLuhan, the triumph of this desacralization is not as complete as Eliade contends.

What Eliade (along with many other contemporary scholars) fails to understand is that the distinction between sacred and profane is obsolete in the electric age. In fact, the sacred has made a comeback. "Modern man," McLuhan writes in *The Gutenberg Galaxy*, "since the electro-magnetic discoveries of more than a century ago, is investing himself with all the dimensions of archaic man *plus*." The paradox that Eliade ignores is that a modern person can embrace archaic (or premodern) attitudes and behaviors. The age of archaic humanity did not disappear with the rise of modern science and secularism. To describe this age as more religious or attuned to the sacred than the present age ignores the fact that every age has its religious myths. Religion and rationality (or the sacred and profane) can coexist simultaneously. By assuming that reason triumphs over religion, Eliade, in McLuhan's judgment, "is in that very large company of literacy victims who have acquiesced in supposing that the 'rational' is the explicitly lineal, sequential, visual."

Eliade could have avoided this misleading distinction if he had devoted more attention to how technological change transforms attitudes toward the universe. As McLuhan explains in *Understanding Media*, a "sacred universe" is one that is "dominated by the spoken word and by auditory media. A 'profane' universe, on the other hand, is one dominated by the visual sense." McLuhan believes that one unprecedented benefit arising from the electric age is potential awareness of these contradictory forces jostling alongside each other within the global village. Because we live in an age in which one medium creates a new environment on top of another, we can retrieve every tradition simultaneously.

Orality and Tribalism in History

Is the electric age the only period of history in which awareness of simultaneity occurs? According to McLuhan, there has always been some understanding of this phenomenon. Orality, which is the first stage in the history of media, began when human beings first acquired the power of speech approximately seventy thousand years ago. Because oral communication relies on the ear, McLuhan associates speech with acoustic space, a place in which it is impossible to screen out sounds or noises. As a result, oral cultures consist of human beings who feel intensely involved with their surroundings. As McLuhan explains in *The Gutenberg Galaxy*, nonliterate people "have no detached point of view. They are *wholly* with the object. They go empathically into it." Orality goes hand in hand with tribalism, which insists that human beings belong to a natural or divine order from which there is no escape. Tribal man, McLuhan further explains in *Understanding Media*, "freely extended the form of his body to include the universe. Acting as an organ of the cosmos, tribal man accepted his bodily functions as modes of participation in the divine energies."

This participation also strongly encourages a sense of tribal attachment to one's people precisely because there is no privacy in acoustic space: it is impossible to act as an individual who is separated from nature or society. As McLuhan shows, "Tribal, non-literate man, living under the intense stress on auditory organization of all experience, is, as it were, entranced," or intensely involved with his people within a cosmic order. The ear cannot detach itself from sound any more than a person can leave his tribe. Without this detachment, the tribal human being perceives all time in terms of the present: what happens now is the most important reality precisely because one has to live up constantly to one's sharply defined (and unchanging) role in the cosmos. "For archaic or tribal man, in acoustic space, there is no past, no history—always present," as the McLuhans write in *Laws of Media*. Put simply, McLuhan associates a sense of time as simultaneous (all-at-once) with the "auditory field" characteristic of oral traditions.

None of these claims should suggest that an oral civilization is shallow. An oral tradition, according to McLuhan, can achieve an understanding of the "total, unified field," after all. Because it lacks the means to preserve tradition through the written word, the memorization of stories and histories is essential. What McLuhan calls the tribal "encyclopedia" that every member of the tribe memorized "made education a sort of 'singing commercial.'" For this reason, McLuhan observes, "Natives are often bewildered by their literate teachers and ask: 'Why do you write things down? Can't you remember?'"

The involvement of the tribal human being with an all-encompassing cosmic order exacts a psychic toll. Although McLuhan, we have seen, is critical of a false sense of detachment that deceives human beings into believing that they master their environment from a safe distance, a lack of detachment poses its own problems. From a tribal-oral vantage point, the universe is as it appears to be at a given moment: all time is present time. For this reason, there is an absence of what McLuhan calls "perspective," or cognitive distance from the universe. Yet this apparent clarity about intense involvement with the workings of the universe does not mean that there is an absence of conflict or violence in the tribal cosmos. Because the universe is considered sacred or divinely ordered, the tribal person is under tremendous pressure to serve this order by paying constant attention to its cycles and rhythms. "To the oral man the literal is inclusive, contains all possible meanings and levels," McLuhan observes in *The Gutenberg Galaxy*. Given the intense involvement that this mentality encourages, the tribal man cannot relax or be indifferent to anything that happens in nature, for everything is subject to its authority. Because the ear is "hypersensitive," detachment is elusive. In other words, a fixed point of view (what McLuhan alternately calls a "vanishing point") is impossible for cultures that have not separated the visual sense from other senses. As McLuhan explains in *Understanding Media*, "Primitive man lived in a much more tyrannical cosmic machine than Western literate man has ever invented," because the former obeys time; he does not create it. Whereas tribal man obeyed a "cosmic clock" based on the cycles of nature, modern man invented a clock to visibly measure and control time.

To exist as if time in the cosmic order is all-encompassing and simultaneous goes hand in hand with the tribalist insistence that everyone fulfills a purpose in this order. McLuhan applies the insights of the classicist Eric A. Havelock in this context. According to Havelock, an oral-tribal society demands strict conformity in speech, deed, and thought. Private or individual identity is inconceivable. Even the slightest deviation affects the entire tribe. As McLuhan contends in a 1968 essay on fashion, "No one in a tribe can act, even exist, without affecting everyone else." The pressure to conform with nature is inescapable, a duty that the tribal leadership requires of every member. The cohesion of the tribe ideally reflects the unity of the universe.

This unity goes hand in hand with a fatalistic resignation to the workings of nature, which society inevitably imitates. For this reason, historical change itself is of little interest to tribalists living in a "total field of simultaneous relations" precisely because they have no control over change that happens all at once, independent of their agency. Tribal man must also wear what McLuhan calls a "stolid mask," one that does not show emotion lest he "release a chain reaction that might shatter the togetherness of the tribe." This fatalism does not mean that change is impossible in this order. If the cosmos demands change all at once, then the tribe must mirror this change. Tribal man, McLuhan contends, "conceives of each person as containing, simultaneously, many selves, all in flux, yet each present." The problem is that this flux is not subject to the control of lowly mortals. It is no wonder that McLuhan saw terror as "the normal state of any oral society, for in it everything affects everything all the time."

Writing, Individuality, and Privacy in History

According to McLuhan, the phonetic alphabet is the "break boundary between tribal and individualist man." With the rise of writing, which the alphabet first made possible in Egypt around 2000 BCE, human beings developed an awareness of the difference between what is independent of their existence and what is within their control. Because human beings could make or create words for the first time, they gradually began to understand their separation from the order of things. This distance opened up an awareness of freedom or the capacity to live apart from the cosmic order, however awkwardly. Out of this momentous shift arose the concept of individual responsibility, which posed a deadly threat to tribalism. This break boundary, McLuhan explains, entailed "the point at which individuals began to be held responsible and accountable for their 'private actions.' That was the moment of the collapse of tribal collective authority."

This new focus on making words raised unprecedented questions about the relation between a divinely sanctioned order and human agency. Although the phonetic alphabet was not the only form of writing, it was unique for inspiring a new focus on the visual sense, which insisted on visible evidence for one's understanding of the universe. Whereas oral culture, existing in acoustic space, treats involvement with nature as sufficient proof for a natural order, literate culture existing in visual space seeks verifiable ways of demonstrating whether such an order exists. As McLuhan quipped, phonetic writing gave tribal man "an eye for an ear."

This gift kept on giving. Because the visual sense encouraged a desire for evidence, it also enabled a limited sense of detachment from the universe. One can gather evidence and reject spurious claims if one is acting as an individual who is separate from the cosmos to some degree. For this reason, McLuhan credits the alphabet with bringing into being the "interior monologue," the state of self-reflection made possible by a psychic withdrawal from the world. Like any technological revolution, these effects of the alphabet were transformative. The ancient Greeks, McLuhan observes, developed an idea of "common sense," a faculty that organizes the interaction of the senses with each other and consciousness. Of course, this distinction presupposes a separation between nature—the senses—and thought. McLuhan and his son Eric credit Aristotle with the insight that nature is unintelligible unless one has left behind the "savage or barbaric" first nature to embrace an "individualized and civilized" second nature. (I discuss the differences between the two natures in greater detail in chapter 6.)

The discovery of an individual identity threatened the tribal order's insistence on unity or togetherness within a coherent natural order. This discovery, in McLuhan's judgment, was "terrifying and altogether shattering," as the story of Oedipus Rex illustrated. Oedipus's discovery, as an individual, "that all men were bound so intimately to one another as to be in effect living in a perpetual incest" dealt a near-fatal blow to the tribalist order.

Nevertheless, McLuhan is certain that civilization is "entirely the product of phonetic literacy." Without the written word, there is no metaphor, symbolic language with which one can interpret (as opposed to taking literally) the cosmos. "Metaphor" comes from the Greek word *metapherein*, meaning "to bear or carry across." It is identical in meaning to the Latin word *transferre*, "to transfer." With this meaning in mind, McLuhan contends that civilization begins with the "transfer" of human beings from the world of nature to the world of language. To accept the universe as it is given is to rely on one's natural impulses, a posture that McLuhan warns against: "Until men translated these magical vocal gestures into visual terms, they went in awe and fear of their ordinary breath, their 'winged words.'" Symbolism (from the Greek *symbolon*, meaning "sign"), which is the art form that seeks meaning in an artifact beyond its immediate image, would be impossible without ancient Greek civilization. The genius of symbolism is, according to McLuhan, to "break things into bits and reassemble them into patterns." This process, which is essential to art and poetry as well as science, is impossible unless one is detached, to some extent, from the universe. One cannot understand the hidden effects of human activity if one is uninterested in moving beyond custom and nature. Writing, McLuhan once noted, "turned a spotlight on the high, dim Sierras of speech. . . . It lit up the dark."

Nevertheless, McLuhan's use of simultaneity reminds us that no new period of media ever completely banishes an old one. The tribal preoccupation with the practices of orality did not completely vanish with the rise of writing. The history of ancient Greek philosophy demonstrates this dynamic. In McLuhan's view, Socrates, as presented by his student Plato, introduced the fateful distinction between mind and heart. He "stood on the border between that oral world and the visual and literate culture. But he wrote nothing." Plato also revealed his sympathy with oral tradition by retaining the tribal dream of living in a polis where every citizen "could hear the voice of a public speaker." Still, the new hegemony of the visual sense inspired the philosophies of Plato and Aristotle, who, as literate Greeks, invented the abstraction of *phusis* (Nature) as distinct from *chaos*, the "buzzing confusion" of the sensory world. In the process, they drew a metaphysical distinction between eternity and the changeable. Plato's warning about the impact of writing reflects this distinction. In his dialogue *The Phaedrus*, Plato (through the voice of Socrates) refers to the mythical story of the Egyptian god Theuth, who brought the gift of writing to King Thamus. He recounts this story to warn about the effect of this new medium on the memory: creating forgetfulness in the souls of human beings. Thus, he cautions, they will possess not wisdom but only "the conceit of wisdom." This "conceit" is a mere appearance of the truth, not the permanent truth that philosophers desire to know. According to McLuhan, the "visual mimesis" that writing makes possible must have struck Plato as "an impoverishment of Being." Plato reveals his preoccupation with awareness of the permanent, which writing discourages precisely because it does not require the memory to preserve tradition or history, as is the case in oral cultures. In brief, mortals will forget everything, lose the ability to defend themselves in dialogue, and seek no permanent truth as long as they are able to write it all down. Plato's nod to the tribalist preoccupation with memory is ironic, given the fact that he wrote dialogues, which, McLuhan notes, "come out of an oral rather than a literary culture."

Despite Plato's warning about writing, McLuhan reads him and his great student Aristotle as the first philosophers determined to "purify the tribal encyclopedia" by converting it to written form. Yet he faults Plato for showing "no awareness here or elsewhere of how the phonetic alphabet had altered the sensibility of the Greeks; nor did anybody else in his time or later." This tough judgment arises from McLuhan's perception that even the most sophisticated Greek philosophers lacked not only an understanding of technological change but also an appreciation for the human talent to make and create things (including technologies). By emphasizing the superiority of the permanent, Plato and his heirs attribute little value to what is changeable, which includes the artifacts that human beings create.

At the beginning of *Take Today*, McLuhan and Nevitt write, "Since Plato, philosophers and scientists have attributed constant forms and patterns of action only to the world of 'Nature.'" As a result, these thinkers have ignored the world that human beings actually make, refusing "to recognize any patterns of energy arising from man-made technologies." The irony of this indifference is that Plato does not acknowledge his own act of creation or making. In *The Phaedrus*, as we have seen, he uses writing to condemn the effects of writing! It is doubly ironic that Plato puts written words into the mouth of Socrates, who philosophized through dialogue and never wrote any works of philosophy. This dialogue is not the only work of Plato's in which he is caught in a contradiction of his own making, pointing out the limits of writing through the medium of the written word. In his *Seventh Epistle*, his description of how the teacher and his student jointly pursue the truth casts considerable doubt on the utility of writing: "There is no writing of mine about these matters, nor will there ever be one.

For this knowledge is not something that can be put into words like other sciences; but after long-continued intercourse between teacher and pupil, in joint pursuit of the subject, suddenly, like light flashing forth when a fire is kindled, it is born in the soul and straightaway nourishes itself." (Despite McLuhan's critique of Plato's animus toward writing, he still makes use of Plato's insights into human ignorance. See chapter 9.)

In McLuhan's analysis, Plato also fails to show how his usage of writing is a creation that is just as changeable as any act of human making. By ignoring the full effects of phonetic literacy, he does not acknowledge that his own understanding of nature or the permanent is enabled by the philosophical distance that literacy makes possible. In the process, Plato and his successors studied a permanent reality that they helped to construct. As McLuhan and Nevitt explain, "Having invented 'Nature' as a world of rigorous order and repetition, they studied and observed only 'natural' forms as having power to shape and influence psyche and society." Although Nature itself became a work of art in antiquity, this was not understood at the time. It was not until the Middle Ages, McLuhan observes, that the world of *phusis* appears as "an extension of the glorified art of the scribe lay ahead."

Plato's devaluation of the world of making is echoed in the philosophy of his student Aristotle, who also contends that the creations of humanity should be *like* nature. After quoting Aristotle (from his work *The Physics*) on how art should imitate nature as much as possible, McLuhan and Wilfred Watson conclude in *From Cliché to Archetype* that "Aristotle thus confirms the sacred quality of the cliché or artifact by aligning it with the cosmic forces." Put differently, we mortals should be like the cosmos as much as possible. This striving to mimic nature reveals Aristotle's preference for simile over metaphor, a distinction that parallels his focus on matching at the expense of making. As we have seen, McLuhan teaches that metaphor is a human innovation that would be impossible without some detachment from the universe. Moreover, all words are metaphors or human creations. Yet Aristotle seeks to match creation with nature, without recognizing that the human understanding of nature is itself a creation or metaphor. Metaphors can be understood only in relation to other metaphors or artifacts. In contrast, simile focuses on imitating a reality that is presumably external to human making or creation. In the argot of McLuhan, simile is preoccupied with the figure of nature without attending to its ground, which is a human creation. As he and Bruce R. Powers explain in *The Global Village*, Aristotle's approach to nature "is descriptive rather than structural or perceptual."

In the same work, McLuhan and Powers render this sweeping judgment on why "the fact that the mind of man is structurally active in all human artifacts and hypotheses" received sparse attention from the greatest Hellenic intellects, who showed little interest in technological change. In brief, Plato and Aristotle were determined to match their philosophies with what they perceived to be nature. Yet these perspectives are contingent on a detachment from nature, which is the result of making (not matching).

Predicting History through Formal Causality

Despite its preoccupation with matching reality, the age of writing provided an important pathway toward understanding the coexistence of past, present, and future. Aristotle articulated the idea of formal causality, a metaphysical notion that had a profound influence on McLuhan. As Aristotle explains in his *Metaphysics* (983a–b), every object has four causes: the formal cause (its essence, or what makes it what it is), the material cause (what it is made of), the efficient cause (what directly created it), and the final cause (its end or purpose). Unlike the other causes, formal cause helps human beings understand the effects of a phenomenon before they occur. Consistent with the idea of simultaneity, the study of formal causality helps us understand the future before it happens. In the words of the McLuhans, "Formal cause is coercive, not passive. It *makes* the thing. It, as it were, shoves it into *being*, and it makes it be *thus*." Put simply, formal causality reveals the form of what something is, including its potential effects on the world. With its focus on the effects that spring from the essence of something, formal causality is a philosophical restatement of "the medium is the message." The medium is the form that dramatically alters the message.

Why do the other modes of causality fail to achieve this effect? Material, efficient, and final causes presuppose visual space, or the empirical verification of a phenomenon's effect after it happens. These causes are easy to understand. A material cause is very intelligible because one can point to the material that constitutes an object: a desk is made of wood. An efficient cause poses no mystery because it is simple to trace an effect back to its direct cause: the carpenter made the desk. A final cause answers the question of why the object is created: a desk's function is to enable human beings to do their work in an orderly fashion. All of these causes are intelligible to the visual (or empirical) sense. Moreover, all of them focus on the object as *figure*, minus the ground or environment.

The ancient Greek search for a permanent reality discouraged awareness of the full implications of formal causality, which emphasizes the importance of predicting change. Unlike the other types of causality, it does not operate in a sequential or linear fashion. In *Laws of Media*, the McLuhans briefly observe that "the Greeks made no entelechies (forms) or observations of the effects of man-made technology, but only of what they considered the objects of the natural world." (*Entelechia*, the Greek term for the realization of something's potential, captures the meaning of formal causality.) In "A Garbage Apocalypse," McLuhan refers to the indifference that Greek philosophers displayed toward the myriad ways in which human beings can transform the world. Although these thinkers carefully studied and classified the "vortices of energy," or entelechies, which were observable through nature, they excluded from their study "all those forms of energy generated by the extension of man's own being."

An additional explanation that McLuhan offers for this inattention lay in the dualistic opposition that Greek philosophy imposed on the relation between matter and form. Dualisms, unlike paradoxes, obey the law of noncontradiction, which denies that something and its opposite may be equally valid. (See chapter 8.) As McLuhan explained in private correspondence, the "biggest discovery" that he ever made was that this dualism impeded a proper understanding of technology in antiquity. Because this distinction privileged the eternal nature of form above the temporal flux of matter, Western philosophy ended up excluding "*techne* from its meditations" as well as a serious treatment of entelechy. If matter is inferior to form, why should one care about the material realm in which human beings exist and create?

The importance of formal causality lies in the fact that it reminds humanity of its awesome responsibility for the effects of technology. Just as the reader is the formal cause of a poem, a user of technology is its formal cause. As Eric McLuhan explains, "That is, and I believe this to be crucial, absent human agency or intellect there is no formal cause at all." The study of effects before they happen expands human freedom. As long as human beings make a serious effort to anticipate the trajectory of a new medium, they can control or mitigate its effects. The alternative is rear-view mirror thinking, the tendency to understand these effects long after a technology has taken root. The fact that the form or formal cause of an object reveals an inherent tendency or bias (to use Innis's term) toward an effect does not mean that it fulfills an unavoidable destiny. To use the example of the desk, this object indirectly enables an environment that encourages stationary or sedentary workplaces. In other words, formal cause is the only mode of causality that invites a study of the ground that a medium potentially creates. McLuhan thus doubts that even Aristotle understood the full implications of his own idea of formal cause, especially what it could reveal about the effects of new media. In McLuhan's judgment, it was not until the studies of Eric Havelock and Harold Innis during the electric age that formal causality received the attention that it deserved.

Formal causality fits well into the electric age of instant information because one can more easily predict the effects of a new medium when it moves at the speed of light. Yet McLuhan also urges the users and makers of media to employ formal causality not just for the sake of knowing the future but also in order to create a future that is humane. For McLuhan and Powers, the real question "that could be asked was not whether it was possible to create something but whether it was desirable in human terms." Unfortunately, even the most powerful figures in the worlds of economic and politics rarely ask this question.

4
REAR-VIEW MIRROR POLITICS

"Politics offers yesterday's answers to today's questions," McLuhan writes in *The Medium Is the Massage*. This pithy summary of what he calls rear-view mirror thinking is perfectly understandable in an age of rapid technological change. As he and Parker observe in *Through the Vanishing Point*, for human beings "to recoil from these new environments and to rely on the rear-view mirror as a kind of repeat or *ricorso* of the preceding environment" is unsurprising. The problem is that this instinctive response ensures "total disorientation at all times." McLuhan also carefully avoids claiming that one age of media is superior to another. His focus is on the danger of judging one medium according to the standards of another medium: "It is not that there is anything wrong with the old environment, but it simply will not serve as navigational guide to the new one." The current state of US politics is not exempted from this familiar pattern.

Although McLuhan admired the dynamism of US society, he often indicated that even forward-looking Americans end up judging their political identity and institutions according to an obsolete set of traditions and practices. As a Canadian who lived most of his life outside the United States, McLuhan thought that this vantage point was an advantage that enabled an accurate understanding of the republic. The border between the two nations, he and Powers explain, is "an interval of resonance," not a barrier. At its best, Canada acts as an "anti-environment" to the worldly environment that its powerful neighbor has become. An anti-environment always makes another environment intelligible. As such, Canada can serve as a Distant Early Warning (DEW) system that can inform the US about dangers that otherwise remain invisible to its citizenry. Canada's proximity to its southern neighbor enables Canadians to share "the American way without commitment to American goals or responsibilities," a perspective that "makes the Canadian intellectually detached and observant as an interpreter of the American destiny." What did this Canadian philosopher perceive about US politics that is imperceptible to many Americans? How did he avoid being the fish in the water?

The United States' Identity Crisis

According to McLuhan, there are two features of the American identity that receive little attention in most political debates. First, the US is a nation with eighteenth-century institutions, which have been unable to address the changes that occurred during the nineteenth and twentieth centuries. Because of the nation's eighteenth-century origins, McLuhan believes that it continues to make "desperate efforts to live" in the electric age. Second, the republic is unique for beginning "its national existence as a centralized and literate political entity." Despite its image as a technologically dynamic nation, many of its citizens and leaders still look for its identity through the rear-view mirror and see only the age of the Enlightenment. Even though this defining period of modernity is long gone, the rhetoric and philosophy of this age resonate mythically with the American consciousness. The Enlightenment's focus on individualism, rationality, and mass literacy created a fixed identity in the republic. According to McLuhan and Nevitt, "Anything that is not visually oriented and rationally processed threatens the entire American way of life. Therefore, it is un-American." Moreover, the United States' status as the first literate nation makes it "least able to confront the advent of electric technology, which contradicts every facet of specialist rational order."

Although McLuhan is not claiming that mass literacy in the US existed in the late eighteenth century (which was hardly the case), he is suggesting that the historic association of literacy with private individuality is central to the American identity. It is also difficult to maintain these values or practices in the electric age, which is indifferent to both literacy and privacy. Therefore, it is understandable that many Americans, in accord with the logic of the rear-view mirror, seek reassurance in a past that is already obsolete. Even the most forward-looking individuals will attempt to retrieve a mythical past that does not bear much resemblance to the present. In McLuhan's words, "As we begin to react in depth to the social life and problems of our global village, we become reactionaries. Involvement that goes with our instant technologies transforms the most 'socially conscious' people into conservatives."

It is unsurprising, McLuhan emphasizes, that people who live in an age of rapid change rediscover tradition and conservatism. The pithy phrase "Novelty causes Antiquity" captures this sentiment. The perspective of a reactionary, however, does not guarantee an accurate understanding of this change. As long as the reactionary confuses the present with what he spies in the rear-view mirror, he unconsciously judges the present in terms of the distant past. Understandable as this temptation is, McLuhan warns that we must be aware of its distorting effects on our understanding of media. Nostalgia, after all, comes from a "loss of identity" that is not fully understood or recognized by those who assume that the identity in question still endures. Evidence for this tendency appears in the language of conservatives who insist that the ideals of the American founding are timeless, that they are as relevant to the electric and digital ages as they were to the print age from which they emerged. This inattention to the specific origin and context of these ideals only helps to obscure how much change—especially technological change—has occurred in the United States since the eighteenth century.

The Politics of Print

Although McLuhan did not study US conservatism in detail, his occasional thoughts help us grasp the politics of the rear-view mirror. As we have seen, he understands the United States as the first literate nation. Yet he also emphasizes that the republic's admirable celebration of literacy makes it unable to grasp the full effects of electric (now digital) media. In other words, the US was founded as a republic that was fully committed to the hegemony of print media. The failure to understand this elementary historical truth generates confusion among today's conservatives who are outraged by the fact that most Americans are indifferent to the values and principles that defined the republic's founding. As the conservative journalist Glenn Ellmers writes, "Practically speaking, there is almost nothing left to conserve. What is actually required now is a recovery, or even a refounding, of America as it was long and originally understood but which now exists only in the hearts and minds of a minority of citizens." Is this refounding possible in a postliterate age?

As McLuhan noted in an interview in 1970, "Individualism, in the old nineteenth-century sense, has been scrubbed right off our culture, and many people find themselves completely bewildered by this change." Individualism, or the creation of a private identity, is inseparable from the age of print. In fact, there is no concern for this identity beyond a literate culture. "With print," McLuhan writes in *Understanding Media*, "the private life became of the utmost concern to readers." Looking at the North American context, he contends that the end of literacy as the driving value of culture goes hand in hand with the end of bourgeois individualism and privacy. McLuhan's conclusion is that "private identity has been dissolved. There are no more private people in North America. There are only groups." Despite this revolutionary transformation of a rugged individualistic republic into a group-driven democracy, conservatives display their nostalgia for the lost age of print by making assumptions that overstate the enduring relevance of the founding era.

In an interview with the English literary critic Frank Kermode in 1965, McLuhan reflected on the Republican senator Barry Goldwater's ill-fated bid for the presidency in 1964. Goldwater's desire to restore limited government, McLuhan commented, was a classic example of rear-view mirror thinking: "The Goldwater mood, as it is called, is an attempt to rediscover the old blueprint of culture that they started out with in the eighteenth century, to get back to the old ground rules of culture." He added that this attempt at rediscovery might even help Americans understand their country "in much greater depth than it was ever founded in," even though this attempt "is disturbing the whole image of the American at the present time." McLuhan sought to aid in this process of rediscovery with the proviso that one cannot retrieve the past simply by echoing its rhetoric.

The eighteenth-century mind, as McLuhan interprets it, assumed that only a literate public could treasure a republican regime and its dedication to moral equality. "One obvious feature of the printed book is its republicanism," he observes. "The page of print is not only a leveller of other forms of expression; it is a social leveller as well. Anyone who can read has at least the illusion of associating on equal terms with anyone who has written." This leveling effect reveals the paradox that the individualism that arose out of the eighteenth century also laid the foundation for a particular type of individual—that is to say, a literate one—who studied ideas from the vantage point of rational detachment. As David Hume once put it, "A man reads a book or pamphlet alone and coolly. There is none present from whom he can catch the passion by contagion. He is not hurried away by the force and energy of action." This calmness or dispassion, as the historian Garry Wills has shown, was a pivotal expectation of founders such as Alexander Hamilton and James Madison, who insisted that there be a "cooling off period" during political debates that might otherwise turn unduly acrimonious in the fledgling republic (as they often did).

Anyone who seeks to restore the literate age needs to acknowledge that literacy and its attendant values are not natural phenomena. Rather, they are specific to a historical period. As we have seen, civilizations based on orality alone have always existed. To make matters worse for those who seek to preserve tradition in an age of change, the only way to do so is through the printed word. Building on the ideas of Harold Innis, McLuhan contends that print media are time oriented, or inclined toward the conservation of ideas. In sharp contrast, the age of space-oriented media seeks to conquer distances through instantaneous communication. This media environment makes the restoration of the past impossible, although it certainly fuels nostalgia. The rear-view mirror temptation to judge the present in terms of the past can easily lead to the erroneous conclusion that an idea has outlived its original historical context. More specifically, the hegemonic authority of an idea, as McLuhan constantly shows, reflects the power of a particular medium at the time. Ideas that emerged in the age of print are unlikely to enjoy the degree of influence in the digital age that they once possessed.

One example of what McLuhan describes as the values embedded within a literate culture can be found in *The Federalist* (1787–88), a series of newspaper articles that argued for the ratification of the new US Constitution. In Federalist No. 2, John Jay celebrates the fact that "Providence has been pleased to give this one connected country to one united people—a people descended from the same ancestors, speaking the same language, professing the same religion, attached to the same principles of government, very similar in their manners and customs," all of which enabled the establishment of "general liberty and independence." In short, Jay saw no contradiction between the value of liberty and the importance of unity on matters of culture, faith, and politics. As the political philosopher Leo Strauss argued, both the First Amendment and the US Constitution were a "product of the eighteenth-century" precisely because their authors shared the conventional belief of the time that freedom presupposed considerable agreement on matters such as religion. Believers were free to worship as they saw fit; unbelievers were not free to avoid worship altogether. In Strauss's words, "Tolerance means for all practical purposes tolerance for every religion, but not for *irreligion*." McLuhan would be the first to point out here that the paradox of freedom coexisting with conformity is a feature of a modern literate culture.

It is unsurprising that the first literate nation-state in history required, as Jay insisted, considerable homogeneity among a citizenry dedicated to natural rights, individualism, and the patriotic love of country. Even before the dawn of the Enlightenment, the fact that the printing press made possible the reading of books in the vernacular also facilitated the rise of mass conformity. People from the same culture could read the same books in the same language. In fact, individualism is inseparable from this sense of conformity or sameness. The "melting pot" of the nineteenth century paradoxically demanded that all new immigrants conform to the standards of bourgeois individuality or morality. The values specific to this era were naturally identified as the universal values of humanity. In McLuhan's words, "The literate liberal is convinced all real values are private, personal, individual."

The "scabrous paradox" that McLuhan associates with the literate age leads to apparently contradictory effects such as the drilling of soldiers, the rise of private initiative, and a politically homogeneous population. There is nothing mysterious, he argues, about the reversal that occurs "when Western man fought the harder for individuality as he surrendered the idea of unique personal existence." Print media created a "Public," which consisted of "separate individuals, each with his own point of view." (In contrast, electric media create a "Mass" of individuals who are "profoundly involved in one another.") This conformity fosters the side effect that the literate mind attributes almost magical power to ideas, as McLuhan stated in an interview in 1977. "The literate man," he declared, "is the natural sucker for propaganda."

Because the American Revolution and founding were based on philosophical principles, the first citizens of the republic had an appreciation for ideas, a practice that is an obvious manifestation of a print culture. Jay takes this attitude for granted when he writes that "the people must cede to it (the federal government) some of their natural rights, in order to vest it with requisite powers." This knowledge of natural rights should, ideally, lead to the conclusion that the practical application of these rights is best accomplished under a federal system of centralized government, not divided confederacies. Despite the tensions over the limits of rights and state power that have emerged throughout US history, it would not surprise McLuhan that Jay and other founders exemplified a fixed viewpoint, one that assumes in this case that the American people would think and act as literate citizens for the duration of the republic. Although this viewpoint, McLuhan notes, "can be collective or individual or both, causing great diversity of clash and outlook," the "written-visual fixity of the American Constitution" is designed to put an end, ideally, to the need for any future revolutionary change. In short, the original intent of the founders assumed that the hegemony of literate values would remain unaltered. It is safe to assume that the founders did not anticipate a time when most members of Congress would refrain from reading the texts of important bills.

McLuhan warns against the conflation of nostalgia with an accurate grasp of history and technological change. In contrast, many American conservatives insist that the founding tenets of the republic are eternally true and valid, regardless of historical context. The very suggestion that the founders endorsed the dominant assumptions of their age, as opposed to eternal truths that are valid for every age, is, to these conservatives, a false and dangerous notion. Robert R. Reilly, for example, has warned against the doctrine of historicism, which teaches that there are no eternal standards outside of history. "Gone are the tenets that Nature and reason are *not* temporal and that they supply truths which are right everywhere and always."

Given McLuhan's focus on the relation between ideas and technological change, it is unsurprising that some of his critics have classified his own work as an embodiment of this historicism. Yet he would reject the crude historicist view that historical context dominates humanity in a monocausal manner. He would also likely respond that human beings create (and are created by) history, to recall Marx. We act on history as much as history acts on us. When we read the eternal truths of the Bible, for example, it is important to understand how God, humanity, and the world, McLuhan writes, "subsist together, and act and react upon one another at the same time." History is not some frozen reality that dictates the destiny of passive human beings. Rather, it happens simultaneously, shaping and being reshaped by human agency. For these reasons, McLuhan follows Vico in the avoidance of what Vico calls "imaginative universals"—namely, spurious claims that a historical artifact is identical to a universal truth. (This mentality reflects what Vico elsewhere calls the "conceit" of scholars, as I have already noted.) Every universal archetype begins with a specific cliché, as McLuhan and Wilfred Watson emphasize throughout *From Cliché to Archetype*.

What is critically important to understand, McLuhan always cautions, is how the history of media shapes ideas in ways that even experienced scholars do not appreciate. The contemporary conservative dream of restoring the old US republic mirrors a lack of interest in the importance of literacy in the eighteenth century, a reality that helps to explain the love of philosophical ideas in that historical period. The American political scientist James W. Ceaser perhaps unwittingly exemplifies this mentality. He praises the founders for making the momentous "turn from History to Nature." In the process, they elevated the power of philosophical principles to a level not seen before in history. "This shift in foundations," according to Ceaser, "marked a revolution in the realm of ideas that was as momentous as were the events at Lexington and Concord in the realm of politics. It was the thought heard around the world." Although McLuhan would agree with the novelty of a revolution that privileges ideas over traditions, it is Ceaser's next claim that would provoke his disagreement: "Americans were the first to bring nature down from the realm of philosophy and introduce it into the political world as a foundation of a full nation." The public philosophy that resulted from this momentous event referred to the authority of nature for a very specific reason. Nature, Ceaser writes, "refers to the permanent and unchanging character of things." McLuhan would likely respond that this inattention to the historical or temporal reflects what Innis calls a space-oriented bias, which seeks the end of all barriers between cultures and civilizations. Although he never suggests that the bias toward time is necessarily superior to a bias toward space, it is important to understand how each bias can shape one's understanding of history.

This devaluation or denial of historical context is an important premise in current American conservative thought. As Sohrab Ahmari explains, many voices on the right elevate the documents of the founding "to the status of holy writ." Referring to this attitude as "Founders-ism," Ahmari argues that "it is a sin in some conservative circles to treat the Founding as the product of a given material conjuncture, reflecting the power relations of its time, even as it also reflects the high genius of some of the greatest practical statesmen who ever lived." This kind of textual fundamentalism that Ahmari describes, McLuhan would be the first to point out, is unintelligible apart from print culture. The danger inherent in this rear-view mirror thinking is that it does not take into account the monumental changes that have displaced the hegemony of print since the eighteenth century.

Americans on the political right who lament what they take to be the persistent influence of liberalism are similarly oblivious to the near vanishing of the technological preconditions that made liberalism possible in the first place. The conservative academic Patrick Deneen has denounced the nineteenth-century liberal philosopher John Stuart Mill's classic *On Liberty* (1859) for identifying "liberty" with ideals that threaten to dissolve conservative community and tradition. In Deneen's words, "Liberty was never its main object; rather, liberty was the mechanism that would transform a traditional, bottom-up social order into a top-down progressive liberal regime. His text sought to align the extant liberal political order, based in theories of radical individual autonomy, with a yet-unrealised progressive social order dominated by those at liberty to engage in ever-more radical 'experiments in living.'" Deneen is looking through the same rear-view mirror as conservatives who seek a return to the ideals of the eighteenth century. His analysis ignores the fact that Mill counted on the longevity of a *literate* citizenry that would engage in reading, discussion, and rigorous debate in the marketplace of ideas, in the hope that some measure of truth and "progress" would be the happy result of this intellectual exchange. A democracy that no longer looks to print media as the source of truth was not the regime that Mill had in mind. The sort of individualism that could inspire "radical experiments in living" has yielded to postliterate tribalism, which is indifferent or even hostile to the realm of bourgeois privacy that Mill valued. McLuhan predicted in the 1960s that while the emerging tribal society might allow the young to "have free rein to experiment," anyone who violated accepted norms on infidelity and divorce would be banished from the tribe. The #MeToo movement, which emerged in the late 2010s as a campaign against sexual abuse in the entertainment industry, is a stark reminder of how the global village punishes in a very public way powerful individuals who have disregarded these norms. As McLuhan anticipated, there is no such thing as a "private deviation" in a tribal society.

In this context, it is also unsurprising that there are myriad attempts by governments to suppress freedom of speech, including controversial ideas that may spread "misinformation" on the internet. Unlike Mill, so-called "liberal parties" today do not believe that every idea deserves a fair hearing in the marketplace of ideas. In sharp contrast to the Millian principle of equating harm with actual physical violence or clear threats of such violence, the "Online Harms Act" (2024) passed by the Canadian Parliament allows someone who fears being victimized by a "hate crime" to ask a judge to "summon the preemptively accused for a sort of precrime trial." The accused individual need not have committed any crime; he must only provoke the fear of the accuser that he *may* commit one. Despite this legislation having been introduced by a government led by the Canadian Liberal Party, it is hard to spy any trace of the old liberalism within it. If liberalism died with the print age, as McLuhan contends, then Deneen and other antiliberal voices on the right are kicking a dead horse.

The US Enters the Postliterate Age

According to the conservative political scientists Willmoore Kendall and George W. Carey, the authors of the Federalist Papers insisted that all political debates in the new republic would require "*deliberation*, that is, dialogue back and forth among members of the assembly and among the 'branches' of the government, as the be-all-end-all of the democratic process," leading to decisions that, ideally, "will produce the 'sense' (*not* the will) of the people as a whole." But this deliberation would not lead to quick decisions. Kendall and Carey write, "It postpones actual decisions concerning policy issues until a relatively tardy moment in the process of deliberations."

This sort of painstaking deliberation made perfect sense in the founding era, when a fixed viewpoint frowned on the very possibility of rapid and unsettling change. In short, the "tardy" nature of debate fits the print age very well. As McLuhan pointed out during a conversation with Tom Brokaw and Edwin Newman on the *Today Show* in 1976, the medium of debate is too "hot" for the modern age of television. Commenting on the televised debate between Gerald Ford and Jimmy Carter in 1976, McLuhan blasted the "most stupid arrangement of any debate in the history of debating," precisely because those who set up this event failed to grasp that "TV is not a debating medium." Instead "they had arranged it as if it were a newspaper set-up or a radio set-up." As we have seen, McLuhan describes radio and newspapers as hot media because they have the effect of rendering their users passive. Debate works the same way, providing a great deal of information to an audience that simply listens. The hapless debaters themselves, asserted McLuhan, acted as if they were not on TV, "looking absolutely like some straightjacketed characters" while operating within "absolutely the hottest type of medium you could imagine." Only when the technology underpinning the Ford-Carter debate broke down did the audience get involved, McLuhan added.

The fact that debate and print media do not *involve* the audience, McLuhan writes in *The Gutenberg Galaxy*, helps to explain why the "new urban or bourgeois man is centre-margin oriented. That is, he is visual, concerned about appearances and conformity or respectability. As he becomes individual or uniform, he becomes homogeneous." Following the insights of Harold Innis, McLuhan saw the War of Independence as an example of "the clash between centre and margin, which is identical with the conflict between conformity and non-conformity." Once the US republic became the new center, it was possible to find new margins to explore and conquer. (The myth of the frontier validates this desire, as I explain in chapter 7.) This fixed identity, which the bourgeois desire for homogeneity manifests, eventually fosters centralism. It also encourages nationalism, or love of one's nation. From this apparent distance, it becomes possible for the literate mind to fantasize about extending civilization to what McLuhan calls the "most backward areas" of the world and "to the least literate minds." The ability to distinguish between the literate and illiterate also reinforced the idea of progress, which distinguishes between civilized and uncivilized cultures. The mechanized conformity that the print age demanded provoked resistance. The rise of the book club reflects the assumption that everyone should read the same books, despite the fragmented desires of the literate public. As McLuhan notes in *The Mechanical Bride*, the very idea of a book club levels down public taste "until it is taken for granted that a President and his stenographers will read the same books," a desire that fosters only boredom and indifference.

Around the same time that the bourgeoisie was imposing its identity on the rest of the world, the new electric age was undermining this vision. McLuhan observes that the telegraph, the very first electric medium, decentralized the "newspaper world so thoroughly that uniform national views were quite impossible, even before the Civil War." The print age also eventually brought about other side effects that contributed to its dissolution or transformation. The "bourgeois spirit of individual separateness or points of view," McLuhan writes, was ill suited to deal with technologies and ideas that foster "total social involvement." As the newspaper publisher William Randolph Hearst presciently understood, nothing is more involving than a war that the media can report on around the clock, even if a war has to be invented. Hearst famously demonstrated McLuhan's contention that technology has the power "to create its own world of demand" when he allegedly told a reporter covering the 1898 insurrection in Cuba, "You furnish the pictures. I'll furnish the war."

The sense of privacy that accompanies the bourgeois mind does not come naturally to human beings who may crave community or membership within a tribe. The psychological pressures that result from living as a private self are unsettling. One effect is apparent in the history of the print age, as McLuhan explains. The bourgeois mind's desire to reconcile individualism and conformity did not succeed in the long run. In private, one can practice "habits of individualism," while in public one must embrace a "role of absolute conformity." This outward conformity allows one to engage in "inner deviation," or the committing of crimes in thought. Reflecting on the identity politics of the postbourgeois era, McLuhan still credited the age of print with creating an identity that eludes the electric age. (See chapter 8.)

The focus of the nineteenth century on the mechanization of human existence eventually inspired growing opposition to the bourgeois preoccupation with individual responsibility. Instead, according to McLuhan, "the entire attention of men turned to the associative and the corporate," as the machine replaced human beings in performing what was once backbreaking toil. What McLuhan means by "the associative and the corporate" refers to an increased appreciation of the interconnectedness of reality, an attitude that clashed with the old distinction between centers and margins. Authority, he declares, is no longer a "one-way pattern."

The breakdown of the center-margin distinction near the end of the bourgeois era is most evident in the transformed image of the US president. The old bourgeois conception of the presidency was that of an office severely limited by the power of Congress. Consistent with the values of the print age, the president was required to uphold the Constitution without exception. While the president was commander in chief of the armed forces, only Congress had the legal power to declare war. Congress also had complete control of the purse strings. Although it is tempting to believe that this original arrangement of power has not changed, McLuhan would caution against focusing on the figure (the founding documents and the institutions of government) while ignoring the ground (the new environment in which the president governs).

According to McLuhan, this "separation of powers had been a technique for restraining action in a centralist structure radiating out to remote margins." Yet the postbourgeois age gradually abolished this distinction. With the advent of radio in the twentieth century, tribalism reemerged as the successor to individualism. Although both print and radio are hot media that provide plenty of content to their users, the radio is still more involving than literature, affecting "most people intimately, person-to-person, offering a world of unspoken communication between writer-speaker and the listener." The effect of radio depends, of course, on how hot or cool the personality on this medium happens to be. Adolf

Hitler, as a tribal man, had a sharply defined or "hot" image that had the same haunting and explosive effect on listeners in Germany as the Orson Welles "War of the Worlds" broadcast in 1938, which triggered mass panic over a Martian invasion. "It was Hitler who gave radio the Orson Welles treatment for *real*," McLuhan notes.

In sharp contrast, the "cool" personality of Franklin Delano Roosevelt had a different effect through the magic of radio. According to McLuhan, FDR was the first president to grasp the hot-cool distinction. Because his enemies in the press portrayed him as a hot character, which was an image that he relished within this medium, he portrayed himself as a cool character on radio through his popular fireside chats. The president "had to hot up the press media against himself in order to create the right atmosphere for his radio chats."

Although McLuhan doubted that either FDR or Hitler had an image suitable for TV, this speculation is less important than the fact that electric media have managed to create a new political leader: the tribal chieftain. McLuhan and Bruce R. Powers predicted that the "last part of this century will see a war of icons not bombs, a conflict governed by impulse, already begun for us by Roosevelt, Churchill, and Stalin at Yalta." Unlike the detached politician whose speeches were read in the newspapers of the bourgeois era, this new leader communicates directly to his listeners. He is involving in a manner that would be inconceivable to the age of print. A leader who gives the impression that his audience is involved in his decision-making is unlikely to have much tolerance for dividing up people according to centers and margins or noting the limits of his power in relation to Congress. Margins are intolerable in the age of space-driven media. The leader in this age, McLuhan said, has to "put on his audience as he would a suit of clothes and become a corporate tribal image—like Mussolini, Hitler, and F.D.R. in the days of radio, and Jack Kennedy in the television era." Whatever their ideological differences, all these leaders "were tribal emperors on a scale theretofore unknown in the world, because they all mastered their media." In the case of FDR, it is hard to explain his political achievement of being reelected three times without attributing some of this success to his acute understanding of different media. It is, however, easy to explain the rise of the imperial presidency in this context. What McLuhan describes as the new "personal and monarchical" style of inclusive presidents is a direct effect of electric media. The simultaneous involvement that a tribal era demands helps to explain why TV networks project a victor in a presidential race before the polls even close.

The risk that a tribal emperor faces is that his audience will think of itself in tribal terms that challenge his shaky authority. Tribalism in this sense blurs the divide between politics and entertainment, realms that were sharply demarcated in the bourgeois print age. As McLuhan predicted in 1966, there is "far more political reality in the Hollywood scene than there ever has been in the so-called political scene." The desire for instant recognition and inclusion has now been fully democratized in the digital age. Whereas the hot medium of radio enhanced the power of the politician along with the passivity of the audience, the coolness of social media creates an inclusive two-way street for dueling tribes. In the all-at-once environment of the electric age, it is unsurprising that politicians court the favor of actors, singers, and athletes. Politicians in the digital age fear celebrities in the entertainment industry who threaten their popularity with a random tweet. In mid-2024, Donald Trump's advisers openly worried about the influence of the popular singer Taylor Swift, a critic of Trump, on her tribe—namely, her millions of fans who might be swayed to vote against him in the November election. For a country that was founded on the values of print and literacy, this is a sea change.

Although Americans are not the only people who see their politicians as chieftains, their system of government is not built for this kind of leadership. Consistent with his focus on rear-view mirror thinking, McLuhan warns that most people rarely notice this transformation until it is too late: "The power of radio to retribalize mankind, its almost instant reversal of individualism into collectivism, Fascist or Marxist, has gone unnoticed." In the case of the United States, a tribalist democracy clashes with the individualism and mass conformity that the bourgeois era once demanded. As he ominously predicted in 1969, the "U.S., which was the first nation in history to begin its national existence as a centralized and literate political entity, will now play the historical film backward, reeling into a multiplicity" of decentralized tribal states.

The managerial, centralized, bureaucratic state, which FDR brought into existence to impose some mass conformity after the breakdown of the bourgeois state during the Great Depression, will also fail to stem the tide of decentralism that tribal groups favor. The mass state will face the demand of debureaucratization, given the fact that tribes and bureaucracy, as McLuhan put it, "are antithetical means of social organization and can never co-exist peacefully; one must destroy and supplant the other, or neither will survive." Rising dissatisfaction with this state currently coincides with the increasing political usage of media for direct communication with the citizenry. Voters who feel powerless in the face of this administrative machinery may desire, according to some analysts, a "Caesar" who can impose his own will on this bloated bureaucracy to act on behalf of the people. Politicians on the left and the right employ X (formerly known as Twitter) to make their case to the voters, presenting themselves as the strong leaders who will take back their country from a corrupt oligarchy that disdains the masses. The current wave of populism is a quest for involvement and participation. Daily tweets by politicians retrieve the fireside chats of the FDR era. Whether these fears or hopes for a new Caesar reflect hysteria would be less important to McLuhan than the fact that these sentiments are appearing at all in the postliterate age. Minus a private self, the "mass man" of the postliterate age wants to merge with everyone else at the speed of light. What could be a more involving or engaging politics than direct communication with an imperial leader in cyberspace? Digitalized populism is the ultimate put-on.

The bourgeois age counted on the power of ideas over a citizenry dedicated to painstaking constitutional deliberation and a restrained presidency. These attitudes reflect the literate age. In an age in which most voters have often refrained from making the effort to read or understand the documents of the founding, the popular preference for charismatic leaders who reflect their own "tribes" or voting blocs suggests that a literate population that prefers deliberation over imagery has vanished. For this reason, the involving nature of the global village yields to the "global theater." This theater, according to McLuhan and Watson, "is the use of public space for 'doing one's thing.'" Like any dramatic performance, this has nothing to do with the decision-making and debates that are supposed to characterize the political realm. Even a child, as McLuhan and Watson note, can understand the reality of the global theater. Instead of believing that the Lord is his shepherd (Psalm 23), the postliterate child looks to this new world and says, "The globe is my theater. I shall not want for parts nor pastures."

The temptation to do "one's thing" on the stage of a theater that is visible to the entire world not only explains the predictable antics of elected politicians who put on a show for their voters through social media but also explains grassroots politics. The politics of statue removal is a case in point. From 2020 onward, protesters across the Western world have removed numerous statues of historic figures on the grounds that these individuals either supported slavery or held racist opinions. The accusers of these figures not only remove these statues in a very public manner, as would befit a theater, but also engage in the rear-view mirror behavior to which McLuhan alludes. The antistatue movement is catching up with the legacy of an institution that was abolished in the United States in the nineteenth century. Now that slavery is a distant memory in the annals of Western civilization, it does not take much moral courage to call for the removal of a statue that is associated with this history. Like any theatrical performance, these removals are purely symbolic. They do not necessarily lead to any improvement in the lives of poor Americans who continue to suffer from the effects of poverty and discrimination.

In accord with the rear-view mirror, the radical Left also judges the US solely according to its racist past. Thus, the purging of figures who opposed and abolished slavery but still fall short of present-day standards of racial equality has begun as well. This activism has been applied to President Abraham Lincoln, whom McLuhan admired (along with Thomas Jefferson) for possessing a mind that was "aristocratic, legalistic, encyclopedic, forensic, habitually expressing itself in the mode of an eloquent wisdom." On Columbus Day in 2020, protesters pulled down a statue of Lincoln in Portland, Oregon. Two years later, a bust of the sixteenth president and a plaque of the Gettysburg Address were removed from a Cornell University library. The leftist social historian Richard Slotkin laments this "indiscriminate iconoclasm" because it makes it more difficult to develop a myth or narrative that could justify the securing of "economic justice for the working and middle classes," based on the inspirational efforts of these same figures, like Lincoln, who combated injustice in their own time. Like McLuhan, Slotkin believes that myth at its best retrieves insights and themes that can enlighten and improve the lives of human beings. At its worst, a myth can selectively ignore the complexity of history altogether.

The best advice that McLuhan gives to counter the pattern of rear-view mirror politics is this brief statement: "Control over change would seem to consist in moving not with it but ahead of it." Yet he never expected this advice to be put into practice. In the postliterate age, it is far more tempting to comprehend technology based on the obsolete patterns of the past rather than the potential effects on the future.

5

MOTHER GOOSE AND PETER PAN EXECUTIVES

One of McLuhan's bedrock assumptions is that the usage of media does not typically coincide with an understanding of their effects. Consistent with this assumption, he further argues that ownership of media does not guarantee understanding. The fact that human beings in the electric and digital ages are involved with media to a degree that is unprecedented in history did not persuade McLuhan that greater awareness of those media's impact was bound to happen. Counterintuitive as it may sound, those who are most involved with the media may often have the least awareness of these subtle influences, particularly if they are looking into the rear-view mirror. As he pointedly asks in *Culture Is Our Business*, "Surely, it is not unbelievable that decision-makers are totally out of touch with the world they live in? How could any contemporary person in any age be entrusted with powers carefully developed and monopolized by people from the previous age?" For this reason, McLuhan urged businesses and corporations to rethink their long relationship to technologies and avoid the assumption that their comprehension of these devices is assured.

From Moralizing to Understanding

McLuhan did not always have these concerns about the disconnect between corporate ownership and understanding of media. In *The Mechanical Bride*, he draws a sharp distinction between businesses that create ads for products and the consumers who passively accept them. The advertising, magazine, and movie industries consciously apply manipulative techniques for the purpose of persuading the masses to buy goods they do not need. McLuhan demonstrates this premise with a format that places various clippings of advertisements and other media alongside McLuhan's critical commentaries that decode the hidden meaning of their messages. Although the style of the book is playful and unconventional, *The Mechanical Bride* (which McLuhan originally entitled *Guide to Chaos*) was meant to be a serious guide to the "chaos" that these media fostered by dulling the critical awareness of consumers so that they would confuse freedom with conformity to the imagery produced by capitalist industry. The real "tyrant" in the early Cold War era, according to McLuhan, was the market researcher who "shepherds his flocks in the ways of utility and market." Writing in the early 1950s, McLuhan was certain that the ad agencies and Hollywood knew what they were doing when they sought the control of the public's unconscious, all for the sake of profit. By flooding "the daytime world of conscious purpose and control with erotic imagery from the night world," these firms succeeded in breaking down the resistance of the consumer. The most effective ads reflected formal causality by "simultaneously anticipating causes with effects and effects with causes." The good news that the book announced was that careful study of these media could help one navigate the vortex of technological change. McLuhan compared the careful student of media to the sailor in Edgar Allan Poe's story "A Descent into the Maelstrom," who survived a violent storm at sea by studying and adjusting to its movements.

As television displaced the hegemony of the printed ad, McLuhan replaced this moralistic attitude toward the owners of media in favor of one that focused on their lack of understanding of the media's unintended effects. The rise of the TV age persuaded him that there was little point in judging capitalists when they themselves were often unaware of the media's full power. As McLuhan writes in *Counterblast*, "The media are not toys; they should not be in the hands of Mother Goose and Peter Pan executives." These corporatists live in a make-believe world where they mistakenly assume that they control the effects of the objects that they create or utilize. Yet harsh moral judgments make sense only if conscious intent is present, as he thought was the case in post–World War II advertising. By the mid-1960s, McLuhan was taking an even tougher line, insisting that the most prestigious and successful corporations had a flawed understanding of their own products and creations. Corporations have no more comprehension of technological change than the scholastic philosophers of early modernity who witnessed the rise of the printed book. Mere self-interest does not guarantee a greater awareness of the process of change unleashed by a company's creations. The successors of Henry Ford in the automobile industry fared no better than he did in grasping this process. As McLuhan pointedly asks in *Understanding Media*,

"Yet does General Motors, for example, know, or even suspect, anything about the effect of the TV image on the users of motorcars?" Even the ad industry that McLuhan once grudgingly admired lacked "any 'literacy' in any medium but its own," reinforcing a somnambulistic ignorance of revolutionary changes wrought by new media.

What exactly do these powerful industries fail to understand about technological change? Like most human beings, corporations focus on the content, not the form, of a new medium. In other words, they do not grasp that the medium is the message. Every new technology creates an environment that reflects primarily its form (or formal cause), not the actual information that it provides. McLuhan faulted Bell Telephone for failing to understand how its product inevitably alters the intended message. With greater understanding of the phone, it could have enhanced education. Because the literate person is visually oriented, the learning of a new language is hard work, given the fact that the act of seeing offers at best fragmented attention. By learning languages along with math and physics through the telephone, one's attention would be more focused or concentrated. McLuhan doubted that this innovative thinking would persuade the masters of the phone industry, given the fact that even more obvious effects of their product eluded their awareness. For example, the phone replaced red-light-district prostitution with the call girl.

McLuhan's post–*Mechanical Bride* focus on the ignorance of corporate executives regarding technology should not imply that he became uninterested in the power that corporate ownership of the media wields. Nor should his willingness to speak to numerous corporate audiences in the 1960s suggest that he became a shill for capitalist interests, as several critics on the left have argued. McLuhan was determined to reach as many audiences as the electric media age allowed. His role as an occasional adviser to corporations did not convert him to the cause of capitalism. In *The Gutenberg Galaxy*, he pointedly quoted "Commodity, the bias of the world" from Shakespeare's play *King John* (act 2, scene 1) to underscore the power of capitalism. In a 1971 letter to Jim Davey, an adviser to Pierre Trudeau, McLuhan complained that "cities are hi-jacked every day by developers who simply pressure the bureaucracy into 'landing' in areas favourable to the developers. Countries can be hi-jacked as readily as a big business."

McLuhan rejects the assumption that ownership of the media guarantees understanding of their effects. In *Understanding Media*, he writes, "Wedded as they [Marxists] are to nineteenth-century industrial technology as the basis of class liberation, nothing could be more subversive of the Marxian dialectic than the idea that linguistic media shape social development, as much as do the means of production." The fact that a medium has properties and effects independent of capitalist power structures usually escapes the notice of scholars who are focused on ownership alone. McLuhan urges scholars to study the mutual interface between one force and another. This task means studying how one institution can influence the other while being influenced in turn. By "interface," McLuhan has in mind the invisible ways in which environments complement or shape one another. Although corporations certainly influence the impact of new media, it is equally true that the environments resulting from these technologies influence corporations in subtle ways.

None of this amounts to a categorical critique of capitalism per se, an ideological project that McLuhan would have associated with the moralistic judgment of his *Mechanical Bride* stage. To be sure, the young McLuhan was sympathetic with the American South's hostility to the soulless and anticommunitarian biases of Northern capitalism. Yet capitalism came with unprecedented benefits as well. Although it turned art into a commodity that robbed it of its critical power, the mass marketing of art also made it accessible to all human beings. In short, "the public became the patron," McLuhan writes in *The Gutenberg Galaxy*. Despite the rapidity of technological change under capitalism, it has become possible for the first time in history to notice and predict these changes with enough effort, given the sheer access to instantaneous information that corporate media make possible.

With their focus on the future, capitalists may pride themselves on understanding the dynamic nature of media better than anybody else does. Steve Jobs, the late CEO of Apple, admitted in an interview shortly before his death in 2012 that he did not allow his own children to use the iPad that he invented, presumably because of its inherent addictive properties (or biases, to use Innis's term). Other tech billionaires have imposed similar restrictions on their children's usage of technology. The Waldorf School of the Peninsula, where the children of Silicon Valley's high-tech bourgeoisie often study, forbids the use of technology in the classroom until seventh grade, precisely because, in the words of the school's directors, "the lure of electronic entertainment in our media-infused society influences the emotional and physical development of children and adolescents on many levels, and can detract from their capacity to create a meaningful connection with others and the world around them." Nevertheless, these billionaires seem unconcerned with the impact that addictive media have on human nature as a whole. In his 1967 article "The Future of Sex," McLuhan takes aim at wealthy futurists like these for assuming that "'human nature' will hold firm. They ignore the fact that technological change has always struck human life right at the heart, changing people just as it changes things." A study of how media leave nothing untouched is imperative, even though it will require participation from those who are not subject to the influence of the technology industries.

Bourgeois Capitalism, the Print Age, and the Bias of Time

The meaning of human nature has always been of great interest to capitalists. The earliest defenders of capitalism insisted that the new market economy is a natural or eternal phenomenon, operating outside history. Yet this assumption ignores that what McLuhan calls the "artificial perception and arbitrary values" that all media foster only appear to be natural, not historical, in origin. McLuhan exposed this ahistorical thinking from the very beginning of his media studies. In *The Mechanical Bride*, he takes note of the tendency within eighteenth- and nineteenth-century classical economics to associate the "laws of the market" with the mathematical universe (or Newtonian laws) that divine providence had sanctioned. According to this ideology, McLuhan explains, "The laws of the market are God's providential and primary machinery for expressing His will to the people."

Despite the seductive fallacy of equating the natural with the historical, it is still possible to cut through this deception. According to McLuhan, capitalism is no more natural than literacy. In fact, one development presupposes the other. In *The Gutenberg Galaxy*, he examines the folly of trying to impose capitalism on oral cultures with strong remnants of feudalism in the twentieth century. Without the transformative effect of the printing press, which enabled the organizing and measuring of reality, the preconditions for modern capitalism could not have emerged. The idea of exchanging commodities through a fixed-price system could not have happened unless these phenomena were treated as if they objectively exist in a self-regulating universe. Thanks to Gutenberg's invention, the saying "Every man has his price" became an irrefutable truth under the circumstances. In short, the print-oriented literate individual or private self was also critical to the rise of capitalism and the bourgeoisie (or property-owning class).

The imposition of capitalism on a literate culture is violent enough. In a Monday-night seminar that McLuhan conducted with Barrington Nevitt in 1977, McLuhan remarked that the Industrial Revolution in Britain was "much bloodier than 1789" in France, given its creation of an economic system "whereby the work ability of anybody could be marketed for money." To this day, capitalists sometimes even celebrate this destructive potential. In May 2024, Apple rolled out its new iPad with a commercial featuring a hydraulic press that crushed musical instruments, art, and other human artifacts. Tribal-oral cultures find it even more difficult to adjust to this mode of production. The psychic involvement with nature that characterizes these cultures discourages the detachment that is needed for capitalism. From a print-oriented perspective, commodities and pricing are uniform and repeatable phenomena that require the private individual to step back and take stock of economic movements that are seemingly beyond his control. Although this fixed point of view unleashed unprecedented wealth, it also required enormous conformity and homogeneity as a precondition to make this system work. As McLuhan notes, "Competition is based on the principle of absolute conformity."

The print age's redefinition of the meaning of time illustrates this pattern of conformity. In tribal-oral cultures, time is cyclical, based on the movements of nature. Time moves humanity along, not vice versa. With the advent of the printing press, it became possible to measure time. In a linear framework it was possible to understand time in terms of a discernible past, present, and future. The measurement of time went hand in hand with the detachment of the bourgeois mind, which saw time as a phenomenon subject to mechanical control. After the invention of the clock in the seventeenth century, the possibility of measuring the time spent in the factory or workplace became a reality. The owners of industry could evaluate their workers according to their punctuality and productivity. Even the private habits of eating and sleeping necessarily accommodated the clock, a dramatic vindication of human subservience to its creations. Time zones fostered uniformity across regions. It was the tyranny of measuring time in sequential units, McLuhan contends, that "damned the bourgeoisie in the nineteenth century," leaving it unprepared to deal with the advent of simultaneous time during the electric age.

The conformity that bourgeois capitalism required from its citizenry had advantages as well as drawbacks. On the positive side, conformity broke down differences between the classes, a phenomenon that was most evident in the United States. Literacy required conformity even within a university setting. As George Santayana put it, "It doesn't matter *what* so long as they all *read* the same thing." According to McLuhan, the wealthiest classes in the nineteenth-century US adhered to the same values as other classes. They abided by the standards of clock time as rigorously as any other class did. Europeans who traveled to the United States during the bourgeois era were shocked to discover that the rich "not only ate cornflakes and hot dogs, but really thought of themselves as middle-class people." None of this was surprising to Americans, who equated equality with conformity in this era.

Yet this conformity came with a psychological toll. The bourgeois mind was forced to live in a dichotomy that juxtaposed money with morals. Just as the print age made the measurement of time actual, it reduced human nature to the status of a measurable machine. The print age, McLuhan notes, had shaped a "new kind of man," one that valued knowledge solely in terms of its utility and application in visual terms. If it could not be visualized (and thus measured), it had little value. The bourgeois inclination to divorce ethics from economics led to other consequences. As McLuhan observes in his 1946 essay "Footprints in the Sands of Crime," the bourgeois mind seemingly solved the dichotomy of money and morals through the slogan "Private Vices, Publick Benefits," the subtitle of Bernard Mandeville's *The Fable of the Bees* (1714). In Mandeville's words, "Thus every part was full of vice / Yet the whole mass a paradise." Despite his satirical intent, this message became the dogma of the rising capitalist class. So long as private self-interest or the desire for money led to measurable benefits for the rest of society, there was no necessary conflict between individual immorality and the common good. As McLuhan explains, "Of course, what men like Swift, Gay, and Mandeville saw as a symbolic monstrosity was seized upon by Adam Smith as a happy formula for solving the Manichean psychological split of the time." This reconciliation persisted so long as people conformed to the "individuality" of the print age.

It was in the interests of early modern capitalists to conserve this bourgeois ethos as a venerable tradition. Because literature "is a relatively time-binding medium," its formal cause encouraged a conservative mentality. So long as literacy was the driving force of capitalist culture, particularly in North America, there was no reason to doubt the endurance of bourgeois civilization. Unfortunately, capitalism is as changeable as the technologies that it unleashes.

Postbourgeois Capitalism, the Electric Age, and the Bias of Space

Electric media are inherently space oriented. They have no tolerance for distinctions between centers and margins. McLuhan agrees with Innis that these technologies create "a kind of organic interdependence among all the institutions of society" as well as in the global village. As a result, electric media, beginning with the invention of the telegraph in 1844, have the effect of involving people in the world all at once. There is no possibility of detachment in this context. For this reason, McLuhan associated electricity primarily with the tactile sense to convey the effect of breaking down any separation between the user and the medium. Like any new medium, electric technology unwittingly threatens to demolish the media that historically preceded it. In this case, McLuhan warned in the 1960s that "our own entire investment in the preelectric technology of the literate and mechanical kind" may be wiped out. This sobering prediction applies to the economic system as well. With the rise of the electric age, capitalism is no longer time oriented. The invention of the credit card put an end to the bourgeois Protestant work ethic, which stressed the importance of patiently earning and saving money to buy goods. A new business community emerged, one that, according to McLuhan, "operates on the very short-run and exists mainly by the control of *space*."

The false conflation of involvement in media with understanding media can lead to a dangerous inattention to the overall power of electric media. Some detachment is necessary, although hard to obtain. For this reason, the literate mind struggles to overcome the instinctive human desire to be involved. The privacy and detachment that reading requires do not arise naturally. "The man of print culture is necessarily a self-educated man," McLuhan observes. "You can't acquire book culture by oral means. You have to struggle alone and in silence against a distracting social environment which looks askance at your solitary quest." As he further explains, "Man works when he is partially involved. When he is totally involved he is at play or leisure." Instant access to information coincides with people becoming "instant, too, in their response of pity or of fury when they must share the common extension of the central nervous system with the whole of mankind." One of the most serious consequences of this involvement is the vanishing of print-oriented values such as objective truth, privacy, and individualism. As long as one is constantly involved with the rest of the world, it is impossibly difficult to muster the detachment needed to think about that world.

In the bourgeois age of literacy, it was a common assumption that journalism should provide both sides of a story; this was known as "objective" journalism. Walter Cronkite summed up this attitude with his famous parting line at the end of his nightly newscast on CBS: "And that's the way it is." Even though it was hardly the case that newspapers in this age were free of bias, they acted as if they were the detached sources of information that their reading public would passively consume. With a time-oriented bias, readers had no choice but to wait for the news that the newspapers saw fit to print. They also had the time to develop a point of view based on the available facts.

In sharp contrast, the journalism of the electric or digital age is meant to involve the person in the news as it happens. With a space-oriented bias, there is no possibility of a point of view that allows for detached reflection. News that is reported as it happens encourages involvement, not thought. As McLuhan put it, "Mardi Gras is a happening. You cannot have objective journalism about a Mardi Gras. You just have to immerse." News, including bad news, that is suited for entertainment alone fits perfectly into this environment. Without the bad news that keeps the audience's attention, no one would pay attention to the good news (e.g., advertising).

Reality itself is up for grabs in this new environment. Politicians are not the only ones compelled to create a charismatic image that involves the audience as much as possible. Businesses must also "put on" their customers and employees as well if they are to succeed. Whereas the nineteenth-century executive sought to control and manipulate the less powerful members of his organizational hierarchy in smoky back rooms, the new executive must put on an image that makes him likable or at least visible in the face of the electric spotlight. Although the bourgeois merchant probably followed Machiavelli's advice not to "care about a name for meanness" as long as he achieves "great things" (albeit with ruthless means at times), the digital age of business demands, *contra* Mandeville, private *and* public virtues. Building one's popularity through virtue signaling in favor of a fashionable cause is an essential strategy. "Now the name of the game," McLuhan and Barrington Nevitt write in *Take Today*, "has changed from manipulation to participation." The old bourgeois hierarchy that was based on governance from the center is obsolete, whether corporate executives fully understand this or not. An age of instantaneous information requires the involvement of all parties concerned, and a system of delegated authority is hard to reconcile with the leveling effects of the telephone or Zoom screen. "Speed," according to McLuhan, "requires that the decisions made be inclusive, not fragmentary or partial." The executive is even tempted to be a "dropout" from the corporate world to become an educator on topics ranging from free speech to climate change. As McLuhan and Nevitt prophesied in *Take Today*, "As all monopolies of knowledge break down in our world of information speed-up, the role of executive opens up to Everyman. There are managers galore for the global theater. By their deeds you will know them—the instant catalysts."

In sharp contrast to the bourgeois Machiavellian age, the acquisition of wealth is often not the prime objective for today's billionaires, who seek inclusion and involvement as much as anybody in the digital age. *Contra* Machiavelli, capitalists in this context prefer to be loved, not feared. As McLuhan once quipped, "Thus in the mechanical age a man was famous for having done something. Today (in the electric age), he is famous for being well known." The necessary ruthlessness implied in Mandeville's slogan "Private Vices, Publick Benefits" now takes second place to a likeable image. Elon Musk did not purchase Twitter in 2022 simply to enrich his vast fortune. Rather, he wanted an audience for the role that he was playing as public savior or visionary. Musk was so stung by the dwindling number of people reading his tweets that he ordered his engineers to investigate whether the algorithm on the site was biased against him. In a classic case of shooting the messenger, Musk fired them after they reported that they found no such evidence.

McLuhan is not naively suggesting that this new decentralized way of corporate governance eliminates centralized hierarchy altogether. As he often reminds his audience, the obsolescence of an old structure is not the same as its disappearance or irrelevance. The downside of the obsession with speed is that corporations rush products to market without anticipating side effects. A rash of attacks by robotic coworkers on human employees at Amazon and Tesla facilities led to the criticism that management irresponsibly encouraged "speedy integration" of this new technology without any thought for dangerous consequences. Daniel Kokotajlo quit his job as governance researcher at OpenAI because of his deepening worry over the speed with which the firm was developing artificial general intelligence (AGI), or technology that can allegedly surpass human cognition. In a written statement, Kokotajlo provided a pithy description of speed as the formal cause embedded within AGI: "They [OpenAI executives] and others have bought into the 'move fast and break things' approach and that is the opposite of what is needed for technology this powerful and this poorly understood."

In short, corporations persist in *attempting* to control or recreate reality. Yet the sobering evidence that McLuhan presents in this context is that big business unleashes new realities that it cannot easily control or understand. The attempt to bring some order to this chaos, McLuhan and Wilfred Watson argue, has contributed to the eradication of the traditional bourgeois "boundaries between private and corporate." In the print age, as we have seen, it was possible to maintain a distinction between the private self and one's public image. One could at least think of oneself as an individual, detached from an objective, rational universe. The owners of large corporate enterprises no longer see themselves in this way, given the vanishing of the private realm under the conditions of acoustic space. The end of the distinction between private and corporate (public) coincides with the distinction between consciousness and the unconscious, resulting in a state in which, as McLuhan and Watson put it, "we begin to 'dream awake.'" The willingness of space-oriented business to demolish all boundaries between the private and public realms encourages self-destructive behavior that may lead to capitalism's demise. Fifty years after McLuhan uttered this prophecy, prominent opinion leaders are issuing the same warning in the context of statist pressure on banks to surveil the private data of customers with unpopular political views. The public intellectual Jordan Peterson testified before Congress in March 2024 about the dangers of a "potential 'superstate' in which collusion between government and corporations may be 'eliminating the private sphere.'"

Consciously or unconsciously, the corporate class of the twentieth century already put an end to the values of the bourgeois era. While this class moved forward, it was still looking backward, in accordance with the rear-view mirror way of perception. In *The Mechanical Bride*, McLuhan explains how the most influential representatives of big business describe capitalism as if it were still identical to the Jeffersonian ideal of "a self-regulating democracy based on a farmer-craftsman economy." The reality, which should have been obvious in the age of concentrated ownership of capital, is that big business has always embraced Hamilton's prescription for a strong central government that aids private interests in their acquisition of wealth. Rhetoric painfully clashes with reality. "The Jeffersonian path," McLuhan writes, "remained the national dream and the National Association of Manufacturers try to have it both ways. They talk Jefferson and follow Hamilton." In the electric-digital age, a new kind of capitalism replaces both Jefferson and Hamilton.

With the rise of instantaneous information in the electric and digital ages, it has become unrealistic to expect the single owner of a firm to manage and process a bewildering amount of information alone. As the "connected stability" of visual space yielded to the all-at-once bias of acoustic space, it became imperative to rely on a bureaucratic class that could master this blizzard of facts. As McLuhan explains, "The old job-holder, secure in his niche in the organization chart, finds himself an Ishmael wandering about in a chaos of unrelated data."

Drawing on James Burnham's *The Managerial Revolution* (1941), McLuhan and Watson take note of the rise of a new class of "managers" who would end up making the most important decisions on behalf of the large firms that employed them. This revolution reversed the traditional relationship between owners and managers. In the bourgeois era, the owners of a firm told the managers what to do; in the postbourgeois era, the owners became so dependent on managerial expertise in analyzing an endless stream of instantaneous data that the real decision-making power in the firm now belongs to the managers. As McLuhan and Watson describe it, "Ownership had long been the environment of the manager, but under electric conditions of information and knowledge it has become quite impossible for owners to know or to decide the great range of matters that needed hourly attention." Even though the executive may "*put on his public*," McLuhan and Nevitt explain in *Take Today*, this act does not alter the fact that his "first job is to select and train several men who can replace him instantly."

Corporate executives who fail to understand these changes often act as if they are still living in the bourgeois print era. Once again, they "dream awake." The best evidence of this somnambulism is the persistent belief that business and the state operate in distinct domains, separate from each other. Although it was possible to maintain this fiction in the age of laissez-faire capitalism, it is no longer credible today. Given the fact that the new managers of corporations rarely own any significant assets tied to their firms, they have little interest in protecting the corporation from the intrusions of the state. McLuhan sees little evidence for the relevance of the old adversarial relationship between capitalists and statists. The electric age's focus on image rendered this history obsolete. Instead, politicians lean so heavily on the corporate technique of public relations that the state often looks like a corporation. In McLuhan and Watson's words, "With the coming of film and TV, representative government itself has been transformed into image-making, a subculture of Madison Avenue PR."

The breakdown of the distinction between big government and big business is coincident with other phenomena of the digital age. Specifically, if information is the most important commodity in this age, then the search for this information is equally imperative. The space-oriented bias tolerates no boundaries between center and margin, private and public, business and state.

The desire to hunt for "Man" is one that is common to both big business and the big state as well. In a 1977 interview, McLuhan observed that "watching the other guy" is the main business of mankind. The act of spying on the rest of the world is inconceivable without the global village. In a conversation with the journalist Peter C. Newman in 1971, McLuhan remarked that the "new human occupation of the electronic age has become surveillance, CIA-style. Espionage is now the total human activity—whether you call it audience rating, consumer surveys, and so on—all men are now engaged as hunters of information." The old bourgeois desire to maintain secrecy and privacy is long gone. Business is just as determined as government to put everyone under surveillance. In the process, people lose not only their privacy but also their identity. As McLuhan and Watson explain, "Data banks know more about individual people than the people do themselves. The more the data banks record about each one of us, the less we exist."

McLuhan would not be shocked in the least that the high-tech industry actively cooperates with the state to spy on the posts of millions of users on Facebook and X (formerly Twitter). Nor would it be a surprise to him that the US Supreme Court in June 2024 saw nothing wrong or illegal about the Biden administration's contacts with media firms to remove "contentious content." Social media are the perfect technology for obsolescing the private-public distinction of the old print era. The fact that "Big Tech" acts like a government when it bans users based on their political opinions further vindicates McLuhan's prediction that the old separation between state and corporation has vanished as well. Privacy is not only invaded: it is ignored. In a subtle dig at Western ethnocentrism, McLuhan and Nevitt note the irony that Western democratic nations try to counter the illiberal influence of the "inscrutable" East while they "have lost the much larger struggle with invisible bureaucracies on the domestic front." The vote by the House of Representatives in April 2024 to ban TikTok in the United States unless ByteDance, the Chinese owner of the popular social media platform, sold its stake is a recent illustration of this pattern. Lawmakers were worried that TikTok could be used as a tool by the Chinese regime (with which ByteDance is presumably aligned) to advance its interests. They have also accused TikTok of data harvesting, spying on its users, and suppressing content that is critical of the

Chinese Communist Party. Although these concerns relating to national security and civil liberties are valid, other accusations reveal a lack of awareness about the form that drives *all* social media platforms, not just TikTok. Nicolas Chaillan, a former air force and space force chief software officer, told the *New York Post* in February 2023 that TikTok's "algorithm is vastly different, promoting science, educational and historical content in China while making our citizens watch stupid dance videos with the main goal of making us imbeciles." While singling out TikTok, this official did not provide any evidence that the bureaucracies in charge of YouTube, Facebook, and Twitter (now X) were posting only videos that educate and enlighten impressionable youth. It is also unclear how a social media platform can "make" anyone watch its videos or transform them into imbeciles against their will.

McLuhan would likely remind this software expert that the bias that animates every example of this medium is to entertain youth who seek their identity in cyberspace, not public libraries. They are the willing somnambulistic content of social media, wherever they exist in the global village.

Warning Signs: Cancel Culture and Artificial Intelligence

Unbeknownst to the corporations that get rich through spying, they are creating a reality that is alien to the formative traditions of capitalism, one that may prove to be fatal to this system. Whether they know it or not, corporations endanger their own economic freedom as long as they uncritically mirror the values of this age. The bourgeois preoccupation with "rights" to the private sphere of economy and leisure is obsolete. As McLuhan warned back in the 1960s, we "don't really have any rights left" after we surrender our senses and nervous systems to the "private manipulation" of those who benefit from this fateful decision. The fact that business thinks in the short run, a reflection of a space-oriented bias, further discourages any deep considerations of the side effects resulting from the usage of new media.

A contemporary example of short-run, space-biased thinking in business is the "cancel culture" phenomenon. In the past decade, Amazon and other booksellers have refused to sell books that offend a certain demographic, even though the books in question are often popular and profitable. "Sensitivity revision" has been applied to popular novels by Ian Fleming and Roald Dahl. Moreover, the publishers have often voluntarily made these changes. This act would be inconceivable to the bourgeois mind that valued the sanctity of freedom and property. Capitalists must now "put on" their consumers or audience. McLuhan's distinction between "job" and "role" helps us understand what motivates these firms. Eschewing the bourgeois preoccupation with earning plenty of money in a job, the corporate executive plays a role that, he believes, creates an image to please demographic groups that may otherwise seek to embarrass the firm publicly. McLuhan and Nevitt write, "In this new situation the market itself has returned to theater—a place to haggle rather than a place to stand."

The danger that results from the corporate practice of cancel culture is that the economic freedom cherished by business is bound to disappear, if by freedom one means the liberty to sell products on the market for a profit. The old bourgeois "public" that consisted of fragmented individuals has yielded to a tribal "all-at-once culture" consisting of diverse groups that track institutions at every step. In short, those who spy and cancel may reap the consequences of this behavior.

Even education does not escape the corporate put-on. For McLuhan, it is a grave mistake to teach as if a school is separate from its environment. What he writes about Plato could just as easily apply to contemporary teachers: "Plato, in all his striving to imagine an ideal training school, failed to notice that Athens was a greater school than any university even he could dream up." Ideally, he adds, one should think about media before they are applied to human existence: "Their being put outside us tends to cancel the possibility of their being thought of at all." The corporatization of education illustrates this pattern. In *City as Classroom: Understanding Language and Media* (1977), McLuhan and his coauthors, Kathryn Hutchon and Eric McLuhan, warn that the encroachment of business into the realm of education turns schools into an extension of the economy. In an exercise, the authors suggest that students ask critical questions about how "school courses can be programmed by computers and the experience they provide directed toward the job market. Does this encourage employers to enter the educational world in order to influence curriculum?" In short, business puts on the role of educator while insisting on the conflation of education with job training for the economy, even though it threatens the replacement of teachers with computer-programmed courses.

The billionaire Bill Gates's support and funding of the Common Core initiative in public schools is a case in point. In the early 2000s, Gates warned that an innovative economy requires citizens with significant literacy in math, science, and engineering. (The humanities and social sciences would presumably receive far less attention.) To achieve this goal, the Gates Foundation has lobbied governments to amplify the use of computers and other technologies in the classroom. In McLuhanesque terms, this effort is an example of a corporation creating its own demand for its product, which requires the leasing of one's senses to private interest. "What the public wants" is an obsolete notion in this context. The usage of this technology would not be confined to the completion of coursework online; it would also dramatically expand the amount of data about the learning abilities of millions of students, who would be required to wear "Galvanic Response Bracelets" or wireless biosensors that measure their attention, anxiety, and emotional arousal while they conduct their online learning. Additionally, based on this mass of data, the computer can predict how to teach each student, leading to a situation in which schools and teachers are unnecessary. In the words of the public school teacher Anthony Cody (who is also a critic of the Gates Foundation), "All a student needs is some sort of computer and a connection to the internet." The recurrent pattern in the history of capitalism whereby machines replace human beings continues to cause unease over the impact of new media.

The growing alarm over the deeply entrenched effects of artificial intelligence (AI), or technology that aims to achieve (or improve on) the same results as human intelligence, is only the latest example of this reaction. The fact that its products, including those that are popular or in demand, are often rushed to market without taking full account of their potential effects illustrates the tyranny of the space-oriented bias. The AI program known as ChatGPT (Chat Generative Pre-Trained Transformer) has demonstrated that it can write documents in the business world (and beyond) that mimic the language of corporate reports based on vast amounts of information extracted or scraped from the internet. Many university students who struggle to write papers have welcomed these programs as well. AI can also compose popular music by imitating the voices of celebrities, dead or alive. Paul McCartney admitted in June 2023 that AI "wrote" a Beatles song that featured the voice of the late John Lennon. AI capitalism threatens to violate copyright laws on a massive scale, flying in the face of long-entrenched property rights.

It would not require a painstaking application of formal causality to AI to anticipate the increasing usage of this technology as a means of surveilling and spying on employees in the workplace. Several Fortune 500 companies now use AI to render judgments on the hiring, firing, and retention of employees, a practice that demolishes the old bourgeois ideal of a sovereign boss making the most important decisions. All five senses are also under surveillance in the workplace. The electronic monitoring that AI enables can include functions as diverse as listening to employee conversations, timing bathroom breaks, and assessing the happiness of a worker in front of a computer screen. As McLuhan prophesied in the 1960s, human beings do not have total control over their minds or bodies as long as electric technology involves the entire central nervous system. The consequence is that we become "servo-mechanisms." The most astute corporations stand to benefit from this unequal arrangement of power. "Leasing our eyes and ears and nerves to commercial interests," McLuhan warns, "is like handing over the common speech to a private corporation, or like giving the earth's atmosphere to a company as a monopoly."

Mira Murati, one of the creators of AI, has belatedly expressed concerns over the "misuse" of this technology and argued in favor of its regulation. In McLuhan's argot, Murati is ignoring the bias or formal cause of her own invention, which is inclined to render obsolete activities once considered the sole domain of human agency and intelligence. For decades a few scholars have predicted that AI raises questions about the viability of the traditional distinction between man and machine. Since the age of Descartes, philosophers have confidently insisted that machines cannot think or develop self-awareness. Yet AI's creators try to break down this distinction by identifying thinking or learning with the processing of information. From a business perspective in the digital age, it is tempting to conflate the two. The unanticipated consequence of this somnambulism is that business is unprepared to deal with the computerized takeover of writing as a result of ChatGPT. As long as the possibility exists of replacing human information processing with a computerized version of the same, there is no reason to believe that one can successfully reverse this trend. In a McLuhanesque tone, the Canadian Conservative MP Rempel Garner has provided some needed historical perspective on the belated tendency of governments' attempts to control AI after the fact: "It's kind of like trying to regulate scribes after the printing press has gone into widespread distribution."

What is required is a rethinking of what thought actually is, independent of information processing. In the AI context, McLuhan would probably call attention to the confusion over the industry's desire to simulate consciousness, which "would by-pass speech in a kind of massive extrasensory perception." That is to say, if AI programs can *appear* to be as conscious as their users, there is little reason for human beings to communicate with others about the tasks of the day. Once an AI program proves that it can draft contracts, policies, and other legal documents more efficiently than lawyers can, the advantage is obvious. Yet an overdependence on this technology can leave a law firm exposed to AI "hallucinations," where a program simply "makes things up." As long as lawyers do not directly speak to each other about the tedious minutiae that make up these documents, they leave themselves vulnerable to a technology that does not need speech. Aristotle once argued that speech is a faculty that sets humanity apart from animals. Given this fact, it would follow that AI may not need human beings at all.

What McLuhan describes as the process of "handing over" common speech to a private corporation is already a development that corporate defenders of transhumanism welcome. Tom Oxley, the CEO of Synchron (a brain-computer interface company), looks forward to the day when advanced brain implants will allow his customers to exchange their emotions with others, without the need for speech. As Oxley put it to a TED Talk audience in June 2022, "So what if rather than using your own words, you could throw your emotions? At that moment, we would have realized that the necessary use of words to express our current state of being was always going to fall short. The full potential of the brain would then be unlocked."

McLuhan would obviously not welcome the prospect of speechlessness and the colonization of minds. As he foresaw in the mid-1950s, the rise of the information economy in the electric age has had effects that go well beyond the creation of commodities for the human estate. Yet he would probably not treat the AI revolution and transhumanism as unequivocal threats to humanity. The computer, McLuhan predicted in the late 1960s, held out the "promise of a technologically engendered state of universal understanding and unity, a state of absorption in the logos that could knit mankind into one family and create a perpetuity of collective harmony and peace."

There are a few other reasons for hope amid this uncertainty. First, in the history of computer technology, the attempt to imitate the human mind has usually hit a brick wall. Although the futurist and Google engineer Ray Kurzweil has confidently stated that computers "know everything," McLuhan would have his doubts. As he once remarked, it remains "one of the mysteries of cybernation that it is forever challenged by the need to simulate consciousness." There is growing evidence that ChatGPT cannot solve logical puzzles, including the detection of changes in grid patterns, which most human beings can solve (although this could change with improved programming). Despite the desire of many companies to use AI for the purpose of content moderation, it is far from evident that a machine has what McLuhan calls the "critical faculties" to interpret the context of this content. A symbol typically has more than one meaning that fits a larger historical context. As Thomas Stackpole writes, "Someone might see the Black Sun, a Nazi symbol, as just a geometric design unless they were familiar with its context, as well as the context in which it is being deployed. Machines cannot match humans in this regard." To recall McLuhan's distinction between matching and making, the attempt to match machine intelligence with human thought ignores how human beings make the reality—including the context or environment—in which machines operate. At best, computers match but cannot make anything. In an optimistic vein, McLuhan assures us that we need not be "helpless" in the face of computers, which still mirror the "cultural assumptions" of their makers. The plethora of emerging evidence points to the biased nature of AI programs. Even ChatGPT has confessed its racial bias!

Second, the possibility that AI can do most jobs that human beings already do should not necessarily provoke alarm as long as this effect is managed with compassion and insight. In the 1960s, McLuhan already predicted that a "guaranteed income" would be needed for human beings who would lose their jobs to automation. This program could bring about enough leisure time to inspire a resurgence of human creativity. At present, a few billionaires in the high-tech industries have called for a "universal basic income" to address the potential poverty caused by this unprecedented automation. Elon Musk has even predicted the creation of a "universal high income" for people whose jobs AI would render obsolete. This income would presumably be the result of a highly prosperous economy run by AI.

The haunting question that remains is this: Do the firms that unleash these changes also have the wisdom and moral decency to navigate their revolutionary effects? In the 1950s, McLuhan declared, "We have switched from the problem of production to the packaging of information. It is not markets we now invade but cultures and the minds of men. And this process is furthest advanced here in North America." It is far from obvious that political and corporate elites have addressed or anticipated the destabilizing effects of this transformation since McLuhan first spoke these words. The media remain toys in the hands of Mother Goose and Peter Pan executives.

6

NEW MEDIA ARE NATURE

The impact of new media on every aspect of life, we have seen McLuhan claim, is typically undeniable and incomprehensible at the time of transformation. This paradox is compatible with another paradox that he employs to demonstrate the extent to which media alter reality. In 1969, he remarked, "The new media are not bridges between man and nature; they are nature." This statement is paradoxical precisely because we create media, whereas nature supposedly exists independently of our creation. The traditional understanding of nature to which McLuhan alludes in this aphorism is that human beings must build bridges to nature because nature exists outside us. Yet he suggests that this distinction is obsolete. The question that McLuhan raises here is whether there is such a thing as nature anymore. This question has great importance because nature includes *human* nature. Are human beings simply passive effects of the media in a given age? Is human nature just a construct of a new technology? If media can treat nature as their own creation, what is left of human nature?

McLuhan's focus on the extent to which human beings are oblivious to the effects of new media may initially suggest that human nature is not a stable or unchanging phenomenon that can comprehend or withstand technological change. As already mentioned, McLuhan compares this mentality to the fish that is immersed in water. In *War and Peace in the Global Village* (1968), he elaborates on the process by which this pattern occurs. Fish know nothing about water because they lack an "anti-environment" with which they could perceive the dominant environment (water). Although their auditory sense helps them function, it does not help them understand the environment that creates the sounds they hear. McLuhan explains, "It appears that they can hear pretty well but have scarcely any power of directional location for the origin of the sounds they hear." The good news for the fish is that their essential nature remains unaltered despite their lack of comprehension. Despite "a very limited sensory life, the fish has an essence or built-in potential which eliminates all problems from its universe. It is always a fish and always manages to continue to be a fish while it exists at all. Such is not, by any means, the case with man."

In this last haunting comment, McLuhan alludes to the instability of human identity in an age of rapid technological change. Unlike the fish, we cannot rely on our senses to help us grasp the origins of new media. In McLuhan's words, "Every environment that we make and assume is a mask that can become a crushing weight distorting our sensibilities, unless countervailed by imaginative response." Moreover, if we cannot understand the origins of these media, then we cannot comprehend their effects. Although McLuhan advises that it is necessary to find these causes by focusing on the effects first (as formal causality stipulates), it is far more common for human beings to avoid this reflective process altogether. Commenting on the "flip" from objective to immersive reporting, McLuhan notes, "Many people would rather die than defend themselves against these effects." As a result, the users of electric media are inclined to react with bewilderment to this transformational change. The good news that McLuhan offers is that it is possible to study how the world of new media is "metamorphosing man." In the process, we can also understand the limits that nature imposes on the technological will to reconstruct human nature.

The Media's Transformation of Nature and Identity

It has never been easy for human beings to find a secure identity. In *War and Peace in the Global Village*, McLuhan declares, "Unlike animals man has no nature but his own history—his total history." Yet not all civilizations in history have interpreted nature and human nature as changeable phenomena subject to historical change. Preliterate tribal humanity, as we have seen in chapter 3, was resigned to the workings of the cosmos and a fixed purpose within a divinely sanctioned order from which there was no escape. With the advent of literacy, the prospect of objectively studying nature from a distance became a reality, one that raised the possibility that the private individual could master nature. With the rise of print media in modernity, the capitalist measurement and control of nature by means of technology intensified this sense of mastery. In the nineteenth century, as we have seen, it was fashionable to identify nature with the laws of laissez-faire capitalism. What happens to identity in the electric and digital ages of media?

"Radical changes of identity, happening suddenly and in very brief intervals of time, have proved more deadly and destructive of human values than wars fought with hardware weapons," the McLuhans ominously observe in *Laws of Media*. It is safe to assume that he has in mind changes that occur at the speed of light in the electric age. The speed with which social media follow trends that can go viral instantaneously makes meaningful content moderation almost impossible. In 2020, a video of a suicide went viral on TikTok, whose internal video creation features made it impossible to scrub the video from the platform before numerous users had already uploaded it.

Moreover, the changes that are of greatest interest to McLuhan involve the recurrent transformation of nature and human nature into objects that are reshaped at will. Nothing is safe from this endless reinvention. As he once remarked, "The human body is now a probe, a laboratory for experiments." This process has unsettling implications for anyone who is nostalgic for a stable identity, as McLuhan notes: "The present fragmented civilization seems on its way out, and what 'being a man' means could swiftly change."

McLuhan often pointed out that the human encroachment into nature has effects that threaten human survival, whether this is understood or not. These effects reverse or contradict the original intent of the intervention. The farther we push into the natural environment for the sake of our own enrichment, the more likely we will suffer unintended consequences. In a 1978 lecture entitled "On Nature and Media: A Dialogue of Effects," he observed that "diseases are human artifacts. . . . Diseases are not something that nature produces. They're made by man." The violence that human beings do to external nature parallels that which we inflict on our internal nature. Human beings use violence to find a new identity that does actual harm to themselves. This violence, according to McLuhan, "doesn't have to be a punch in the face. It can be violence one does to one's *own nature*." Within the electric age, the search for identity is particularly violent in an unprecedented way, given the fact that the media saturate every sense or faculty of human nature. "Electronic man wears his brain outside his skull and his nervous system on top of his skin," McLuhan and Bruce R. Powers contend. "Such a creature is ill-tempered, eschewing overt violence." Nature's interface with humanity is not a one-way street: nature affects humanity as much as humanity affects nature.

As McLuhan points out in a different work, "The fact that with modern technology the entire material of the globe as well as the thoughts and feelings of its human inhabitants have become the matter of art and of man's factive intelligence means that there is no more nature." But then McLuhan adds this qualification: "At least there is no more external nature." This comment seems to imply that there may be an internal nature, one that severely constricts human understanding and control of technology.

This constant reconstruction of nature and human nature does not foster peace of mind. Instead, the new "nature" causes new, unintended stresses for human beings. "Man-made nature, fashioned according to life as art, may tax human creativity far beyond anything levied on presatellite (Sputnik) man," write McLuhan and Barrington Nevitt in *Take Today*. The ascendancy of the postliterate age under electric conditions returns us to the orality and acoustic space of the preliterate age as well as an all-involving understanding of the world. The *Sputnik* event in 1957 illustrated this dramatic shift. With the rise of satellite communications, we could no longer objectively view nature as an extension of economic interests, one that is open to unbiased study. This fixed economistic position fell prey to the new awareness that human environments can envelop nature, which is now the subject of worship, not the object of usage. "As soon as the planet went inside a man-made environment," McLuhan argues, "the occupants of the planet began to hum and sing the ecological theme song without any further prompting." The fact that an idea can "flip" implies a reversal that has implications for the stability of identity in the digital age. Unfortunately, this process is usually not well understood as it happens. "This feature of organized ignorance," writes McLuhan, "is a typical flip of the situation in which we live." Immersion within this "man-made environment" fosters the illusion that one can escape from nature by creating new identities. The manifestations of "organized ignorance" in this context include the revival of the belief in magic, which fosters the temptation to create new identities that seem to be natural ("second natures") or identities that do not require nature at all ("discarnate identities").

Do You Believe in Magic?

Once again, McLuhan is neither celebrating nor condemning these changes. Rather, he is urging us to understand them. This is no easy task if one assumes that there is necessarily a logical or rational explanation for these patterns of behavior. If rationality is identical to bourgeois self-interest and detachment, then it provides little understanding of the environment in which we are immersed. Nor does greater involvement guarantee understanding. The postliterate human being who inhabits the electric and digital ages arguably has more in common with the preliterate tribalist. Both personalities are utterly involved in (and uncritical of) their surrounding environments. "There never was a sceptic or an agnostic in a pre-literate society," McLuhan notes, "so the post-literate society in which we now live is also much involved in religion and the inner trip." But although McLuhan sometimes associates the preliterate and the postliterate in this limited sense, his distinction between the two is more relevant to the task of understanding how the electric age destabilizes identity. As McLuhan puts it, "we are post-literate and more primitive than the pre-Socratics (the pre-literate) ever dreamed of being." What does he mean by this?

The new reality of the electric age, according to McLuhan, is more "primitive" because it encourages belief in magic. This version of magic is far more radical than the incantations of the preliterate mind, which practiced magic to make sense of a preestablished and unchanging cosmos. The postliterate mind, in sharp contrast, dreams of reconstructing this cosmos over and over again by means of technology. In the electric age, McLuhan explains, just as government and politics have become music and entertainment, commerce "has become incantation and magical gesture. Science and magic have married each other. Technology and the arts meet and mingle." Why is this magical? McLuhan associates magic with art, or the powerful temptation to create new realities that allegedly replace the old ones. From a magical-artistic vantage point, nature itself is constantly susceptible to transformation through technology. None of this, however, implies that human beings have the wisdom to construct reality anew. McLuhan asks, "Are there sufficient signs that technological man is prepared to manipulate, as his matter, both earth and spirit? Have the ancient boundaries between art and nature been erased?" Preliterate humanity respected these boundaries. Postliterate humanity seeks to extinguish them.

To unpack these concerns posed by McLuhan, we need to understand how exactly media after the print age encourage this magical transformation of nature and, in the process, identity or human nature. McLuhan's use of the word "magical" is carefully chosen because it illustrates the irrationality of human beings that is evident in their engagement with technology. In his 1967 essay "The Future of Sex," he observes that human beings usually push a technology to its utmost limits. Consistent with formal causality, the form of a technology will likely produce unintended effects. In simple terms, if a technology can be used for a specific purpose, no matter how unsettling this purpose is, the odds are good that it will be used for this end. According to McLuhan, "Extremes create opposite extremes. . . . Grotesque and distorted extremes tend to pop out just at the end of any era." In short, human beings are not by nature moderate beings in their treatment of technology. What makes this pattern even more fantastic is that a technology that is pushed to an extreme will reverse or "flip" into its opposite. The McLuhans may have predicted transgenderism when they used the logic of the tetrad to explain how feminism reverses into maleness while it obsolesces individual or distinct sexes. If every gender identity is a construct independent of nature, as feminism claims, then no identity can be condemned for being "unnatural."

The conflicts that new media engender have magical effects. McLuhan and Powers write in *The Global Village*, "Whenever two cultures, or two events, or two ideas are set in proximity to one another, an interplay takes place, a sort of *magical* change. The more unlike the interface, the greater the tension of the interchange." The close attention to a figure coincides with even greater inattention to a ground, resulting in "a continual state of abrasive interplay." The abrasive nature of this magical interplay has deep roots in history. McLuhan warned about Gnosticism, an ancient belief that still persists as an influence on politics today. He sympathized with the philosopher Eric Voegelin's definition of Gnosticism as a mentality that despises the material nature of the world and seeks to replace it with a higher spiritual identity. McLuhan was so preoccupied with the resurgence of Gnosticism in a modern guise that he shared this worry with Voegelin. In a brief exchange of letters in 1953, he expressed his concern that "cults and secret societies" in the arts and academia were spreading Gnostic influences.

In a 1955 review of Hugh Kenner's study of Wyndham Lewis, McLuhan went so far as to spy the spread of these influences within Hollywood and movie culture, which he said had revived the "nihilist philosophies of neo-Platonism and gnosticism." In scathing prose, McLuhan accused the entertainment industry and other new media of making palatable and mainstream the attitude that existence "is an empty machine, a cheap art work." The triumph of this nihilism was attributable to an age "when nature has been abolished by art and engineering, when government has become entertainment and entertainment has become the art of government." Put differently, the crude materialism of these industries has flipped into its opposite extreme—namely, a desire for a spiritualist escape. As a result, "the gnostic and neo-Platonist and Buddhist can gloat: 'I told you so! This gimcrack mechanism is all that there ever was in the illusion of human existence. Let us rejoin the One.'" If the Gnostic is correct to claim that nature is merely an illusion that new identities can replace and surpass, how do electric and digital media contribute to this transformational project?

Second Natures

McLuhan's distinction between "first nature" and "second nature" is pivotal to understanding this project. The McLuhans associate first or primordial nature with a "savage or barbaric state" or "wild body" full of instincts and desires that have not yet undergone the leavening effects of civilization. As we have seen, McLuhan warns against relying on our instinctual responses to media, which will destroy us. First nature has little understanding of how human beings can remake themselves through technology. Second nature, in contrast, is "nature made and remade by man as man remakes himself with his extensions," the McLuhans assert in *Laws of Media*. Language is the first attempt to transcend this primitive existence. Ever since human beings began to learn how to talk to each other, there has been a gradual movement away from first nature. As McLuhan explains, "Language does for intelligence what the wheel does for the feet and the body," enabling them "to move from thing to thing with greater ease and speed and ever less involvement." The rise of a second nature is not a bad thing in itself: it is the mark of civilization. The McLuhans credit Aristotle for realizing that ancient Greeks could understand nature only when they had left behind the violence of first nature and put on "an individualized and civilized" second nature.

Yet it is dangerous to assume that this first nature disappears altogether. Consistent with the traditional language of Christian theology, the fact that second nature belongs to the civil or social state of humanity does not mean that the animalistic first nature vanishes. Nevertheless, the temptation to believe in the extinction of first nature gained currency with the rise of the modern era, which opened the door to the utopian fantasy of reshaping human nature at will. Although the modern defender of political realism Machiavelli is not usually associated with utopianism, McLuhan believes that the Florentine philosopher tried to legitimize in empirical terms the fantasy of controlling humanity's instinctual first nature. Machiavelli, as McLuhan reads him, dangerously overestimates how easy this mastery is, assuming that a prudent political ruler (or "Prince") can extract good results from this wild nature as long as it is under his control. As Machiavelli puts it in *The Discourses* (1.57), the multitude will "run to obey" a prince who threatens to punish them. The modern intellectual, McLuhan argues, has been easily seduced into accepting Machiavelli's contention that human nature is so malleable: "And at all times he [the modern intellectual] finds it hard to remember the *common human nature* which persists intact beneath all the modes of mental hysteria" in the modern age that commenced with Machiavelli. Yet even the Florentine did not anticipate, in McLuhan's judgment, how the elevation of humanity's most destructive "psychic powers" opens the door "to the totalitarian remaking of human nature." As McLuhan constantly reminds his audience, control of human beings and the media they create is the greatest illusion of all.

In the age of electric and digital media, it is particularly tempting to believe that this first nature is extinguishable. Our "inner existence," which is McLuhan's occasional synonym for first nature, never disappears amid a plethora of newly created second natures. As McLuhan warns in his essay "Space, Time, and Poetry," "The new media have blurred the boundaries of inner and outer existence. The omnipresence of news and views has merged man's inner and outer life. Uninhibited mechanization is totalitarian at many levels," returning humanity "to the state of collectivized, emotional consciousness of archaic man." In accord with the laws of media, the electric age enables the reversal of second nature (individualism) into first nature (tribalism). Put simply, electric and digital media reawaken first nature.

Judging first or second nature on moral grounds is not what McLuhan has in mind. What is important to his purpose is to understand why humanity living in the electric age is so determined to replace first nature with second nature. Before the present age, second nature was an innocuous reality, one that represented the ways that humanity uses technologies as extensions of the senses. Yet users of media in the electric age are so determined to liberate themselves from first nature that they magically create a second nature through technological means. Unless one thinks like an artist who can bridge the gap between this inheritance and the new environment created by technological change, second nature becomes a novel form of control. The McLuhans explain, "Without the artist's intervention man merely *adapts* to his technologies and become [sic] their servo-mechanism." The only way to avoid this fate is to study the "relations between second and first natures: which organs or faculties are extended or stressed or numbed and in which pattern or degree by each one of our artifacts." Out of this study a "new science" devoted to understanding the hidden effects of new media environments will ideally emerge. Otherwise we will remain like fish, unaware of the water all around them.

The problem that practitioners of this new science face is that it is hard to persuade people that liberation from "servitude to [first] Nature" leads to enslavement "to the vagaries of second nature." Although the idea of being enslaved to a nature that human beings create sounds puzzling, McLuhan is determined to explain why it is not so mysterious. The fact that human beings act as if a new identity is natural reveals the depth of their immersion in a new environment that is not natural in the least. Try as they may, the creators of a second nature do not escape nature altogether. First nature does not disappear amid this change. (A quick glance at the myriad savage outbursts on social media will find sufficient evidence for the existence of first nature.) As McLuhan and Powers advise, understanding the way that "natural man" relates to a man-made environment is as important as understanding how he relates to the natural environment. The failure to make this distinction leads to the magical desire to ignore the limits that first nature imposes on the creation of second nature.

The all-at-once news environment of the postliterate age encourages the replacement of the old second natures with new ones. With the rise of the global village, human beings no longer have the freedom to detach themselves from a world that involves them through the dissemination of instant information. In this "theater of the absurd," people look to electric media to escape from privacy. As McLuhan shows, these media generate the impression that a private self may as well be a "nobody" on the frontier. The need to get "noticed" becomes paramount, even if it takes a dramatic form (e.g., terrorism).

In a less dramatic context, the desire for gainful employment provides another example of second nature. McLuhan's distinction between working a job and playing a role is relevant here. In the print age, self-interested individuals worked often pointless jobs for the sake of survival and comfort (private vices lead to public benefits, as Mandeville explains in *The Fable of the Bees*); in the digital age, people seek roles that provide meaning. They no more wish to match a given reality with their self-interest than desire to preserve their inner selves. Rather, they want to make a reality in which they can play a role as participants. This role becomes second nature to millions of people in the age of instant information.

Consistent with his "fish in the water" metaphor, McLuhan always notes that most human beings, apart from the artist, understand that change has occurred without comprehending how the environment they have made has enabled this change. At best, people in the digital age can understand that reality is no longer fixed or unchanging while being oblivious to the fact that the technologies fashioned by their own hands have fostered this attitude. In short, their acceptance of reality as fluid mirrors their uncritical dependence on the categories of electric media. As McLuhan once noted, the rise of worker absenteeism in the automobile industry is an effect of media. These workers rebel against a tightly structured work schedule based on the assembly line, which does not match the speed of information that characterizes the electric age. The one-thing-at-a-time mentality that characterizes the assembly line is out of sync with the all-at-once world of mass media. As a result, absenteeism rises and quality falls. "Two or three days a week seems to be as much as the Detroit worker feels necessary to be involved in gainful employment," McLuhan wrote. "Absenteeism means that most of the cars now turned out on Fridays and Mondays are duds." The routinization of jobs in the industrial age is not suited to workers who want to complete their tasks as soon as possible so that they can "drop out" and "tune in" on themselves through greater leisure time.

Once people are focused on playing roles, they will no longer feel any loyalty to their jobs unless these occupations involve them in the transformation of the world. McLuhan often calls attention to young workers who increasingly "drop out" of the economy so that they can find a profession that fulfills them on an existential level, as opposed to providing a paycheck for survival. They must see themselves as actors seeking meaningful work. One effect of the COVID-19 lockdowns in 2020–21 was to persuade many workers to reject the traditional distinction between work and home, a phenomenon that McLuhan anticipated as far back as the 1960s when he declared in a televised appearance, "Documents, contracts, data. All of these materials could be just as available on closed-circuit at home." Once workers got used to working at home during the lockdown, they no longer meekly accepted the idea of returning to the workplace after the lockdown ended. Working remotely at home allowed them to be as involved with the world as with working at the office. In the process, employees had the time to watch events such as the death of George Floyd in 2020, which led many to make demands on their employers to advance racial justice and equity. With the breakdown of the private-public dichotomy, human beings pay attention to events that were often ignored in the past. Events like these can no longer be "*contained* in the political sense of limited association," as McLuhan warned back in the 1960s.

Although the playing of a role, or second nature, is not necessarily a bad thing, it can come with a cost. If this second nature (the external self) becomes blurred with one's first nature (the inner self), the results can be disastrous. In April 2023, the FBI arrested Jack Teixeira for leaking hundreds of classified documents on a popular online gaming platform called Discord. These documents contained information about the Ukraine conflict, including the battlefield positions of soldiers in the Ukrainian army. Teixeira was an information technology specialist and national guardsman who imagined that his fellow gamers could become "super soldiers," armed with access to these sensitive documents. The motive that explains this young man's illegal espionage activities had nothing to do with money or ideology, which were prominent factors during the Cold War. In the bourgeois print age, these motives manifested rational self-interest. Yet Teixeira did not use his job as a mere journeyman, tasked with protecting cybernetworks from external attacks, in the service of foreign interests. Rather, he and his fellow gamers were playing the roles of imaginary combatants in this global theater. As McLuhan put it, this theater is suited to the "man of action who appears not to be involved in the action." The absurdity of this mode of being is dramatically illustrated in Teixeira's actions, which had more to do with fantasy than dreams. As McLuhan and Powers explain, "Dreams have some connection to the real world because they have a frame of actual time and place (usually in real time); fantasy has no such commitment." The "super soldier" fantasy in which Teixeira participated illustrates the danger of creating a second nature that blurs fantasy with reality without any awareness of the unnerving consequences that follow.

Discarnate Identity

The magical creation of second natures correlates with McLuhan's later reflections about the rise of "discarnate" identity in the electric age. As he explained in a Monday night seminar at his center in the mid-1970s, "One of the peculiarities of radio and electric technology is that it moves you instantaneously: you are everywhere at the speed of light, without a body. People using telephone, TV, or radio, or any other electric service do not have bodies; they are discarnate beings." While the convenience of accessing and sending information at the speed of light is undeniable, McLuhan astutely pointed to the unintended side effect of a diminished identity in this context. Although he admitted in this seminar that he had not fully studied this new phenomenon, he offered this observation: "I would venture off-hand to say that people without bodies tend to be very weak in private identity, that a private identity tends to form in an interfacing of social surround. But, minus a body, the social interfacing or encounters are very weak." Put differently, we abolish our first nature when we abolish the body.

Discarnate existence threatens to intensify the dualism within first nature, one that pits the inner self against the outer body. This false opposition has plagued human existence throughout history. In "Nihilism Exposed," McLuhan contends that "on the plane of applied science we have fashioned a Plotinian world-culture which implements the non-human and super-human doctrines of neo-Platonic angelism to the point where the human dimension is obliterated by sensuality at one end of the spectrum, and by sheer abstraction at the other." "Angelism," a term coined by the Catholic philosopher Jacques Maritain, does not rely on God for revealing knowledge of the world. Rather, as Paul Edwards explains, "it arrogates to the human mind an 'angelic' *a priori* knowledge through direct access to the divine ideas that create reality." In the process, it subordinates the realm of matter to the control of the intellect, a dualism that has characterized a great deal of Western philosophy.

This dualistic divide between the sensual (the body) and the abstract (the mind) is a doctrine that McLuhan, as a Christian celebrant of body *and* soul, rejects. Generally, he understands Christianity as a faith that rejects all dualisms or false oppositions. For this reason, he advises his brethren to understand the true message of their savior Jesus Christ, which is to close the "distance or separation between the medium and the message: it is the one case where we can say that the medium and the message are one and the same." In the Incarnation, body and soul became one, a reconciliation that is inconceivable to neo-Platonists and Gnostics. Similarly, the medium is the form (ground, environment) or body that envelops the mind, or the intention that creates the content of a medium. As much as possible, McLuhan believes, they must be related, not opposed, to each other.

McLuhan's concern with angelism parallels his interest in the pernicious effects of these dualisms (body vs. mind, form vs. content, medium vs. message) in the age of discarnate identity. A bodiless existence encouraged people to act as if they are spiritual (or magical) beings. As McLuhan and Powers put it in *The Global Village*, "Angelism, sometimes called discarnatism, allows technology to move as a dumb force, because without perceiving all four-fold processes [of the tetrad] we are unconscious of its effects. Discarnatism floats in the abstract clouds, without any relation to ground, or environment—the besetting sin of academic hypothesis." In less cryptic terms, McLuhan elsewhere distinguishes angelism from discarnatism by observing that being "on the air," or everywhere at once, surpasses the power of angels: "This is a power beyond that of the angels, according to Thomas Aquinas, for they can only be in one place at a time." (In chapter 10, I discuss what McLuhan considers to be the apocalyptic implications of discarnate identity.)

McLuhan laments the fact that the church has ignorantly neglected the danger posed by this new creation. In a 1977 interview with Pierre Babin, he warned that a "discarnate world, like the one we now live in, is a tremendous menace to an incarnate Church, and its theologians haven't even deemed it worthwhile to examine the fact." This was a "menace" precisely because human beings could seemingly experience the age-old dream of existing universally and eternally, a power that only God enjoys. Until the rise of discarnatism, only God existed "with centres everywhere and boundaries nowhere." This desire is far more radical than ancient Gnosticism, which seeks knowledge that leaves a flawed physical world behind. The avatars of transhumanism do not free the mind from matter. As Joe Allen explains, they force "the imagination into physical form, or encoding a fabricated spiritual realm out of voodoo algorithms." The upshot is that a computerized god "will eliminate death and suffering via biological longevity and digital immortality." Even death will not be a boundary that impedes the new digitalized deity.

The absence of a private and embodied identity leads to the lack of a sense of private guilt, even though, McLuhan notes in *Understanding Media*, we have feelings of guilt expressed in terms of a "social consciousness." In a world in which everyone is involved with everyone else, guilt is not the expression of an individual self. "The new feeling that people have about guilt," McLuhan writes, "is not something that can be privately assigned to some individual, but is, rather, something shared by everybody, in some mysterious way." As a result, "nobody can really imagine what private guilt can be anymore." Although no one feels responsible in an individual sense, one can experience a vague feeling of collective guilt. Commenting on the trial of the Nazi war criminal Adolf Eichmann in 1961, McLuhan believed that the coverage of this trial "involves the audience so completely in the process of his action that they begin to feel far more guilty than he did."

The panic that often characterized behavior during the COVID-19 lockdowns in 2020–21 illustrates McLuhan's thoughts on the magical breakdown of the distinction between private and collective guilt. This period also illustrates his view that "panic terrors" go hand in hand with a world devoid of privacy, a world that is instead "a small world of tribal drums, total interdependence, and superimposed co-existence." First nature roared back with a vengeance. Many citizens expressed panic as a reaction to the nonstop coverage of the pandemic, which led many to spy on their fellow citizens whom they suspected of violating lockdown measures. In Alberta, McLuhan's home province, many individuals turned to "snitch lines" for this purpose in 2020. They were not acting as private individuals who struggled with guilt over their own actions. Rather, they were anxiously exposing the guilt of others to demonstrate their own morally superior innocence in the process. They could prove this status by complaining about their neighbors in the safety of discarnate space (e.g., phoning via snitch lines). "Superimposed co-existence" was glaringly obvious. These neighbors were insisting that everyone feel the same degree of guilt or responsibility during this crisis. The tribalist passions mirroring first nature were on full display here. The boundary between privacy and the public realm magically broke down, as did adherence to the facts on the ground. As Barry Cooper and Marco Navarro-Génie have shown, citizens who complained about other citizens often simply fabricated claims about infection cases. In their words, "Between March and August, close to 20,000 complaints were launched in a province with 15,957 confirmed COVID-19 cases by September 16. That there were more citizen-on-citizen complaints than there were actual infection cases in that time frame indicated an epidemic of panic among Albertans, with likely equivalences in the rest of the country." In short, our age insists, however irrationally, that everyone ought to feel guilty in a public sense, not as a private self. The triumph of discarnate identity is complete in these cases.

In *The Global Village*, McLuhan and Powers write, "What may emerge as the most important insight of the twenty-first century is that man was not designed to live at the speed of light." Endless attempts to deny the enduring existence of nature or human nature through magic and the creation of new unstable identities have effects that are not understood while they happen. The recurrent tendencies of human beings to inflict oppression and violence on each other become glaringly obvious in the global village of the electric age.

7
THE DIVIDED GLOBAL VILLAGE

McLuhan's observation that the postliterate world is "the new world of the global village" is arguably the most famous idea that he ever expressed. This metaphor also perfectly illustrates what he means by a cliché, an act of "total consciousness" or "the sum of all the clichés of all the media or technologies we probe with." This total consciousness, McLuhan contends, occurs because the world is one big metropolis in which everyone is involved in everyone else's business, putting an end to the old "center-margin structure." The world is now a "unified cosmic Happening," or a "global melting pot of peoples and cultures which can only end by making of the world a single city." This village even turns the entire planet into Spaceship *Earth*, where "there are no passengers but all are crew." Is this a good thing or a bad thing?

McLuhan gave different answers to this question. At times he predicted that this village might become a place of "harmony" with the overcoming of tribal differences. McLuhan's musings that the new global village of shared information and the vanishing of walls between "peoples, arts, and thoughts" might inspire everyone to become artistic creators of their own environments sometimes generated the popular image of McLuhan as a utopian. Yet the New Age desire to live in a unified and peaceful world free of conflict did not so easily displace old-fashioned tribalism. McLuhan also predicted that this interconnected world would be violent and unstable. Even in the optimistic heyday of the 1960s, he soberly observed, "War, as it were, has become the little red schoolhouse of the global village. It's a gory little schoolhouse at that."

Conflict, McLuhan ultimately believes, is the more probable feature of this new world order. In 1977, at the beginning of his last televised interview, he took aim at the optimistic attitude, which was sometimes attributed to him, that the global village creates a consciousness that wondrously brings everyone together. Instead, he warned, this village is playing history backward by reviving the tribal consciousness. The tribal attitude of hostility toward outsiders is a perfectly intelligible (although not admirable) response to the involving effects of globalization. The more we know about each other, the less we may like each other. "When people get close together," McLuhan explained, "they get more and more savage, impatient with each other." There is not only a lack of evidence that closeness breeds amity; nothing justifies the hope that tolerance of each other's differences will automatically grow out of the global village. Consistent with his notion of simultaneity, cultures that were once separated by time, McLuhan believed, are now violently thrown together, forced to coexist in the eternal here and now. Nor is first nature so easily extinguishable. As McLuhan noted in this interview, "Village people aren't that much in love with each other. The global village is the place of very arduous interfaces and very abrasive situations."

McLuhan was not suggesting that this violence is a new phenomenon, a novelty of the electric age. The quest for identity has always been violent. Nevertheless, living in an age of rapid change intensifies the violence of this quest. If the media of the global village ignore some of its unruly citizens, they may resort to violence to escape the feeling of being nobodies. Terrorists and hijackers are determined to get media coverage to remind others of their existence. The Hamas terrorists who attacked Israel on October 7, 2023, filmed their brutal and vicious acts for the whole world to see. In the cold-blooded words of Hamas leader Yahya Sinwar, "No blood, no news." (Ironically enough, Sinwar's death in a firefight with the Israel Defense Forces in October 2024 made the news.)

Some people may feel that their identity is under threat precisely because the global village pulls them into a new, involving reality for which they are unprepared. In "our time, when things happen very quickly, there's very little time to adjust to new situations at the speed of light," McLuhan warns. Even though the global village has abolished all frontiers, margins, and secrets, the violence does not dissipate.

Tribalism, Old and New

Although McLuhan is aware of the apocalyptic tone that these thoughts imply, he is not putting on the role of the doomsayer. As he explains in his 1969 interview with *Playboy*, while environmental changes can be catastrophic, they need not be overpowering: "It is how we perceive them and react to them that will determine their ultimate psychic and social consequences." Although McLuhan refrains from making moral judgments that privilege the superiority of visual, literate, and individualistic cultures at the expense of acoustic, oral, and tribal ones, he contends that tribalism exerts far more control over speech, thought, and behavior. For all the talk about diversity in the global village, few "rebels" will challenge their own tribe. As McLuhan observes in the first issue of *Explorations*, instantaneous communication makes "free speech and thought difficult if not impossible" as long as only "the most acceptable words and notions" are tolerated. Besides, as he explains in a 1968 interview, the so-called cultural "diversity" of the global village will paradoxically lead to less intellectual diversity, especially if this village imposes conformity on the private realm of life. "There is more diversity, less conformity under a single roof in any family," McLuhan says, "than there is with the thousands of families in the same city."

Electric and digital media also break down not only bourgeois traditions but also loyalties to the nation-state that once enshrined these values. The equality that nation-states extended to their citizens requires a homogeneity of values that does not suit the global village. As McLuhan shows in *The Gutenberg Galaxy*, equal rights make sense only if people share a common culture, language, and set of traditions.

From a tribalist perspective, equality is an alien value. Media that involve the peoples of the world all at once only serve to remind them of how different they actually are. They also provide a reminder of how powerless nation-states are in the face of this involvement. As McLuhan explains in an essay on Harold Innis, "Electric technology creates not the nation but the tribe—not the superficial association of equals but the cohesive depth pattern of the totally involved kinship groups." This "depth" based on greater involvement with the world is not necessarily a good thing. McLuhan gives due credit to nationalism for providing "relief" from the "tribal-global village," a place that is far more divisive and conflicted than any nation-state was. "Village is fission, not fusion, in depth," McLuhan concludes in a 1968 interview.

From this vantage point, it is not surprising that people who have lived on the margins of the bourgeois world would not lament its downfall. In the late 1960s, McLuhan took note of the rising Black power movement in the US, which sought a return to a mythic Africa amid the collapse of the bourgeois print-oriented civilization. This movement, "with its emphasis on Negritude and a return to the tribal pride of African cultural and social roots," mirrored this shift in media. This response also illustrated the quest for identity in an age of fluid identities and total involvement, one that showed a renewed historical awareness of the violence that "has traditionally been directed at the tribal man who challenged visual-mechanical culture, as with the genocide against the Indian and the institutionalized dehumanization of the Negro."

The current debate over identity politics vindicates McLuhan's analysis of the endless quest for identity in the electric age. This politics, as Roger Lancaster contends, arises from the desire of marginalized people to bolster their "stigmatized identities" by creating communities based on "shared attributes and interests." Unlike the bourgeois print age, which extended rights to all *individuals* who assimilated its values, identity politics demands the creation and enforcement of rights that belong to *groups* that reject the pressure of conforming to a dominant (e.g., Eurocentric) understanding of human nature. As Sonia Kruks explains, "The demand is not for inclusion within the field of 'universal humankind' on the basis of shared human attributes; nor is it for respect 'in spite of' one's differences. Rather, what is demanded is respect for oneself as different." In short, some groups demand rights that do not belong to other groups. The clash between groups over which identity deserves the greatest measure of rights creates a politics in which there is little consensus over the meaning of freedom and equality, values that belonged to the bourgeois age. In this tribalist context, it is unsurprising that the media that accompanied these values would be suspect. To give just one example, a diversity, equity, and inclusion (DEI) program at the University of Colorado Boulder stipulates that the "worship of the written word" should be associated with bigotry or "white supremacy."

As a lover of paradox, McLuhan recognizes that civilization's technological progress can coexist with the rejection of civilized mores. For this reason, he does not desire a return to primordial nature under electric conditions. As he writes in *Understanding Media*, "The return to Nature and the return to the tribe are, under electric conditions, fatally simple. We need beware of those who announce programs for restoring man to the original state and language of the race." This return to first nature was already underway before the dawn of television. As McLuhan notes in an aphorism near the end of *Counterblast*, "Radio returns us to the dark of the mind, to the invasions from Mars and Orson Welles. . . . We have evoked a super-civilized sub-primitive man." In *Understanding Media*, he holds up Adolf Hitler as the most infamous example of first nature returning with a vengeance. Hitler, he says, "gave radio the Orson Welles treatment for *real*." In describing Hitler as both a tribal man and a radio man, McLuhan is illustrating the disturbing disjunction between technological innovation and progress in human rationality. He is also pointing to the distinct ways that different media transform politics. Radio does not require a literate or rational audience. As Innis contends in *The Bias of Communication*, the radio reached vast areas, put the literate and illiterate on the same level, and enabled centralized or bureaucratic government.

In *Understanding Media*, McLuhan claims that Hitler's use of radio was far more important than his thoughts, which "were of very little consequence."

The main point that McLuhan is trying to drive home is that radio reawakened tribal feelings (first nature) once thought to be extinct as a result of technological progress. The Germans who most enthusiastically supported the Nazis did not endorse the values associated with literacy or print media: free speech, the right to privacy, individualism. As a tribal man and a radio man, Hitler repudiated a bourgeois literate civilization that had never completely taken root in Germany. McLuhan is not claiming that Germany, which has made a massive contribution to Western philosophy and literature, was a nation of illiterates. His subtle point is that Hitler's success lay in the fact that print media were unable to convey his image as a powerful tribal chieftain. Radio accomplished this feat for him. Although McLuhan never denies that the content of Hitler's speeches played a role, albeit one that was subordinate to the medium, it is safe to assume that the number of Germans who listened to the Führer on the radio far outnumbered those who read his political manifesto, *Mein Kampf*.

Ideologies that reflect the values of the print age cannot explain the rise of tribalism. Marxism, for example, predicted that the class struggle between the bourgeoisie and the proletariat will end with not only the triumph of the impoverished working class but also the decisive proof that economic conflicts trump all others. Yet wars between these classes can lead to conflicts that are not rooted in the unequal distribution of wealth. As McLuhan and Barrington Nevitt write in *Take Today*, "Pushed to extreme, class conflict resumes tribal warfare." Defenders of capitalism embrace the same mistaken approach to the tribal cosmos as Marxists do. Although bourgeois economists used to insist that the rise of capitalist consumption and trade on a global scale will bring peace to earth, this expectation hits the wall of tribalism. In McLuhan's argot, both capitalists and Marxists are still stuck in the era of "hardware," as opposed to "software." The instantaneous information about the global village that electric media (software) enable puts an end to mechanized media (hardware), which assume the universality of an identity preoccupied with economic self-interest. Tribalists, who are suspicious of other tribes in this village, are indifferent to the pleasures of material consumption, as McLuhan and Nevitt note in *Take Today*: "The satisfactions of conspicuous consumption in the age of 'software' are zero. *Homo consumens* in the Western world is dead, just as the *economic man* was killed by Hitler."

The Futility of Imposing Patterns

Given the persistence of tribalism within the electric age, McLuhan doubts that civilizations determined to impose their ideas on others would fare well in the global village. As he writes in *Understanding Media*, the "mark of our time is its revulsion against imposed patterns." Yet nations with deeply rooted identities are often inclined to ignore this fact.

As we have seen, McLuhan contends that the United States' original identity is rooted in literate and bourgeois values. It does not have a tribal past. None of this, however, suggests that literate civilizations are necessarily peaceable ones. As McLuhan and Bruce R. Powers note, the US Civil War was clear proof that the republic had a "strong national identity, reminding Canadians that only the bloody-minded could seriously wish to obtain a group identity by such violence." Conflicts over ideas can be just as violent as tribal ones. As the historian Mark A. Noll has shown, disagreements over what the Bible teaches about the practice of slavery greatly contributed to a "theological crisis" during the Civil War. This conflict over the legitimacy and validity of scripture intensified the struggle between the liberal-minded North and the fundamentalist South.

The use of myth or a grand story is often the foundation of a fixed identity. The American myth of the frontier is one famous example of this pattern. In his 1893 essay "The Significance of the Frontier in American History," the historian Frederick Jackson Turner contended that the modern American character was fully formed by the conquest of the western frontier. As Richard Slotkin explains, "For Turner, it was the economic aspects of the frontier, the free land with its promise of agricultural abundance and broad access to property, that made America exceptional." (This myth also offered an ideological rationale for the military conquest and mass displacement of the Indian tribes living within the western territories.) When the Census Bureau in 1890, according to Slotkin, announced that "there was no longer a substantial reserve of undeveloped arable land," the myth of the frontier seemed to be obsolete. Yet technological change breathed new life into this narrative. With the invention of the telegraph and the creation of instantaneous communication, the discovery (along with the conquest) of new space or territory was sure to follow. The endless need to conquer new frontiers naturally arose out of this momentous change.

Although McLuhan praises Turner for coming up with a "wonderful myth," it was still only a myth, one that paid little attention to the violence associated with frontier expansion (e.g., wars of extermination waged against Indigenous peoples). Yet even myths can transform the world in unintended ways. In McLuhan's judgment, the effect of a myth is far more important to understand than its historical accuracy. Americans who believe that their bourgeois individualist identity ought to be the preeminent one in the world have invoked the myth of the frontier to justify the dissemination of the American identity around the world. Theodore Roosevelt, for example, was anxious that the closing of the western frontier not signal the end of the adventure and conquest that formed the American character. According to Slotkin, the wars against Indigenous peoples provided a basis for the renewal of this myth on a global scale: "Roosevelt's real solution to the problem was to open a new imperial frontier in Asia and Latin America, where a virile new generation of Americans could engage in the regenerative violence of 'savage war' that made their fathers great." The problem is that this frontier identity is one of many, making a clash with other identities in the global village very likely. More seriously, as McLuhan warns, "When our identity is in danger, we feel certain that we have a mandate for war."

That search for new frontiers was one of the driving imperatives behind the Vietnam War. It was also a dramatic attempt to retrieve or repeat a mythical past, one that global communism threatened to destroy. The "new frontier" to which President John F. Kennedy referred in 1960 during the presidential election was presented in this archetypal language. Kennedy proclaimed that the old "pioneers gave up their safety, their comfort, and sometimes their lives to build our new west. They were determined to make the new world strong and free—an example to the world." Yet he also insisted that the United States' embrace of this historic struggle must not slacken: "We stand today on the edge of a new frontier, the frontier of unknown opportunities and perils.... Beyond that frontier are uncharted areas of science and space, unsolved problems of peace and war, unconquered problems of ignorance and prejudice, unanswered questions of poverty and surplus." In short, the US is fulfilling its historic destiny by looking for new frontiers to conquer while demonstrating that its identity is the one that the world must emulate for its own good.

Vietnam would become one of these frontiers. As McLuhan put it in his 1967 Marfleet Lectures, "What is now going on in Vietnam is very much a repeat of what went on in the American frontier for centuries." Yet it was not a literal repeat of the old frontier experience. This time the frontier in question would not be so easily conquered, or even understood, by what some called the "new frontiersmen." McLuhan asserted that Lyndon Johnson's administration, which had inherited all of Kennedy's advisers, was full of "unconscious frontiersmen going through the old motions of being frontiersmen without noticing what they were doing."

The exuberant rhetoric about the new frontiers turned out to be another example of how human beings are "unconscious" of the transformative effects of technological change. JFK, LBJ, and their advisers on Vietnam acted as if the US could simply repeat the conquest of the western frontier on an international scale. Yet the new reality of the global village made this retrieval project unlikely. Unlike the frontier wars of the past, Vietnam was the first *televised* war, a conflict that was visible to the American people on the nightly news. As McLuhan explains in *War and Peace in the Global Village*, this war was being fought in the living room as much as it was on the battlefields of Vietnam: "The public is now participant in every phase of the war, and the main actions of the war are now being fought in the American home itself." Information about wars in previous eras was available through hot media such as newspapers, movies, and radio, which encouraged a sense of objective detachment. With the advent of TV, war became public. Americans were not simply watching the war; they were involved with the conflict in a manner that was unprecedented in US history. As McLuhan wryly observed, "Parents can now see their sons killed in living color. All sons become ours on TV." The implication of this technological feat was striking. It was not so easy to assume that the world desired the American identity when Americans could watch violent resistance to its military intervention around the clock. This total involvement, McLuhan said, was "untakable," making war far less tolerable than it was in the past.

As an anticommunist, McLuhan was not morally opposed to the objective of defeating the totalitarian aggression of the North Vietnamese regime against the people of South Vietnam. Rather, he was highlighting the blinkered assumptions that often influenced the United States' waging of the war. The most erroneous premise was that the electric environment in which the war took place made no difference, even though McLuhan constantly warned that human beings had not yet learned to cope with its effects. The persistence of the frontier myth encouraged the erroneous impression that the US could fight and defeat the "tribal man" in Asia in the same manner as it had during the wars of westward expansion. The war itself, McLuhan argued, was a "form of education," teaching "many hard lessons to people in Vietnam now and with vast cost to ourselves." In fact, this educational intervention was so massive that media reportage of the war became more important than actual combat operations in Vietnam. In a 1970 interview with the journalist Tom Wolfe, McLuhan remarked that more people were covering "Vietnam business" around the world than were actually fighting it, leaving the impression that the war was a "colossal fiction."

Guerrilla warfare in Vietnam pushed back against this odd synthesis of education and "mythic form" provided by TV news. Despite the superiority of US military hardware, the Viet Cong were prepared to sacrifice their lives in the face of this awesome firepower. This self-sacrificing mentality, according to McLuhan, closed the gap "between the advanced American-type technology and their backward technology." The fact that this war was on TV further inspired the Vietnamese communists to use electric media as a "teaching machine," one that highlighted their exploits for the entire world to see. Although traditional tribalists preferred a society closed off to the rest of the world, the new tribalists were "private and tribal," willing to use Western technology to create sympathy for their cause. In short, nothing abolishes the distinction between the center and the margin quite like a televised war. The little red schoolhouse is alive and well in the electric age.

McLuhan was not making moral judgments as to the merits of the West at the expense of the East. What is imperative to understand, in his view, is the difficulty of imposing any pattern on the fractious and diverse global village, particularly if this blueprint does not fit the electric age.

A "Perverse Mimesis"

Despite the Vietnam debacle, the appeal of a global mission to spread American ideals has not dissipated, even in times of political turbulence. What McLuhan describes as the American tendency to "feel a certain obligation to conquer the twentieth century or take full advantage of it" is an enduring influence in the present age. On the third anniversary of the January 6, 2021, riot in the Capitol, President Joe Biden declared, "Democracy is still a sacred cause. And there's no country in the world better positioned to lead the world than America." This collection of claims about US democracy requires some interpretation. First, if democracy is a "sacred cause" (a term that Biden borrowed from George Washington), then it is presumably a regime that has a divine or transcendent origin and legitimacy. It must follow, then, that anyone who questions democracy American-style is on the wrong side of the gods. Second, the United States' leadership of this mission is beyond doubt, given its great power. The US must lead by projecting her great power throughout the world. Although most of Biden's speech was directed at domestic "enemies" of democracy (e.g., Donald Trump and MAGA Republicans), his statement about the natural leadership of the US on a global scale implies that there remain frontiers to conquer or strengthen in the name of democracy. Because democracy is sacred, it is not just an American credo; it is a universal ideal that transcends all cultural differences. Therefore, it is perfectly justified and necessary to fulfill this mission by intervening in regions of the world that resist democracy in theory or practice. In simple terms, the US must lead and the world must follow. The question that would interest McLuhan in this context is this: In attempting to change the world, does the US also change in the process? Put differently, is causality a one-way or two-way street?

As we have seen, McLuhan is convinced that any radical change in identity in a short period of time is unsettling. Moreover, any "interface" or forced intersection between two distinct phenomena is bound to create tremendous "tension." Within this dynamic, each side shapes the other, just as the media that we create also alter who we are. The West's longstanding incursions into the East are dramatic vindications of these truths. As McLuhan explains in his major works, Western civilization began with the advent of the phonetic alphabet and the triumph of literacy over orality. The subsequent rise of bourgeois individualism was an effect of these processes. In contrast, the civilizations of the East, which were originally wedded to orality, did not originally cultivate individualism. The literate mind's distinction between the inside mind (subject) and outside reality (object) reflects a visual orientation. The dualistic attempt of a civilization to act as the center transforming a margin parallels the dualism of a subject discovering an objective reality. This dualistic tendency to match reality clashes with Eastern metaphysics, which emphasizes the fluidity of one reality, one that is not divisible in terms of essences (the mind) and appearances (the outside world). From this perspective, the mind cannot detach itself from an external reality. In short, the Western mind is trapped in dualistic oppositions that are alien to its Eastern counterpart. In the all-encompassing global village, this illusion of detachment breaks down. Yet without this detachment, the conquest of new frontiers becomes an impossibility.

Not only is the West unable to impose these dualisms on the rest of the world, but its intervention into the non-Western world weakens its attachment to its own literate traditions. The law of reversal dramatically illustrates the limitations of any appeal to any universalism, Western or non-Western, within the conflicted global village. The reversal of the West into the East (or the East into the West) is a phenomenon that, in McLuhan's view, is not well understood precisely because this process is not a conscious decision. Whenever one civilization imposes its values on another by means of technology, it unconsciously takes on the features of its enemy or subject. "We become what we fight in the very act of fighting," McLuhan and Nevitt writes in *Take Today*. "There is a kind of perverse mimesis, which causes the thing we fear to come upon us."

Mīmēsis, which is the ancient Greek word for "imitation," is not bad in and of itself. As the high-tech entrepreneur Peter Thiel explains, "The learning of language and the transmission of various cultural institutions" is the conventional way of understanding mimesis. It becomes perverse, to use McLuhan's term, only when enemies imitate each other in violent ways. Thiel writes, "In the process of 'keeping up with the Joneses,' mimesis pushes people into escalating rivalry." In McLuhan's judgment, the East and the West are imitating each other in this sense.

To make this argument about the Western world "going Eastern," McLuhan was fond of quoting the following passage from Joyce's *Finnegans Wake*: "The West shall shake the East awake. While ye have the night for morn." The West's awakening of the East through greater contact and intervention is not leading to a more progressivist future in which the West reshapes the East in its own image and likeness. Rather, the West will reenter "the tribal night" or "Finn cycle." None of this is rational or deliberate, McLuhan notes: "It is like our contemporary consciousness of the Unconscious."

In the process, the West's interventions threaten to upend its bourgeois values. The Vietnam War demonstrated this process, McLuhan believed. "While we are

Westernizing the East, the Orient, by our old technology," he said, "we are Orientalizing ourselves by new technology. The electric age is giving us all the inner trip." This "inner trip" requires the rejection of the old print and individualistic mentality, even though the West believes that it is imparting this ethos. In his 1967 lecture "Open-Mind Surgery," McLuhan associates the inner trip with integral, organic involvement, not the bourgeois "outer trip" of individual specialism. Unlike the West, the East makes no distinction between the inner and outer. In short, once the West abandons its historic adherence to the private self, it will have become Orientalized.

If anyone needs evidence for this radical assessment, McLuhan provides it by looking at the transformation of the modern democratic state during the electric age. In *Take Today*, he and Nevitt discuss how modern warfare has transformed the old bourgeois state into a "warfare-welfare state." This state, which came into being during World War II, has the power to wage war abroad while it provides extensive social insurance for its citizens at home. The authority of the old bourgeois state, in contrast, was confined to maintaining law and order and protecting property rights. With the technological transformation of nature into an artifact, it is easy to believe that this state is all-powerful. During the Cold War, citizens became used to the normality of wartime conditions (e.g., inflation) even during peacetime. "In the warfare state built and experienced during the first part of the twentieth century," McLuhan and Nevitt write, "the ebb and flow of depression and inflation have become a way of life."

Even long after the Cold War ended, the warfare-welfare state continues to grow in size and power. This phenomenon signals the end of bourgeois values. Western corporations and governments no longer abide by the private-public dichotomy that characterized the bourgeois age; instead these entities freely reject the inner-outer distinction that is the basis of privacy and individualism. A perverse mimesis between West and East is taking place. While the West is "sloughing off" old bourgeois values, McLuhan and Nevitt observe in *Take Today*, the East is creating the "nineteenth-century world of consumer services and packages," albeit by authoritarian means. Corporations are just as eager to work with the new surveillance state as their counterparts in China are. While the West turns away from capitalism to embrace statist collectivism, the East's statist collectivism accommodates capitalism on its own terms. Since the establishment of a "social credit" system in 2014, the communist government in China has acted like a capitalist bank or credit union by tracking the purchasing decisions of its citizens. In the process, it also assigns a score that restricts the freedom of citizens based on their behavior in the marketplace or beyond. In short, China is an example of an Eastern civilization using Western technology to reinforce the "forms" of tribal loyalty to the regime.

In the West, corporations such as Meta and PayPal collect information on radical groups that post messages that are ostensibly a threat to political order. This information gathering has led to the censorship and exclusion of these groups from social media as well as from the entire economic system. PayPal has pledged to share this information with other financial services. Banks are also under pressure to submit to statist diktats on the replacement of paper money. The Biden administration's interest in launching a digital currency would allow the federal government to require banks to authorize this currency, with the official aim of helping the disadvantaged (or "unbanked") access banking services. This plan is comparable to banking policy in China, where citizens can access electronic allocations of credit to buy goods and services. In both cases, the reach of the state into the economy would grow as dramatically in the United States as it already has in China. The loss of privacy and individual freedom would be predictable casualties, as the economist Eswar Prasad explains: "The government could also make transacting with certain people difficult or impossible. China already has a social credit system that ranks citizens algorithmically and punishes them in various ways." In short, while increased involvement and interaction between the United States and China have hardly led to greater understanding and affection, they have contributed, paradoxically, to the countries' greater imitation of each other.

The line between state and economy becomes more blurred as the policies of the West and the East converge. The warfare-welfare states of both civilizations employ state and corporate power to "war" against dissenters in the name of protecting the "welfare" of society. The "happiness" of the citizenry is equally the concern of both states and corporations. Commenting on a full page-ad entitled "Happiness Is the Federal Government Doing a Study on Happiness" in the *New York Times* (1968), McLuhan sardonically notes, "If 'Violence' is substituted for 'Happiness,' the result is the same. Government, culture and business are now one." With a nod to formal causality, it is highly probable that corporations and government will continue to maximize the interventionist potential of surveillance technologies.

Will this convergence of perspective and power foster a more peaceful relationship between the West and the East, as opposed to a perverse mimesis? McLuhan was cautious here. In "the last half of the 20th Century," he and Powers predicted, "the East will rush Westward and the West will embrace orientalism, all in a desperate attempt to cope with each other, to avoid violence. But the key to peace is to understand both systems simultaneously." This task is imperative. "Never before has the entire world been organized on two patterns, both of which are in a state of interchange and simultaneous metamorphosis," write McLuhan and Nevitt in *Take Today*. Despite the fact that East and West are involved with each other in unprecedented ways, understanding is not the same as involvement. Is there any nation left in the global village that can provide this understanding and bring about peace?

Is Canada the Exception?

At times, McLuhan presents his own country as an example of how to survive the instability and violence of the global village. Canada is a success story in this age of conflict precisely because it has no fixed identity based on dominant myths. A strong sense of identity, McLuhan insists, usually encourages the violent imposition of this identity onto others. In contrast, the lack of a fixed Canadian identity puts it in a greater position to navigate the electric age than those nations that possess strong identities. This absence has enabled some Canadians, particularly McLuhan, to act as the observer of the American experience, enjoying the benefits of its neighbor without buying into its identity. As McLuhan claims in his 1977 essay "Canada: The Borderline Case," the "Canadian 'nobody' can have the best of two worlds: on the one hand, the human scale of the small country and, on the other hand, the immediate advantages of proximity to massive power."

The qualification that McLuhan adds to this pleasant portrait of the Canadian experience is that Canada's elites should not impose a centralizing fixed identity where none has ever existed. In fact, no nation should attempt to do this in the electric age, which encourages decentralization. Canada serves as a warning against the imposition of an artificial unity or centralism onto a country with vastly different regions and borderlines of its own. McLuhan associates the practice of centralized control with the obsolete bourgeois print era. As long as a center can control the flow of information to the margins, it can maintain control. In the age of acoustic space, where information is instantaneously transmitted, it is not so easy to control this flow, although governments and media firms make an effort to do so. As McLuhan explains, "In the electric age centralism becomes impossible when all services are available everywhere. Canada has never been able to centralize because of its size and small population. The national unity sought by the railway 'hardware' now proves to be irrelevant under electric conditions which yet create an inclusive consciousness." McLuhan thus concludes that the old center-margin distinction is obsolete.

Nevertheless, obsolete is not the same as extinct. As McLuhan once asserted, "Obsolescence never meant the end of anything—it's just the beginning." Put differently, a process has little impact until it has affected every aspect of a society. Even though McLuhan doubted that any return to the old bourgeois period of history was possible, the passing of this era did not put an end to the *desire* to continue the centralization of control over the margins. The federal government's policy of official bilingualism in the federal civil service encouraged similar doubts about the imposition of a fixed identity. In a 1978 letter to Prime Minister Pierre Trudeau, the architect of official bilingualism, McLuhan critically noted that the requirement that all bureaucrats be fluent in English and French would only remind Canadians of what distinguished them, not what united them. The fact that they shared two common languages would not foster a sense of unity. "Do not English Canadians speak American and feel at home in the U.S.A. without the slightest thought of unity?" he asked. McLuhan felt that this policy would be more "acceptable if it grew up naturally from below," in a manner that reflected different traditions and customs, not just language.

McLuhan's qualified praise for Canada's official policy of promoting a "cultural mosaic," which also began in the 1970s, expressed similar doubts about the efficacy of imposing identity from above. The official goal of this mosaic was to avoid the homogenizing effects of the American melting pot by enabling new immigrants to preserve their cultural identities and maintain their ties to their native lands while gently embracing Canadian values. In short, their differences would not "melt" into their new country when they assimilated the Canadian identity, one that McLuhan thought lacked fixity anyway. Like official bilingualism, this policy of multiculturalism was also meant to create unity among established Canadians and new immigrants, or at least discourage conflict between them. In 1977, in his last televised interview, McLuhan discussed this unprecedented approach to immigration by wryly pointing to the likelihood that it would minimize conflict between Canadians without actually encouraging any connections between them. Although he hoped that this unprecedented policy, which no other nation had attempted, would perpetuate Canada's survival in a divided world, he also concluded that the mosaic was "a way of using our available resources in communication to keep people apart and to keep them intact without merging." In other words, the multicultural mosaic was another example of a policy that reminded Canadians of their differences. To impose a unifying identity, even one that celebrates diversity, on a nation without any defining identity is as elusive as expecting unity in the global village. Put differently, the mosaic unwittingly reveals that Canadians have a weak identity. Trudeau later admitted he had not anticipated that new immigrants would put their ethnic identity before the Canadian identity. Trudeau's son Justin perhaps unintentionally reminded his countrymen of the persistent absence of any fixed national ties between Canadians when he declared in 2017 that Canada is the first "postnational" country.

As a Westerner who grew up on the outer reaches of the Canadian imperium, McLuhan had no illusions about the desire of domineering centers to impose their wills on the powerless denizens of the hinterlands. In *Counterblast,* he describes the Maritime provinces as an "impoverished little empire that breeds EAGER EXECUTIVES for all the RAMPANT EMPIRES: Daily Express, Imperial Oil, Bank of Montreal," and he chides western Canada "for its meekness in filling the coffers of Bay Street." McLuhan's feelings of detachment from central Canada never truly vanished. As he later remarked in a conversation with the Canadian journalist Peter C. Newman in the early 1970s, the one thing that unites Canada's diverse regions is hostility toward Toronto "as enemy territory" precisely because "all the decisions are made there on everything and their miseries are invented there."

Central Canada's historic preoccupation with controlling the margins represented an attempt to create a sense of national unity and purpose that was, frankly, impossible in a country that, as McLuhan put it, has a "low-profile identity" amid "multiple borderlines." Moreover, any attempt to control the flow of information that operates at the speed of light will fail. McLuhan believed that the same principle applies to the control of identity. Unlike many Canadian nationalists, he was not overly suspicious or fearful of US influence on Canada. Most Canadians are very grateful, McLuhan contended, for their free access to US media, not least because it "feeds the philosophical attitude of comparison and contrast and critical judgement" within a context of "princely hospitality and neighborly dialogue on the ground." For these reasons, McLuhan was unsympathetic to the attempts of Canadian nationalists to control and restrict the broadcasting of popular American TV shows to shore up the Canadian identity. A western like *Bonanza,* he believed, posed no threat to the national psyche. The popularity of this show in the 1960s demonstrated the universal human desire to "clutch at" a bygone age that provides reassuring images during a period of rapid technological change. As soon as Canadians watched *Bonanza,* its content became Canadian.

The passage of Bill C-11 (the Online Streaming Act) in 2023 allowed the Canadian Radio-Television and Telecommunications Commission to promote "Canadian cultural content" by imposing "conditions on how online streamers support Canadian content and contribute to production funds, as well as ensuring Canadian programs and films show up in search results." McLuhan's contention that Canadians already Canadianize foreign content is apparently lost on the federal government, which assumes that it alone is the sole guardian of a nonexistent national identity. In the electric and digital ages, no single center can control the margins of the global village.

8

THE RETRIEVAL OF THE BOOK

In the late 1940s, McLuhan sternly warned that there are no quick fixes to the "trance-like" effects of media. It was also naive to believe that powerful interests within the state or big business could impose any fix of this kind. "So the process of renewal can't come from above," he wrote. "It can only take the form of reawakened critical faculties." He went on to observe that the shutdown of the press, radio, and movies for six months would reveal the "agony" experienced by masses of people addicted to these media. Was there any medium left that could reawaken critical faculties? McLuhan's answer was the book.

McLuhan often faced the accusation that he was hostile to the medium of the book simply because he supposedly predicted its demise along with the values and culture that accompany it. The essayist Dwight Macdonald faulted him for preferring "speech over writing, for the primitive over the civilized." Macdonald went so far as to suggest that McLuhan was looking forward to the emergence of a new "Noble Savage," one that is "equipped with computers and other electronic devices that make writing, indeed even speech, unnecessary for communication." Like many critics of McLuhan, Macdonald was confusing the medium—the messenger—with the message. The fact that McLuhan noted the weakened status of the book does not mean that he favored this change. In an interview in 1967, he remarked, "The new environment shaped by electric technology is a cannibalistic one that eats people. To survive one must study the habits of cannibals." As he wrote in a letter to the editor of the *Globe and Mail* in 1970, "It is not easy to convince people that if one describes a process, one is not taking a stand, pro or con. As a Professor of Literature, I am entirely on the side of print."

As we shall see, McLuhan also anticipated a viable future for the book after the electric age had knocked it off its perch. In the postliterate age, one can even rediscover an old medium. Electric media can encourage, unwittingly, the *retrieval* of the book. According to McLuhan, "Like the human memory, the process of recall is an act of discovery." In *The Gutenberg Galaxy*, he welcomed the opportunity to study the "positive virtues of print" after the displacement of literacy by radio and television. This act of discovery may lead to a better understanding of what the book can do in the present age. In his essay "The Crack in the Rear-View Mirror" (1966), he makes this prediction: "The book is about to cease being a vehicle of self-expression, and is about to become a corporate probe of society." A successful book does not merely reflect the ideas of its author. Instead it shakes things up, which is exactly what a "probe" is supposed to do, as he once explained: "For me any of the little gestures I make are all tentative probes. That's why I feel free to make them sound as outrageous or extreme as possible. Until you make it extreme, the probe is not very efficient."

Why does the book need to probe or change anything at all? It is not as if people have stopped reading. A 2023 article reports, "In the UK 58% of consumers surveyed prefer reading magazines in print rather than online, and overseas in the US about 1 in 4 American adults buys a print newspaper." The same article points out that many readers have made the transition from social media back to print media. The retrieval of early versions of print media is becoming an actuality as well. A growing movement of scholars is rising against the centralized corporate control of academic journal publishing, which has become a multimillion-dollar industry. Instead of relying on these firms to publish journals that charge exorbitant fees, these scholars are contemplating the retrieval of the self-published pamphlet (a medium that originated in the late Middle Ages), which would be more affordable to impoverished academics and university libraries. It would also enable the decentralization that McLuhan often expected in the electric age by placing decision-making power in the hands of academics.

Still, McLuhan probably would have avoided simplistically predicting a return to books, given the fact that electric and digital media do not generally encourage patient and reflective reading. TikTok drenches its users in images, not words (see chapter 9). Reading within an electric age is an experience that is different from that of reading within a print age. The brief public glance at or perusal of a magazine or newspaper, which the bias of space encourages, is far more comparable to the quick reading of a social media website than it is to the careful private reading of a book. As McLuhan claims in *Understanding Media*, the reading of a paperback in the TV age is a "tactile" experience that permits the reader to enjoy the book anywhere, given its mobile nature (formal cause).

As I show in this chapter, McLuhan values the reading of books that help us understand the world that we have made through media or technology. In his view, the educational establishment needs to understand this reality, lest the very existence of civilization itself be swept up and drowned in the maelstrom of technological change. At its best, McLuhan contends, literacy cultivates "the power of man to act without reaction." The careful reading of *some* books can even assist in this task. McLuhan is very critical of literature and pedagogies that discourage this understanding. Some of the most sophisticated minds in history—particularly Plato and Aristotle—draw his critical scrutiny because their preoccupation with an eternal world independent of human understanding led them to devalue the world that humanity had created. The way that McLuhan presents his own doctoral dissertation as an attempt to "reconsider" the entire intellectual tradition from Greek antiquity to the modern age applies to his entire oeuvre.

What is the reason behind this reconsideration of Western philosophy? In *Laws of Media*, the McLuhans praise the philosophers Francis Bacon and Vico for their focus on what human beings create, particularly idols or false gods of their own making. They approvingly quote Vico, who, writing in *The New Science*, can only "marvel that the philosophers should have bent all their energies to the study of the world of nature, which, since God made it, He alone knows; and that they should have neglected the study of the world of nations or civil world, which, since men made it, men could come to know." (The fact that the subtitle of *Laws of Media* is *The New Science* reveals McLuhan's intellectual debt to Vico.) In short, if we are to understand the world of media adequately, we must turn our attention to what we create and, therefore, potentially control.

An additional benefit that comes from recalling the book is that we can appreciate the importance of paradox, or the coexistence of two opposing forces. We have already seen McLuhan emphasize the coexistence of human ignorance and knowledge in relation to new media. Books that help us understand paradox are particularly important to McLuhan precisely because they resist a long philosophical tradition of "dialectics" that denies paradox. For this reason, he prefers the pre-Socratic philosopher Heraclitus to Aristotle for saying "YES AND NO," as an affirmation of the paradox that something and its opposite can be equally true.

In contrast, Aristotle denies paradox. Instead, he emphasizes the authority of the law of noncontradiction (sometimes called the law of contradiction or the excluded middle). Put differently, Aristotle says "YES OR NO," disregarding any possibility that something and its opposite may be equally correct. The denial of paradox has been a costly one. McLuhan would agree with Sigmund Freud's warning that the "logical laws of thought do not apply in the id, and this is true above all of the law of contradiction. Contrary impulses exist side by side, without cancelling each other out or diminishing each other." The effect of dialectics or logic has been to legitimize false choices, or "dualisms," that split reality into two parts. Plato, Aristotle's great teacher, placed an eternal reality above a changeable one, which led him to attack poetry as a mere fabrication of this higher existence knowable only to philosophers. In accord with the law of noncontradiction, only the thoughts of philosophers can access the eternal, while poets can only feel their way through a changeable reality that they fabricated. McLuhan's interest in the science of cognition stems from his opposition to the false choice between an objective rationality (the left hemisphere of the brain) and creative intuition (the right hemisphere of the brain). What McLuhan and Harley Parker call the "dualism" between the subject (the mind that discovers reality) and the object (the reality that is discovered) must be overcome through education if we are to understand how the creation of technology puts an end to any distinction between what is permanent and what is created.

While recalling paradox through the rediscovery of books, McLuhan, as a grammarian, is also determined to understand the underlying language of the world. More specifically, we can reinterpret the unity between what McLuhan calls the "Book of Nature" and the "Book of Scripture." As a traditional Catholic, he seeks to understand how these two books relate to each other. While the Book of Scripture is the Bible, the Book of Nature is the world that God has created. Both books reveal the truth of God's relation to humanity, as revealed in the Genesis narrative. By studying nature as a God-given book, we can recapture the wisdom of the first Adam, who delighted in nature as the creation of God. After the Fall, the second Adam received the God-given knowledge to create technology. According to McLuhan, human beings must act as if they are both the first and second Adams, equally appreciative of both God-given creation (the Book of Nature) and the awesome power of human creation (as revealed by the Book of Scripture). In the process, we can also learn how essential the Bible is: it is *the* book that inspires us to grasp our awesome responsibility for what we create, usually without understanding in the secular age. None of this can happen, of course, unless people actually *read* the Bible.

The Return of the "Great Books"

The rise of the electric age displaced the authority of the written word. McLuhan often targeted educators or academics who failed to understand this fact. Many, he wrote, imagined that they "could pursue the old ends by the new means" through the introduction of electric media (e.g., television) into classrooms that were used to books and essays. Like the fish in the water, they did not understand the gap between the pedagogy of print and the new media environment. As a result, the classroom felt like a "feudal dungeon." McLuhan believed that students raised on TV wanted to be involved with the happenings of world, not recipients of its information. As a result, he was unsurprised that many of the brightest students were dropping out after encountering a teaching environment that required passivity and detachment. These dropouts, he observed, "are saying that they would rather be involved in the creative processes of production than in the consumer processes of sopping up packaged data."

McLuhan felt that the solution that educators should contemplate is the study of how different phenomena relate to each other. This new pedagogy would have the merit of emphasizing how every human being participates, however unwittingly, as an agent, not a detached observer, in the global village. Instead of encouraging "the absorption of classified and fragmented data," education should focus on "pattern recognition, with all that that implies of grasping interrelationships." Put differently, "total field" study should be the object of an educated person's attention. Although McLuhan was certain that the new media "threaten our entire way of life," he believed that education still plays an essential role in enabling a patient and total understanding of their powers and influences. The role of the book is pivotal in this context. As he confidently declared in a review essay, "The book having lost its monopoly as a channel of information or as an avenue of recreation, now assumes a higher role as tool and trainer of perception in all the arts."

One practical way of creating this new pedagogy of the book is to understand pattern recognition, or the interrelationships between phenomena. McLuhan himself practiced this educational approach by breaking down artificial barriers between disciplines. Much to the chagrin of his colleagues, he was unafraid of using insights and data from disciplines as diverse as literature, history, philosophy, art, and science. This interdisciplinary sleuthing was a rebellion against the print mind, which, according to McLuhan, encouraged narrow specialization. The separation of art from other comparable disciplines was a particularly strong obstacle to the discovery of interrelationships. "In America," McLuhan wrote, "print and book-culture became the dominant form from the beginning, setting walls between literature and art, and art and life, which were less obvious in Europe." Given the importance that McLuhan placed on the role of the artist in helping us understand the nature of technological change, this effect of specialization is particularly troubling.

By studying the relation or interface between one medium and another, McLuhan contends, one can create an "anti-environment" that is most familiar to the artistic temperament. "There is no possible protection from technology except by technology. When you create a new environment with one phase of technology, you have to create an anti-environment with the next." This understanding of dueling environments requires a rigorous education across the disciplines. The proper study of poetry, for example, requires the reader to understand poems as being intelligible to both the visual and auditory senses. One can read and sing the words of a poem, as the preprint age of orality understood well.

For this reason, McLuhan initially welcomed the creation of the "great books" program at the University of Chicago. He credited its founders, Robert Maynard Hutchins and Mortimer Adler, for creating a program that required students to study the great works of philosophy, literature, and other humanistic disciplines to counter the narrow specialization that dominated the university scene. Ideally, McLuhan hoped at the time, this program would put an end to the "ancient quarrel" or dualism that pitted Platonic dialectics and Aristotelian logic against the worthy study of poetry and rhetoric.

As Leo Strauss argued in the 1960s, this great-books pedagogy is a "counterpoison" to the leveling effects of mass culture. The assumption that drives the study of great books is that the authors who wrote these works articulate timeless and uplifting truths about how humanity can resist modern democracy's slouching movement toward the mechanization of human intelligence. A few scholars have expressed the hope that this "liberal education" can overcome the challenge of technologies (e.g., ChatGPT) by reminding universities that their mission is to teach students to ponder what it means to be a human being, not to provide them with practical skills for the marketplace. Programs based on economic necessity and utility (e.g., business) have the most to fear from ChatGPT, which threatens to make those programs obsolete. In contrast, the humanities can achieve what artificial intelligence cannot: the cultivation of the souls of young readers searching for the truth. This prediction is not just the wishful thinking of academics. Robert Goldstein, the chief operating officer of the BlackRock investment firm, has conceded that his firm needs to hire more people with a liberal arts background so that the company can benefit from greater "diversity of thinking." George Lee, co-head of Goldman Sachs's global institute, has predicted that the rise of AI will make "the revenge of the liberal arts" a reality. "Some of the skills that are really salient to cooperate with this new intelligence in the world are critical thinking, understanding logic and rhetoric, the ability to be creative," Lee explains. "It will allow non-technical people to accomplish a lot more—and, by the way, begin to perform what were formerly believed to be technical tasks."

Despite the enduring appeal of great-books programs, not everyone has been convinced that they can fulfill these ambitious goals. In the late 1980s, the conservative author Robert Nisbet cautioned that every age needs fresh thinking that may not be available in a list of great books. "The most important thing in the world," Nisbet wrote, "whether in comparative literature, philosophy, and social studies or in biology, chemistry, and physics, is the induction of the tyro into the living world of problems, not the world of books which have the imprimatur of Great on them."

If anyone qualifies as an exploring tyro in Nisbet's sense, it is Marshall McLuhan, who warns that any attempt to recover the culture of reading without considering the new problems caused by technological change is doomed to failure. McLuhan's early praise of the great-books program at the University of Chicago gradually turned to critique. In *The Mechanical Bride*, he targeted Hutchins and Adler for failing to understand the full effects of media such as the press, radio, and movies on mass education. Although McLuhan acknowledged that Adler and Hutchins recognized how the university cannot easily compete with the "constant storm of triviality and propaganda" that arises from these media, he also pointed to the irony that the great-books program was "an unintentional reflection of the technological world in which he [the educator] lives." By placing the "great ideas" of these works in "coffin-like filing boxes" that an index makes accessible for "immediate use," Hutchins and Adler were unconsciously imitating the values and structures of the mechanized age that they otherwise consciously despised.

McLuhan never opposes the reading of books, including the great books of literature and philosophy. Given his long-held penchant for drawing connections between diverse disciplines, this is not surprising. More importantly, he acknowledges, the book "can never lose its usefulness as a means of arresting thought and language for study." Moreover, the "printed book is thus the only available means of developing habits of private initiative and private goals and objectives in the electric age." In short, civilization based on literacy is worthy of preservation. While watching TV in the 1970s, he confided to a friend, "Do you want to know what I really think about these machines? If we want to save a trace of Graeco-Roman-Christian civilization, we'll have to smash all of them!" What McLuhan does emphasize is the need to relate the great books of civilization to the present age in a *conscious* manner, without unconsciously taking on its biases. As he explains in *The Mechanical Bride*, "The failure to come to grips with the particulars of contemporary existence also becomes a failure to converse with the great minds *via* great books." By employing these books as part of a program dedicated to the study of popular culture, students would be able to attain "a fuller sense of the particularity of human conditions, past and present, without which there is no understanding either of art, philosophy, or society." Before this happens, however, certain dualisms that have pitted timeless truths against timely opinions need critical scrutiny.

Philosophy versus Poetry

As early as his dissertation on Thomas Nashe, McLuhan laments the influence that Plato and his most famous student, Aristotle, have exerted on philosophy. Plato's hostility to sophistry, rhetoric, and poetry as changeable and inferior imitations of the eternal contributed, in McLuhan's judgment, to a "dialectical" picture of philosophy that condemned it to the search for eternal truths. This search has had two unfortunate side effects. First, Platonists and Aristotelians ignore the fact that those ancient philosophers who focused on the temporal were still "strongly, tirelessly moral and political in doctrine and emphasis." Second, Platonism and its successors opened up a dualism between temporal reality and eternal reality, creating a dangerous divide "where the human dimension is obliterated by sensuality at one end of the spectrum, and by sheer abstraction at the other." Taken together, these passages reveal McLuhan's opposition to any scholarly tendency to subordinate the changeable or sensual to the eternal or abstract. Even Plato did not consistently adhere to this dualism. He never achieved the severance of rhetoric and wisdom, McLuhan observes.

Plato's critique of the poets as mythmakers who are oblivious to the eternal order of things is particularly relevant here. The fact that the poets create or fabricate stories provokes Plato's suspicion that they offer nothing more than changeable opinions about the eternal. Plato's famous distinction between the discovery and the making of reality explains his treatment of poetry as a way of life inferior to philosophy. While the philosopher seeks or discovers reality, the poet makes reality by constructing fables or narratives. In book 10 of the *Republic*, Plato more dramatically presses this point by calling for the exile of the poets from his ideal city. The reason for this action dates back to "an old quarrel between philosophy and poetry." In earlier passages, Plato articulates the nature of this quarrel. As he explains through the voice of his teacher Socrates, "Imitation is surely far from the truth; and, as it seems, it is due to this that it produces everything—because it lays hold of a certain small part of each thing, and that part is itself only a phantom." Unlike the philosopher—the lover and seeker of wisdom—the poet confuses wisdom with the stories that he constructs. "Shouldn't we set down all those skilled in making, beginning with Homer, as imitators of phantoms of virtue and of the other subjects of their making?" Plato asks. "They don't lay hold of the truth." Imitation ultimately teaches nothing of worth: "The imitator knows nothing worth mentioning about what he imitates; imitation is a kind of play and not serious."

In McLuhan's view, Plato's banishment of Homer from the republic reflects his preference for dialectics over grammar by asserting that philosophy is concerned with the timeless (e.g., mathematics, logic), while poetry is trapped in the flux of grammar, a mere imitation of eternity. In Platonic terms, the philosopher is somehow able to discover reality or "match" his mind with the eternal, an achievement far beyond the ken of the poet. As McLuhan astutely notes in his dissertation, even Plato does not consistently obey this surgical distinction between philosophy and poetry, given his own usage of poetry and myth "to express his own most significant and esoteric teaching." The irony that results from this dualism is that most philosophers since Plato have tried to match their psyches with an elusive permanent reality that is of their own making. With the advent of the electric age, McLuhan and Barrington Nevitt explain, "it became apparent that 'Nature' was a figure abstracted from a ground of existence that was far from 'natural.'" At best, philosophy in the Platonic-Aristotelian sense can describe the order of the "natural" world without paying due attention to the "effects of man-made technology" that transform this world. Although McLuhan credits Aristotle with the insight that human making or creation *ideally* aligns with nature, this attempt at analogy fails to take account of how human making can not only depart from nature but even dethrone it.

The Left-Right Opposition in the Brain

In fairness to Plato, there is a biological analogue to his distinction between discovering and making reality. In the 1970s, McLuhan became deeply interested in the science of the brain, following the surgery on his brain tumor a few years beforehand. The brain has two distinct hemispheres. The left hemisphere (on the right side of the body) houses the speech and verbal functions of the brain. It also perceives reality in logical, mathematical, and linear terms. Predictably, the left hemisphere gravitates toward the sequential ordering that reading and writing require. This hemisphere also perceives reality as something to discover, match, and analyze. The right hemisphere (on the left side of the body) houses the spatial and musical functions. It perceives reality in artistic, symbolic, and simultaneous terms. Naturally, the right hemisphere gravitates toward the intuitive and creative thinking that art and music encourage. In the process, this hemisphere encourages the making of reality. Ideally, both hemispheres should work together to make sense of reality. If McLuhan is right, it all depends on the environment that people inhabit. In *Laws of Media*, he and his son Eric associate the right hemisphere with the tribal culture that insists on an intuitive and emotional involvement with the environment, one that is "closed" to outside influences. The paradox that everything happens all at once, as in simultaneity, is a given in this environment. The left hemisphere, in sharp contrast, encourages individual thought, detachment from nature, and, implicitly, an intolerance of paradox.

In his portrayal of what has come to be known as the "bi-cameral mind," McLuhan is not suggesting that there is a clean demarcation between the two hemispheres. Rather, it is important to "ask why it is that most individuals and cultures seem to favor one hemisphere at the expense of the other." The answer to this question, according to Robert K. Logan and McLuhan in their book *The Future of the Library*, requires the study of "biases in our thinking processes that result from our communication patterns." A civilization dedicated to what McLuhan calls "matching" reinforces the hegemony of the left hemisphere. The corresponding indifference to "making" that results from this focus leads to a "robotic" existence. In *Through the Vanishing Point*, McLuhan and Parker claim that ancient Greek civilization, particularly fifth-century Athens, fell into this pattern as it began to embrace the alphabet and the visual sense: "In discovering the joys of matching or of realistic representation, the Greeks were not behaving like free men, but like robots." McLuhan's use of the term "robots" is not meant to be a moral judgment, nor is it intended to be a simplistic analogy that identifies human beings with machines. "Robotism" specifically "means the suppression of the conscious 'observer' self or conscience so as to remove all fear and circumspection, all encumbrances to ideal performance." One lives as if one is already dead because one feels "a supreme release from conflict." Even so, as McLuhan elaborates in *The Gutenberg Galaxy*, the early efforts of the Greeks to adapt to the visual sense look in retrospect "timid and tentative," a mentality that Plato exhibits in his warning about the effects of writing on memory.

To be sure, the sense of detachment encouraged by the left hemisphere makes literate civilization and its blessings possible. At the same time, it encourages a lack of appreciation for the making of reality. As a result, it is reasonable to assume that one has no control over one's environment. "Nature" itself becomes the figure, without recognizing that this idea itself has been created. The real environment or ground receives no attention because, paradoxically, human beings have created this ground. As McLuhan and Bruce R. Powers explain, "When the ground moves too fast, a condition endemic to the electronic society, only figure is left. The left-brain-oriented individual substitutes the act of going inside himself for identity. He uses his own figure as his ground." Put differently, the mind sees itself as an autonomous subject matching reality.

This robotic inattention to the ground, the McLuhans contend in *Laws of Media*, is characteristic of preliterate and postliterate civilizations alike. Current attempts to portray AI as superior to human intelligence would confirm, in McLuhan's view, that the desire to match reality—in this case, the matching of artificial intelligence with human intelligence—is so pervasive that it continues to eclipse awareness of making the ground or environment. Although AI can match (or surpass) the quick processing of information by human beings, it does not create anything. It imitates a human environment, one that it does not make. While it may appear to have the robotic intelligence that McLuhan associates with the left hemisphere, the intuition and creativity of the right hemisphere are absent altogether.

The difference between the left and right hemispheres highlights the importance of studying how Western philosophy has been generally intolerant of paradoxes. Because the left hemisphere is devoted to logic, it denies the coexistence of opposites. As Iain McGilchrist explains, "The edifice of rationality (logos), the left-hemisphere type of reason, was weakened by the recognition that (in contravention of the consistency principle) a thing and its opposite may well both be true." Consequently, the inevitable contradictions of life become impossible to grasp. As McLuhan concludes in *The Gutenberg Galaxy*, "What is meant by the irrational and the non-logical in much modern discussion is merely the rediscovery of the ordinary transactions between the self and the world, or between subject and object." It is unsurprising that McLuhan leans on the nondialectical great books of philosophy and literature to make sense of paradox. The literate mind, despite its tendency to privilege the left hemisphere over the right, is still an indispensable means to "discover how we can have the better of two worlds—the left world of analysis and the right world of synthesis."

Back to the Beginning—the Bible

If there is any literary pathway toward overcoming dualisms that McLuhan invites his readers to reconsider, it is the Bible. Although he is sometimes reluctant to bring his faith into discussions of media, "lest perception be diverted from structural processes by doctrinal sectarian passions," he does not downplay his view that Christianity has a superior understanding of creation. As McLuhan once put it, "My own attitude to Christianity is, itself, awareness of process." This "awareness of process" (or creation) illustrates the paradox that human beings fail to understand the effects of what they create, while they ignore the limits of creation imposed by God.

The rediscovery of scripture is no easy task in a postliterate age. As a careful student of history, McLuhan often reminds his religious brethren that Christianity triumphed in the West because it was able to spread its truths through the alphabet. In the process, Christianity invented propaganda, or the technique of "spreading" (*propagare*) doctrine for the purpose of persuading great numbers of people. The ground that facilitated this project was a literate population. For this reason, McLuhan and Powers warn that " people are not only unable to receive but are unable to retain doctrinal teaching without a minimum of phonetic or

Western culture." As he put it more bluntly in his last televised interview, "Religion is a form of indoctrination, which requires a considerable amount of literacy. You cannot get religion into people minus literacy."

Which truths does the Bible reveal in an age of rapid change? The answer to this question is evident in the book of Genesis. As McLuhan explains in *War and Peace in the Global Village*, "the first Adam was an esthete, viewing and naming and enjoying creatures, a resident in a world he never made" (see Gen. 2:20). This Adam gloried in a creation that was not of his making. Even so, the first Adam had the God-given freedom to name things, an indication that Genesis distinguishes between divine and human agency. McLuhan seems to imply that the naming of things by human beings is a biblical notion, in sharp contrast to the ancient Greek belief that this power belongs only to a god, as Plato discusses in his dialogue *The Cratylus*. This Adam was so successful that his naming of creatures inspired medieval and modern scientists to classify nature. By the time of Gutenberg, McLuhan observes, this act of naming had become "old cliché."

The second Adam, after being expelled with Eve from the Garden of Eden, is "like God, knowing good and evil" (Gen. 3:5). As a result, McLuhan remarks, "the second Adam remade His first establishment and conferred on man totally new powers of creativity such as the first Adam had not known." McLuhan implies that the second Adam fatefully inspired the creation of technology. As McLuhan puts it in a different context, all human beings share with the second Adam "the mandatory role of being creative."

This focus on creation goes beyond the book of Genesis. The ultimate message of the Incarnation is that humanity has God-like powers. Jesus, who is sometimes called the "second Adam" (1 Cor. 15:45), had new powers of creation as well. McLuhan concludes his brief discussion of the two Adams with this telling observation: "To the Christian the Incarnation means that all matter was reconstituted at a historical moment and that matter is now capable of quite superhuman manipulation." McLuhan similarly claims that God's creation of the universe enabled humanity to share in this divine power: "The moment God touched matter its very structure was ordered, its potency was enormously enhanced." The question that arises here is this: Are human beings supposed to have these powers, which include the power to reinvent reality itself?

This creative power is not necessarily a good thing, given the fact that it happens after the Fall of man. With the Fall, human knowledge of (and appreciation for) nature disappears. As McLuhan shows in *The Classical Trivium*, before the Fall, Adam could read the Book of Nature "with ease," but after his expulsion, he "lost his ability to read this language of nature." Because almost no one has retrieved this language, it is the business of art "to recover the knowledge of that language which once man held by nature." This study of language goes hand in hand with McLuhan's lifelong appreciation for the medieval trivium (logic, grammar, and rhetoric). The study of paradoxes in grammar, which is neither dialectical nor logical, helps us understand our changing relation to the Book of Nature.

Philosophy and theology also have central roles to play in the interpretation of nature. The Aristotelian idea of formal cause is particularly important, as we have seen. The Christian reinterpretation of formal cause is a momentous innovation all its own in the history of thought, for it rests on the paradox that knowledge inspires both good and evil. Knowledge can coexist with liberating insight as well as sinful ignorance. Because Plato and Aristotle adhere to the law of noncontradiction, they cannot embrace this paradox. Unlike Plato, who, as Vico observes, was ignorant "of the fall of the first man," the Christian believes in a deity who grants even sinful humanity the freedom to use and misuse knowledge of creation. Unlike Aristotle, the Christian believes in a god who allowed a human being not only to name the things of the universe (first Adam) but also to create new things (second Adam). Because post-Fall acts of creation are usually entwined with sinful ignorance, it is essential that the Christian recognize that anything he creates is most likely a potential abuse of nature or the created order. Had human beings not knowingly sinned against this order, the first coming of Jesus Christ would have been unnecessary. As McLuhan wrote in a letter to Fr. John Culkin in 1975, "Fallen man is the formal cause of the Incarnation." McLuhan's focus on the creation of technology as a continuation of the second Adam's legacy is both theological and ethical. Only a Christian consciousness, at its best, grasps that creation is part of our nature. Put simply, we have the God-given freedom to create. In ethical terms, we are also responsible for what we create, including the unknown effects of this creation. This responsibility requires an awareness of formal causes, or the probable misuse of a created thing.

Although it may sound far-fetched to claim that the Christian alone possesses the deepest insight into formal causality, McLuhan occasionally makes sharp distinctions between Christian and non-Christian traditions. In a 1974 public lecture, he went so far as to remark that "Christianity has nothing to do with the Greco-Roman idea of civilization." To be sure, McLuhan admires pagan authors (especially the Roman orator Cicero) for their insights. The concept of an "idol," a false god that becomes the object of blind human worship, is evident within the biblical tradition and Greek myth. As he writes in *Understanding Media*, the "concept of 'idol' for the Hebrew Psalmist is much like that of Narcissus for the Greek mythmaker." He immediately adds the suggestive point that "the Psalmist insists that the *beholding* of idols, or the use of technology, conforms men to them," transforming them into servomechanisms. If the Psalms and the myth of Narcissus understand this truth equally, why is a Christian (or biblical) consciousness so indispensable in understanding the temptations of technology?

The answer to this question lies in McLuhan's distinction between pagan fatalism and Christian (or Judeo-Christian) creation. Whereas the pagan mind perceives change as subject to fate or a destiny beyond the control of humanity, the Christian mind recognizes that human beings can freely change the world for good or ill. (For this reason, McLuhan believed that the Christian missionary understands this truth best because, unlike scholastics who have incorporated pagan ideas, he is acting against a pagan ground.) The Christian is more able to deal with the technological change of the electric age than the old Greco-Roman (e.g., Platonic) mindset that elusively seeks a permanent realm amid endless flux. "For communication is change," McLuhan avers, "and Christianity is concerned above all and at all times with the need for change in man." This "need for change" reflects the understandable desire to justify all changes as ones of which God approves, even though this desire opens the door to the idolatrous worship of technology. By glorifying "their own handiwork as extensions of God," human beings took the momentous step to create technology. "The initial merging of God and His creatures may have begun with art and technology. It led to much technology and to the clouding of the mind." McLuhan quotes William Blake on the paradoxical truth that human beings slavishly worship what they fabricate: "They became what they beheld." Blake's insight, McLuhan notes, is directly indebted to the biblical tradition of the Hebrew prophets and Saint Paul.

The good news that the biblical tradition offers, unlike its pagan counterpart, is that this "clouding of the mind" is not fated or inevitable. Human beings still possess the freedom and insight to anticipate and thus control the effects that arise from their creations. Although humanity's inability to understand how media affect the psyche, McLuhan acknowledges, may lead to the conclusion that "this sounds like a classical or pagan instance of fate and *hubris*," it does not have to be this way. In fact, this inability is a deliberate choice that the biblical tradition reveals. In a brief discussion of John Milton's *Paradise Lost*, McLuhan and Wilfred Watson credit Milton with the insight that a highly intelligent being such as Satan can deliberately obscure his understanding of the depths of sin and his subordination to God's authority by using language "to confuse his mind" about his defeat at the hands of God. As McLuhan once remarked to a graduate student, "'Sin' might also be defined as lack of 'awareness.'" McLuhan never exempts his fellow Christians from displaying a gnostic "contempt for the world as a wreck or middenheap," an attitude that contradicts the celebration of the Book of Nature as God's creation.

Can Christianity overcome the dualism that separates the Book of Nature from the Book of Scripture? McLuhan's answer to this question is steeped in his study of the history of the Middle Ages and modernity. This dualism was inconceivable until the nineteenth century. McLuhan greatly admires Saint Thomas Aquinas for his influential teaching that the senses are "properly analogous" with the world, a philosophical premise that repudiates any inevitable conflict between human nature and God-given nature. The unity of the Book of Nature and the Book of Scripture was not merely a medieval metaphor or belief. Deep into the eighteenth-century Enlightenment, philosophers interpreted the symbolism of the first creation story as a narrative that saw all creatures—both human and animal—as naturally and divinely created. The desacralization of nature that began with Descartes in the seventeenth century did not immediately demolish this unity. The exegesis of the two books in tandem, McLuhan contends, represents "an unbroken tradition from the (Church) Fathers to the *Novum Organum* of Francis Bacon."

The modern animus toward the "primitive" Book of Nature came, ironically, without a recognition of its own mythic content. In his early essay on G. K. Chesterton, McLuhan takes aim at the idea of progress as a modern dogma that devalued both the eternal and historical in one fell swoop. One fateful effect of this idea was to turn history into a "toboggan slide," or a process that celebrates the goal of rapid change while rejecting the past as obsolete. This change was neither thoughtful nor desirable. (Besides, the idea of progress is an example of rear-view mirror thinking that relies on ideas made obsolete by technological change.)

Fortunately, Christianity can counter this destructive influence. As a young man, McLuhan credited Chesterton for having exposed "the Christless cynicism of the supposedly iron laws of economics and shown that history is a road that must often be reconsidered and even retraced." The crude modern attempt to replace God with economic determinism led to a fatalistic embrace of "iron laws" of capitalism that devalued not just human agency but also human creation in history. The deterministic necessity that progressivism associated with the forces of history, McLuhan argues, simply fostered "an excuse for procrastination."

McLuhan's appreciation for the unity of the Books of Nature and Scripture explains why he did not worry about theologians in the 1960s who declared "the death of God" or "the death of Christianity." These theologians who seemed to embrace atheism were understanding God as a being detached from creation, just as nineteenth-century figures severed the Book of Scripture from that of Nature. The only deity that was truly dead was the Newtonian God, the "cosmic clockmaker" who is detached from his creation. This reduced God to the status of a lifeless "concept" that exists "out there," replicating the visual dualism between inner and outer reality. Instead, according to McLuhan, God should be understood as a "percept" whom we understand through his effects. One of these effects includes the revelation that we must act as if we are the two Adams, equally respectful of the two books.

None of this guarantees that anyone, including Christians, will understand this unity, especially if they are uninterested in retrieving the values of literacy. It is far more likely that human beings will play God instead of obeying God, a temptation that the globalization of technology makes all too real.

9

THE ELECTRIC CAVE

Marshall McLuhan never lost hope that human beings may be able to grapple with the effects of technological change. They will not succeed, however, if they seek a return to a mythical golden age that is superior to the present. This nostalgic attitude reflects the temptation to judge the media on moral grounds, which impedes a practical understanding of the media's effects. Despite McLuhan's love for the literature and philosophy of the late Middle Ages and the early modern era, he rejected the criticism that he was advocating a return to these periods of history. As he explained to Gerald Stearn in a 1967 interview, "The moralist has instinctively translated my forward-looking discovery into backward-looking misanthropy." This mode of discovery, however, is not the same as the expectation that humanity is progressing toward a blissful state. McLuhan rejected any tendency to restore the past as vehemently as he repudiated the temptation to assume that utopia is waiting in the wings. Archaism and futurism are equally false, although understandable in an age of rapid change. To "point back to the day of the horse or to look forward to the coming of antigravitational vehicles is not an adequate response to the challenge of the motorcar," he writes in *Understanding Media*. The only viable alternative to these attitudes is to adopt the position of the dedicated artist who "seems to have the power for encountering the present actuality."

This last observation reflects a recurrent theme in McLuhan's thought. As he and Harley Parker note in *Through the Vanishing Point*, the artist is uniquely aware of new environments wrought by media: "Whereas the ordinary person seeks security by numbing his perceptions against the impact of new experience, the artist delights in this novelty and instinctively creates situations that both reveal it and compensate for it." Put differently, the artist is best suited to apply formal causality by anticipating the effects of media before they happen. Nevertheless, McLuhan and Parker stop short of expecting any utopian result from the efforts of the artist, who is, after all, a frail human being like everyone else. "The function of the artist in correcting the unconscious bias of perception in any given culture can be betrayed if he merely repeats the bias of the culture instead of readjusting it" through the creation of counterenvironments. Can the individual artist inspire in the public an awareness of the effects of media?

This is certainly the hope of McLuhan, who sometimes contends that the "mass audience" can be involved as "participants and co-creators rather than as consumers" in the electric age. While admirable, this is, of course, easier said than done. To generate this awareness within human beings who have been numbed or massaged by the maelstrom of technological change would require studying these effects without being swept up in the process. In his last taped lecture, delivered at York University (Toronto) in 1979, McLuhan soberly noted, "The huge vortices of energy created by our media present us with similar possibilities of evasion of consequences of destruction." Armed with this study of these vortices' effects, it may "be possible to program a strategy of evasion and survival." McLuhan's brief allusion to "vortices" probably echoes his typical celebration of the artist who comprehends change before it happens. As the vorticist artist reveals, one must understand the vortex from different vantage points while remaining somehow unchanged in the process. Because change occurs at the speed of light during the electric age, the application of formal causality on an unprecedented scale may be possible. Still, how likely is this understanding, given the enormity of the task? Can everyone enjoy the vantage point of the artist?

McLuhan believes that certain intellectual obstacles stand in the way of transforming ignorance into knowledge. The metaphorical meaning of Plato's cave allegory in the *Republic* provides the framework for this chapter precisely because this story stresses the intractable nature of human ignorance. This account provides a cautionary tale for McLuhan's hope that ignorance of one's environment is not inevitable. Machiavelli's teaching on the rational or self-interested use of power in politics is another intellectual influence that, in McLuhan's judgment, impedes the task of educating human beings about the impact of technology today. While this modernist teaching fits the age of print media, it is obsolete in the electric and digital media of the present age. Machiavelli's reliance on the rationality of political rulers and the ignorance of the ruled conflicts with McLuhan's contention that the elites are no more enlightened than the masses in their approach to technology. Whereas McLuhan disagrees with Plato that the ignorance of the prisoners in the cave is inevitable, he also disagrees with Machiavelli that the rational self-interest of the ruling elite will liberate us from this cave. Faith in democracy as the regime best suited to navigating the impact of new media is another idea that McLuhan cautions against, given his grave doubts about the ability of postliterate tribalists to muster the intellectual and moral stamina necessary for a healthy democracy. McLuhan believes that the only way to convey the importance of studying (and therefore controlling) the effects of media in the age of digitalized democracy is to retrieve the populist myth of a wise democratic citizenry dedicated to anticipating the effects of media before they happen. If enough people take on this role, which is hardly guaranteed, then it may be possible to slow down technological innovation before it wreaks havoc on the body politic.

The New Platonic Cave

Plato's famous parable of the cave in book 7 of the *Republic* is a useful way of understanding the difficulty of changing humanity on a mass scale. It also articulates in mythical form how we can best understand human ignorance of its environment, a task that is dear to McLuhan's heart. As the English sociologist John O'Neill explains, while this dialogue beautifully and logically constructs an ordered cosmos, it is also "terrifying because it is severe with those who do not understand the cosmos and whose ignorance necessarily confines them to its lower levels, to a world of shadows and selective ignorance" that is analogous to the world of electric media.

Through the voice of Socrates, Plato compares the ignorance that characterizes human beings to the lives of people who have inhabited an underground cave from childhood. The cave has an entrance that leads out to the light and a long passage leading downward. Because their thighs and necks are bound by chains, they cannot leave the cave. They are also forced to focus on what is immediately in front of them because their chains prevent them from turning their heads around (*periagôgê*) and toward the light. A fire is the only light that is dimly provided inside the cave. A walkway runs between the fire and the prisoners. Next to this walkway runs a wall, alongside which people carry statues and other objects. The cave dwellers see only the shadows of these artifacts, which the light from the fire casts onto the wall of the cave facing them. If one of the prisoners is dragged out by force "into the light of the sun" outside the cave, he will feel great pain while realizing that the things he once thought were real were in fact mere shadows. This lucky person who emerges from the cave is the philosopher, who is understandably reluctant to return to its darkness. If he makes such a return with the intention of enlightening his fellow cave dwellers, he risks ridicule, hostility, and even death. Socrates asks, "Wouldn't he be the source of laughter, and wouldn't it be said of him that he went up and came back with his eyes corrupted, and that it's not even worth trying to go up? And if they were somehow able to get their hands on him and kill the man who attempts to release and lead up, wouldn't they kill him?"

Although McLuhan, we have seen, is critical of Plato for his attack on poetry as well as his dualistic distinction between the eternal and the changeable, at times he makes use of themes reminiscent of the cave allegory. Like Plato, McLuhan doubts that the senses can reveal reality in an adequate way. "Survival cannot be trusted to natural response or natural instinct," he warns. Moreover, both agree that the transition from ignorance to knowledge, which progressivists interpret as the direction of history, does not inevitably happen as a result of advances in the sciences and technology. Indeed, those who endlessly search for an identity in cyberspace do so precisely because they do not know who they are, fatefully demonstrating Plato's contention that one can never find something unless one has knowledge of it in the first place. Finally, the degree of ridicule and hostility that McLuhan incurred for pointing out the ignorance of technology's effects that even the most powerful people in the world exhibit is uncannily similar to the reception that the philosopher experiences upon his return to the cave.

There are some places in McLuhan's oeuvre that reveal a more subtle debt to Plato's allegory. In his dissertation on Thomas Nashe, he gives due credit to Plato, notwithstanding the latter's animus toward poetry, for insisting on the importance of understanding the relationship "between the order of speech and language and the order of nature." The problem is that this relationship can elude those who focus on image at the expense of nature. As McLuhan shows, advertising is in the business of making the image associated with a product, not the product itself, the real message. In Platonic terms, the shadows on the walls of the cave perform this function as well. The shadows are more compelling than the higher reality outside the cave.

Although McLuhan's later comparison of prehistoric cave art and "the stone age world of ads provided by Madison Avenue" does not explicitly refer to Plato, his analysis is reminiscent of the message within this allegory. "Like the art in the Altamira caves," he writes in *Culture Is Our Business*, "ads are not intended to be seen but to produce an *effect*. The cave paintings were carefully hidden. They were a magic form, intended to affect events at a distance. They were of corporate, not private, origin." In Platonic terms, this art is a magical imitation of reality that only a tribal (corporate) consciousness could take for real. The philosophical (private, individual) self can see through this second reality. In a more explicitly Platonic vein, McLuhan interprets cinema "as the exact embodiment of Plato's Cave" precisely because the "dreaming eye of the movie god casting his images on the dark screen corresponds to that image of human life offered to us by Plato in the *Republic*: existence is a kind of cave or cellar on the back wall of which we watch the shadows of real things from the outside world of reality." As a result, this medium provides "merely a dream world which is a substitute for reality rather than a means of proving reality."

Does this dream world apply to other media? According to McLuhan, the cave-like movie provides a lesson that is analogous to other electric media. Like any mass medium, films must "parrot the world in order to hold our attention." They do so by rolling up the "carpet of the external world"—a carpet that "becomes the magic carpet of dreams, carrying us instantly anywhere." Although every electric medium, including cinema, moves us at the speed of light, this speed does not enlighten; rather, it has darkening effects. One cannot think at the speed of light. The phenomenon known as "TikTok brain" illustrates this fact. As Michael Manos, the clinical director of the Center for Attention and Learning at Cleveland Clinic, explains, "Directed attention is the ability to inhibit distractions and sustain attention and to shift attention appropriately. . . . If kids' brains become accustomed to constant changes, the brain finds it difficult to adapt to a non-digital activity where things don't move quite as fast."

In tetradic terms, social media platforms obviously enhance instantaneous communication. Yet they also reverse creation into imitation (parroting the world) by enabling users to construct and post videos that mirror or reproduce the most popular fashions of the time. Furthermore, they obsolesce patient self-reflection by equating the individual self with an online identity that craves constant recognition. Finally, these media retrieve the world of magic by constructing a dream world that is an escape from reality. In short, TikTok is the pocket cave of our times.

Users of social media are more addicted to these media than they realize. In Platonic terms, they are ignorant of their own ignorance. Like the fish in the water, they are unaware of the electric cave. As the Canadian political philosopher John von Heyking observes, "Our students inhabit a technologically mediated world dominated by fabricated objects, including not only their digital devices but the devices through which they encounter the world. The medium is the message, as Marshall McLuhan said." Additionally, this ignorance coexists with anxiety and loneliness, which drive young people to these platforms. Von Heyking writes, "For example, millennial students frequently express high levels of anxiety as well as loneliness while acting in every manner, like being addicted to social media, that perpetuates that loneliness and anxiety. They inhabit their souls as caves and need to be liberated because they lack their own means of liberation." The instantaneous creation of images simply reminds users of their loneliness and anxiety while they reside in an eternal present, increasingly disconnected from the past or future. "To the blind all things are sudden," McLuhan observes.

Although Plato and McLuhan disagree on the ability of the poet "to arrest the intake of experience and to reverse the flow," they would concur that this dream world is analogous to the cave described in the *Republic*. The real world is accessible through patient thought and study, not mere imitation of popular, ever-changing fashions and images. As McLuhan often emphasizes, simultaneous communication abolishes logic and history, both past and future. Communication at the speed of light makes a casualty of the attention span required for studying anything with care: a "weak identity" goes hand in hand with a weak attention span.

Do most human beings want to be freed from their chains within the new electric cave? In Platonic terms, can their souls be turned around (*periagôgê*) in the cave and toward the light outside it? Given McLuhan's meticulous analysis of the recurrent pattern of ignorance that humanity has displayed toward the media's effects throughout history, it is tempting to conclude that most human beings do not desire this freedom until it is too late for them to reverse these effects. Plato's tough judgment is that the ignorance of the prisoners within the cave is natural, a condition that is inherent within human nature. To quote von Heyking again on the relevance of Platonic teaching in this context, "Our natural condition is like a baby who wishes to know and communicate but gets angry and frustrated for being unable to do so." The implication of this judgment is that only a small number of individuals can overcome their natural ignorance by escaping from the cave.

McLuhan would agree that the digital age transports us back to this manifestation of preliterate infancy. As I showed in chapter 6, electric media reawaken what McLuhan calls "first nature." Nothing is more natural, he argues, than the sensory response to electric technology, which is "directly related to our central nervous system." This bombardment of the senses in auditory space recreates tribalism (or what McLuhan sometimes calls the "primitive") in electric form. McLuhan would, however, disagree with Plato that an escape from the cave is even necessary. The cave, after all, is a human creation. (For this reason, Francis Bacon in his *Novum Organum* referred to the man-made "idols" of the cave.) Plato, in contrast, is silent on whether the origin of the cave is natural or man-made. Creation, as the story of Genesis reveals, presupposes knowledge. Because human beings have created their caves or dream worlds, they can also potentially overcome their ignorance of the effects that these fabricated realities have on their psyches. According to McLuhan, Plato dismisses the value of human making or creativity precisely because it does nothing to transform humans' ignorance into knowledge. The possibility that the cave itself contains resources that could liberate its prisoners does not occur to Plato. In the process, he leaves his cave dwellers trapped in ignorance: the woeful state of his public, according to McLuhan, "is the formal cause of his philosophy." As an adherent of the law of noncontradiction, Plato denies that knowledge and ignorance can coexist in the cave. One acquires the light of knowledge only after leaving this darkness.

The good news, McLuhan and Wilfred Watson explain in *From Cliché to Archetype*, is that Plato's "cave is the first 'rag-and-bone shop,' to use Yeats's phrase, the first archetypal storehouse." Although this shop contains discarded materials that Plato does not value, these are ideas that the prisoners can utilize to win their freedom. Plato is too quick, McLuhan and Watson believe, to toss "all the multileveled phenomena of the world into his cave." How can mortals interpret their reality if they do not start with a multileveled phenomenon, such as language or grammar, that reflects the world they have actually created? As we have seen, McLuhan faults Plato for dismissing the medium of writing that he himself uses in his dialogues. Indeed, the irony is that Plato's written teachings, including the parable of the cave, are invaluable resources within the cave! In short, only media, including the artifacts of the cave, can make sense of other media.

McLuhan's distinction between "light through" and "light on" is relevant here. "Light through" is his metaphor for how different senses interact with media. All of these senses require attention and study. "Light on" refers to the mistaken tendency to judge other senses from the vantage point of just one sense, which is analogous to how the left hemisphere of the brain devalues the right hemisphere. McLuhan doubts that a "philosopher king" in the Platonic sense could single-handedly bring this light into the darkness. In one of his early essays, he muses that "once the bulk of society has been pulped into passivity by industrial logic, then the greatest philosopher-king would be a tyrant such as Priscus Tarquin." To be sure, McLuhan's own fame as a public intellectual in the 1960s provided him with the opportunity to single-handedly enlighten the public about media. He and Parker once even contemplated the need for a "corporate" hero who could educate the public in a democratic manner. Be that as it may, McLuhan does not pin his hopes on a single intellectual master who will shed light on the ever-changing phenomena of mass media.

Instead of waiting for such a figure who has somehow miraculously escaped the effects of media and reentered the cave to cast the "light" of his reason (that is, visual sense) on his ignorant brethren, the denizens of this cavern should take it upon themselves to study how their senses relate "through" each other within the electric-digital cave they have made. To recall another one of McLuhan's distinctions, instead of *matching* reality with just one sense, we should study how the senses relate to a reality of our *making*. The "light" of knowledge is not outside our cave-like human experience. To deny this truth is to "adopt the Narcissus attitude of regarding the extensions of our own bodies as really *out there* and really independent of us," an attitude that meets "all technological challenges with the same sort of banana-skin pirouette and collapse."

In practical terms, though, can every human being accomplish this task? Can anyone help to liberate others from unwittingly acting as prisoners (or servo-mechanisms) of the media that they themselves have constructed? Surprisingly, McLuhan's positive answer to this question reflects a partial debt to Plato, even though he also seeks to transform the world to a degree that would have been inconceivable to the Greek philosopher. In "Roles, Masks, and Performances," McLuhan refers to the Platonic love of dialogue as the starting point for this project: "Perhaps I will be permitted the role of the 'stranger' used by Plato to promote the ends of dialogue and to avoid the specialist exchanges of an 'in-group.'" Although Plato usually restricts dialogue to a select few (just as only a few can escape from the cave), McLuhan is cautiously optimistic that anyone can play the role of the philosophically astute stranger. A stranger (alien, foreigner) who does not belong to any clique or tribe can still be a participant in a dialogue. Even Plato at times suggests that the stranger or alien is a worthy human being who may deserve the greatest sympathy and attention, as he observes in *The Laws* (729e): "For the alien, being without friends or kinsmen, has the greater claim on pity, human and divine." McLuhan appears to agree with this understanding of the stranger's role. "The function of the 'stranger' as the trigger for dialogue," he notes, "appears even in the self-appointed role of cab-drivers as philosophers. There is usually a stranger in the back seat." This use of dialogue may require the stranger to use probes and puns that provoke attention. This person may also have to "put on" the audience by understanding the limitations and biases of the people whom one is addressing while involving them. With a nod to the laws of media, a person who escapes the cave may have to engage in a *reversal* that means returning to the darkness to liberate others through patient dialogue, even if ridicule and ignorance will greet this brave individual, as McLuhan personally discovered. As he explained to Gerald Stearn, "I'm quite prepared to live the life of Confucius or Plato, day in, day out, in my conversations."

McLuhan is confident that these techniques are available to anyone, not just an enlightened minority. We need not assume that only the artist has the ability to educate others when, as McLuhan told an interviewer, "the new environment of electric information makes possible a new degree of perception and critical awareness by nonartists." Anyone can play the role of the stranger, McLuhan argues: "The 'stranger' has become the guide; the passenger, the driver. Since this multi-role playing is inevitable in an electronic world, one hopes that the put-on has also been a turn-on." In a brief discussion of Plato's dream of a small polis whose citizenry would regularly listen to public speakers, McLuhan muses that the decentralizing effects of electric media "could easily implement the Platonic political dream on a world scale." In short, whereas Plato calls on the wise few to transcend the cave, McLuhan seeks to transform it.

True to form, McLuhan offers qualifications to his own hopes and predictions. A new birth of dialogue on a global scale may, in theory, liberate human beings from the numbing effects of new media. The problem is that electric or digital media do not necessarily encourage rational dialogue of the sort that Plato favors. As mentioned in chapter 5, AI capitalism encourages speechlessness—the opposite of dialogue. A 2024 study by the Google subsidiary Jigsaw Research (UK) of the online habits demonstrated by a group of Gen Z users (thirteen-to-twenty-four-year-olds) revealed that they were far more interested in being part of the "in-group" to which McLuhan refers. Specifically, these users preferred to look at the comments after an article, not the article itself, so that their views would align with the "influencers" who wrote those comments. The search for truth has yielded to the search for an identity within a group online.

McLuhan would probably agree with Leo Strauss that the denizens of the "second, much deeper cave" of the present age need "a propaedeutic, which the Greeks did not need, namely, learning through reading." As we have seen, however, discarnate identity, transhumanism, and artificial intelligence do not require the stable sense of self that speech (along with reading) requires. McLuhan warned in the 1960s that an "immediate simulation of consciousness would by-pass speech in a kind of massive extrasensory perception." Simulation in this context sounds eerily similar to Plato's idea of imitation or mimesis. The mere imitation of the human falls far short of the essence of what is human—namely, thought itself. As von Heyking explains, the soul that "slavishly imitates what it receives" is not one that is "capable of self-direction and self-reflection." Notwithstanding McLuhan's misgivings about Plato's elitism, he would agree with the Platonist analysis offered by von Heyking that any media that bypasses the most essential qualities of human identity—thought, consciousness, and speech—by simulating them keeps human beings in a cave of their own making. Despite McLuhan's hopes for transforming the cave through dialogue and reflection, he never promises that this liberation from ignorance will automatically happen.

Will Machiavellian Rationality Liberate Us from the Cave?

McLuhan's sober observations may provoke readers who assume that dialogue about the media is guaranteed as long as human beings have the capacity to reason. Put differently, if citizens have the freedom to study and discuss the effects of media, then why should they share the caution about mass enlightenment that McLuhan sometimes expresses? The answer to this question depends on what we mean by "reason." Does the modern understanding of reason, which places trust in the rational self-interest of powerful elites, help or hinder our comprehension of the media today?

According to McLuhan, this modern understanding owes its greatest intellectual debt to Machiavelli. It is impossible to understand the trajectory of modern political thought without comprehending his indelible influence. McLuhan often associates the Florentine philosopher with the most important ideas of modernity. In *From Cliché to Archetype*, he and Watson emphasize the massive influence of Machiavelli's distinction between the private intent of the leader (the "prince") and the public ends that he attains. Inspiring Mandeville's famous slogan "Private Vices, Publick Benefits" in *The Fable of the Bees*, Machiavelli, according to McLuhan and Watson, "saw the new private morality created by the new specialist technology of print as creating new political goals. The theme echoes through all the situations of the culture." McLuhan and Watson have in mind Machiavelli's surgical distinction between the prince who uses immoral means to secure power and the citizenry (the "vulgar") who are deceived into believing that these means are moral, particularly if the ends are beneficial to all. Machiavelli writes in chapter 18 of *The Prince*: "So let a prince win and maintain his state: the means will always be judged honorable, and will be praised by everyone. For the vulgar are taken in by the appearance and the outcome of a thing." In the all-at-once age of electric and digital media, is Machiavelli's distinction between a rational leader and the gullible masses still relevant?

In his early writings, McLuhan maintains that the influence of this Machiavellian teaching does, unfortunately, persist. Like most conservative readers, McLuhan generally sees Machiavelli as a teacher of evil, the most infamous advocate of "the end justifies the means" politics. McLuhan contends, in his dissertation on Thomas Nashe, that Machiavelli sought to weaken nature as the moral standard by which to judge human action. Machiavelli "looked on nature as shut off from grace and as shut in upon itself, and abandoned to the interplay of its own distorted forces." Machiavelli also cynically employed biblical theology to achieve this aim, so that his immoralist approach to politics would enjoy more respectability: "There is much of the Old Testament attitude in Machiavelli—the attitude of trust in the prince as one who cooperates with God to bring good out of evil, having regard to the passionate and blind violence of men." The modern intersection between capitalism and Protestantism further demonstrates the subtle influence of Machiavelli. To bring good out of evil is identical to Mandeville's transformation of private vices into public benefits. The American puritan of New England, McLuhan quipped, "made the transition from high theology to high finance."

The success of this *realpolitik* all depends on whether the ruler is able to persuade the ruled that they should follow him and not their own reason. Machiavelli,

McLuhan explains, "has no place for eloquence in his education since he has no trust in men's capacity to be persuaded to follow right reason, or any reason. The state must compel man to espouse a useful life free from the anarchy of the passions, and for this purpose eloquence is useless." In short, reason belongs only to the prince, who inflicts force and fraud on the irrational multitude.

If McLuhan were simply pointing out that Machiavelli is a teacher of evil as it applies to politics, he would not be adding anything novel to the conventional image of this political philosopher. The originality of McLuhan, however, lies in his provocative thesis that Machiavelli's ideas are no longer as important in the present age as they were in early modernity, the age of print. McLuhan states throughout his major works that the thought of the Renaissance philosopher *once* enjoyed tremendous importance, albeit in a sinister sense. In *The Mechanical Bride*, he restates the meaning of "the end justifies the means" by noting that "Machiavelli stands at the gate of the modern age, divorcing technique from social purpose." In a lecture that he gave three years after the publication of that book, McLuhan mused that Machiavelli's influence in the United States had become normalized: "It has been noted how Machiavelli in the sixteenth century created the crisis in which we persist today by raising an age-old truth to a new level of awareness. Practical politics had always had a very shabby side. But Machiavelli made of these imperfections the basis of the art and grammar of power." Specifically, his focus on power had turned into a virtue through the rise of the "self-improvement" ideology that Dale Carnegie made famous. Whether he knew it or not, Carnegie transformed Machiavelli's study of human frailty and insecurity into a practical technique to boost one's self-esteem. "On this discovery of the abyss of human vanity and self-deception," McLuhan asserts, "Carnegie, like Machiavelli, erects his system for obtaining power." According to McLuhan, Machiavelli's enduring success lies in discovering "how man's factive intelligence could be turned to artistic use in fashioning cities and states." Although Machiavelli was not the first to show that political leaders engaged in "techniques of power manipulation," he "enabled men to use this age-old instrument quite impersonally and with a clear conscience."

Even in this "moralistic" phase of McLuhan's thought, he implies that Machiavelli's thought is losing much of its power, presumably because of technological change. "Today with the revelation of the poetic process which is involved in ordinary cognition," McLuhan writes, "we stand on a very different threshold from that wherein Machiavelli stood." Whereas Machiavelli opened the "door into negation and human weakness," the present age opens the "door to the positive powers of the human spirit in its natural creativity." These new powers, if ruthlessly developed, could even create a "possible path to the totalitarian remaking of human nature," one that showed "the way to a new circle of the Inferno." The attempts of the transhumanist industry to amplify the "natural creativity" of human beings by separating their thoughts and speech from their emotions through advanced brain implants (see chapter 5) may prove Machiavelli more prophetic than he knew.

The fact that McLuhan notes the temporal difference between Machiavelli's original threshold and the one in which he was speaking in 1954 suggests that Machiavelli's influence is not as great as it once was. Although he opened the door to a new era of possibilities, these changes go beyond his intent. Machiavelli's portrayal of human nature as frail and wicked does not mean that he necessarily considered the "remaking of human nature" possible. As we have seen in chapter 6, his philosophy at most seeks the control, not the replacement, of humanity's "first nature." Yet this aim depends on the Machiavellian distinction between the prince and the vulgar multitude, a dichotomy that McLuhan believes the electric age renders obsolete.

As McLuhan explains in *The Gutenberg Galaxy*, the old Machiavellian mindset of the print era tackled the problem of identity by making sharp distinctions between ruler and ruled, producer and consumer, and writer and reader. These distinctions generated "conflicting interests" because they enshrined an unequal arrangement of power. The merchant class applied the Machiavellian "power technique" of equating knowledge with the solving of technical problems. In the process, human beings were treated as machines that had the job of solving these problems. As we have seen, the rationale behind these divisions is that private vices lead to public benefits, to recall Mandeville. In this vein, Machiavelli's influence was rendered conventional, acceptable, and rational. Moreover, this regime, because of its disdain for moral idealism and utopianism, was stable enough to withstand the challenges of *fortuna*.

The normalization of the Machiavellian influence is impossible to understand without considering its subtle relation to other forces. As McLuhan suggests in his dissertation on Nashe, the fact that Machiavelli sounds Protestant in his attack on nature as a moral authority helps to explain his success. If Machiavellian thought could be associated with a major faith tradition, then it would be more respectable than it actually is. More specifically, Machiavellianism requires a certain measure of secrecy or subtlety so that its immoral aims are not fully revealed to the masses. The fact that Protestantism, particularly Calvinism, embraced capitalism and print media further advanced the influence of the Florentine. It is little wonder that McLuhan associates the influence of Machiavelli and Calvin with the modern desire to master nature and human nature, freed from God's benevolent wisdom. He groups Machiavelli with Luther and Calvin as lethal exponents of the "violent scission of nature and grace." Elsewhere, McLuhan contends that the "common human nature" that moderns tried to suppress and reshape "persists intact beneath all the modes of mental hysteria rampant from Machiavelli and Calvin until our own day."

Despite the various ideological attempts to normalize Machiavelli's influence, McLuhan doubts that it would endure indefinitely. Even in *The Mechanical Bride*, he points to art or artistic criticism as the one mode of inquiry that could expose the inherent instability of the Machiavellian system, although it could also be co-opted: "As such, with regard to the modern state, it [art] can be a citadel of inclusive awareness amid the dim dreams of collective consciousness." In his later studies of media, McLuhan is even more dubious about the survival of Machiavelli's influence in the electric age.

The Machiavellian preoccupation with secrecy has become obsolete in the age of instantaneous communication and global sleuthing. Although McLuhan never denies that the most powerful elites would persist in trying to conceal, in good Machiavellian fashion, their sins or crimes, this effort was futile. Commenting on the popularity of the song "Behind Closed Doors" (with its lyric "No one knows what goes on behind closed doors") during the Watergate break-ins, McLuhan offered two reasons for doubting this message. First, "everyone knows what's going on behind closed doors nowadays in Washington and Ottawa because of investigative reporting and electronic eavesdropping." Second, the "real problem is that people can't see what is happening all around them—things that are really destroying our society!—the hidden environment or 'ground.'"

McLuhan was subtly relating these two observations by pointing, once again, to the deliberate ignorance or indifference that the "people" show toward the effects of technological change. The fact that citizens are privy to the bad deeds of politicians has not led to a greater understanding of how this environment encourages popular tolerance of rampant misbehavior. Moreover, the constant exposure of these vices conditions human beings to believe that these events are normal or tolerable. In fact, the media's coverage of the tawdriest secrets dilutes those secrets' impact and significance. The relentless spotlight on the sexual dalliances of politicians (e.g., Bill Clinton, Donald Trump) often generates the public's sympathy or indifference. This phenomenon would not surprise McLuhan at all. "Only puny secrets need protection," he writes. "BIG SECRETS are protected by public incredulity. You can actually dissipate a situation by giving it maximal coverage. As to alarming people, that's done by rumors, not by coverage." Nothing demonstrates the obsolete nature of Machiavelli's ruler-ruled dichotomy more than the fact that the inability of modern princes to keep secrets from the masses has greatly diminished. Most tellingly, the preoccupation with exposing ever more secrets through online sleuthing has not necessarily led to mass moral outrage against the powerful. In an age where everyone plays a role or "puts on" an audience, the regular discovery of deception at the political level is bound to provoke a numbed response.

Can Democracy Liberate Us from the Cave?

If citizens have become habituated to the misbehavior of political elites in the age of instantaneous information, what does this pattern reveal about the spiritual health of democracy? As McLuhan noted in his Marfleet Lectures, the "democratic principle is more fragmented and more skeptical and assumes that anything that looks like power is almost certainly corrupt." A citizen will naturally try "to dig it out, search it out, and to wreck that institution as soon as possible." In the electric age, this cynicism leads to the replacement of bourgeois democracy with something quite different. The involvement of citizens in the tawdry and secret affairs of their leaders encourages the former to act in a tribal fashion, favoring those leaders who interact simultaneously with them through media. In his Platonic analysis of modern democracy, von Heyking warns that the inhabitants of the democratic cave can encourage an "obsequious submission to democratic public opinion and slogans." Some citizens even forgive leaders who seem to offer a personal or online connection with them. The leader who publicly jokes about the airing of his dirty laundry (e.g., Donald Trump) may be more charismatic and seductive than one who hopelessly tries to conceal his misbehavior. To be sure, other citizens are not so forgiving of these actions. Nevertheless, one haunting question arises: If a substantial number of citizens discovers repeatedly that "anything that looks like power is almost certainly corrupt," as McLuhan puts it, then why is a corrupt regime worth preserving at all?

The decentralization that McLuhan expected from electric media certainly has the potential of advancing democracy in a direction that he occasionally welcomed. "Psychological decentralization" is possible through the formation of small communities that have weaned themselves from their dependence on centralized media. Decentralized media, in principle, advance the cause of democracy and decentralization. In McLuhanesque terms, electric media are the perfect extension of democracy precisely because they enhance our natural desire to create worlds of our own choosing. The ability of AI products to engage in "hyperpersonalization"—to advertise and create products that specifically reflect a consumer's preferences—boosts the sovereignty of consumers. Yet the increasing accessibility of technologies like AI can yield the perversely democratic result of enabling users to fabricate a reality of their choosing. The technology journalist

Laurie Segall discovered this fact to her horror when she asked a chatbot to "create a deepfake campaign" to tarnish her reputation. This test of AI's capability led to the creation of an elaborate (and false) story about her having an alleged affair with the high-tech titan Mark Zuckerberg. In Segall's words, the democratic potential of this technology is part of the problem, not the solution: "We are entering a world where in the next couple of years, so much of what we see online because of the democratization of these AI tools, because of some of that stuff . . . it's going to be so easy for anyone to make a believable campaign, make anyone do anything." It is little wonder that McLuhan believed that democracy is only as healthy as the citizenry that constitutes it.

To be sure, McLuhan was not as opposed to democracy as Plato was. Still, there is considerable evidence of a deep-seated skepticism in his writings about this regime. The denizens of the postliterate era did not reassure McLuhan that they even favored democratic ideals. In his 1969 *Playboy* interview, he went so far as to declare that "political democracy as we know it today is finished," precisely because the new tribalists of the electric age had no use for bourgeois values such as privacy and intellectual liberty. Anyone who understands the law of reversal, as McLuhan and Barrington Nevitt explain in their 1973 essay on causality in the electric world, would also grasp the paradox that "the medium can reverse the roles of producer and consumer by making the reader or audience not only the 'content' but also the comaker of the work."

This prescient assessment enjoys even more relevance in the digital age. Postliterate tribalists raised on social media can identify themselves as producers of their own content: videos posted on TikTok, Instagram, YouTube, and Rumble all illustrate this fact. They can also consume the videos of their fellow producers. The point is that they are playing roles that require a mass audience. Nothing could be less natural to the nomad on social media than a desire for privacy. The fact that social media platforms share the private information of users is far less important to these consumers than the need to be visible on the digital stage. To disappear from these media altogether through "deplatforming" is the greatest source of anxiety. For example, political activists who voice unpopular views are justifiably worried about the removal of their platforms on YouTube. What the media scholar Taina Bucher writes about Facebook could apply to any platform today: "In Facebook there is not so much a 'threat of visibility' as there is a 'threat of invisibility' that seems to govern the actions of its subjects. The problem as it appears is not the possibility of constantly being observed, but the possibility of constantly disappearing, of not being considered important enough." As McLuhan anticipated, users who play the public roles of producer and consumer are inclined to view the right to privacy as an archaic and incomprehensible notion best forgotten.

The freedom to debate competing ideas within a democratic context is also not a practice that suits the mentality of a generation raised on social media. At a conference at Cambridge University in 2023, Alex Mahon, the CEO of the British network Channel 4, blamed the influence of these media for the inability of members of Gen Z to discuss and differ with each other. Taking aim at TikTok, Instagram, and YouTube, Mahon called these social media platforms "echo chambers" that feed the preconceptions of their users instead of exposing them to ideas that may challenge their assumptions. As a result, Mahon noted, "They [Gen Z] haven't got the skills to discuss, they haven't got the skills to disagree and commit because they haven't been raised, particularly with being out of colleges to have those kind of debates, to get to the point where you've got people with a difference of opinion to you and you're happy to work alongside that, and that is a really dangerous step change in my view that we are seeing." In short, these echo chambers are the perfect medium for postliterate tribalists who need their opinions validated, not deconstructed.

Can religion save democracy? As a Christian, McLuhan occasionally suggests that a democracy based on the biblical morality of "love thy neighbor as thyself" would be superior to secular versions of democracy. In his 1967 interview with Gerald Stearn, he remarked, "I think of human charity as a total responsibility of all, for all," and he immediately cautioned that the historic roots of modern democracy are already obsolete: "Democracy as a by-product of certain technologies, like literacy and mechanical industry, is not something that I would take very seriously." Still, if democracy somehow retrieves its Christian character, there may be hope for this political order. "Democracy as it belongs very profoundly with Christianity is something I take very seriously indeed," McLuhan said, precisely because the electric age could fulfill the egalitarian and Christian concept of the mystical body in which all human beings are "members of the body of Christ."

Is any version of Christianity, however, suited to inspire the moral fortitude of a democracy? Protestantism was no longer an option in the electric age, given its historic attachment to literacy and individualism. Yet this judgment about the obsolete nature of Protestantism is not the same as predicting its demise altogether. As McLuhan noted in a 1977 interview with Pierre Babin, postliterate people may even manifest the old Protestant suspicion of authority: "Acoustic or tribal man reacts like a deviant or Protestant, a rebel, when he opposes the centralized bureaucracies and legalistic hierarchies which we inherited from the alphabet." Nevertheless, a loosely Protestant temperament is no substitute for the traditional Protestant determination to discover the God-given meaning of scripture, free of human sinfulness or bias. Instead of relying on the priest to interpret the Bible, every literate individual could be his own interpreter, thanks to Gutenberg's printing press. All of these historic conditions presupposed the primacy of the visual sense, which encourages detachment, privacy, and individualism. It is no wonder, McLuhan notes, that the egalitarian idea of individual interpretation multiplied the number of sects under Protestantism. "This slide toward the visual explains the appearance of sects," he told Babin. "The word sect evokes visual fragmentation. Sects separated from one another according to visual criteria."

Once the visual sense gives way to the all-at-once world of digital media, however, adherence to the strict truths of the Bible yields to new substitutes that do not require literacy or any other sacrificial effort on the part of believers. The narcissism that McLuhan and Bruce R. Powers associate with acoustic space characterizes religious belief among postliterate youth. The pathological selfishness at the core of narcissism is directly opposite to the ethic of sacrifice that all traditional religions demand. Without a strong sense of identity, what is there to sacrifice? As Christian Smith and Melinda Lundquist Denton persuasively show, a high number of American adolescents understand God as a deity who wants people to be "nice" to each other as well as feel happy and good about themselves. Subjective well-being, not repentance from sin, is a key goal of this belief system. "Moralistic therapeutic deism" is the new religion of democracy. In turn, adherents to this manner of belief expect God to be nice to them. The popularity of Bible apps that select a "verse of the day" often performs the therapeutic function of choosing only passages from scripture that make the user feel happy and content. This "algorithmic spirituality" not only discourages a sustained reading of the Bible, as opposed to reading randomly selected passages, but also fosters the illusion that the purpose of faith is to make us feel good about ourselves. In Platonic terms, these postliterate citizens are imitating shadowy and changeable opinions, not examining thoughts, within the democratic cave.

McLuhan already anticipated this new version of faith in the early 1970s. Given the fragmenting effects of Protestantism that become more intense in the electric age, it did not surprise McLuhan that anyone could interpret biblical morality according to their own self-serving intent. Once the Protestant undermining of authority takes root, it is tempting to conflate "love thy neighbor" with love of one's almighty self, as McLuhan and Nevitt write in *Take Today*: "Today, the Golden Rule has dropped out. It has become do unto others what they want done unto them. This means the right of every man to be himself and to be recognized as such, whereas the Golden Rule assumed that people knew who they were and you did unto them as they did unto you. . . . Identity now changes faster than rules." This narcissistic adulteration of biblical morality does not provide any moral fortification for democracy.

The Retrieval of Myth and Formal Causality

If a democracy can no longer rely on rationality (Machiavellian or otherwise) among its rulers and ruled, which other option for enlightenment is available? With another nod to Plato, myth, including the parable of the cave, is an essential means of educating the uneducated. McLuhan, we have seen, repudiates the modern or progressivist notion that myth is an archaism that belongs to a less enlightened age. Myth is never obsolete. McLuhan further suggests that the use of myth can always awaken consciousness. A digitalized democracy retrieves the power of myth with even greater effect than in previous periods of media. "Instant awareness of all the varieties of human expression," McLuhan writes, "reconstitutes the mythic type of consciousness, of *once-upon-a-time*-ness, which means all-time, out of time." The advantage of myth is that it is intelligible to anyone, even within the electric age, which enables inclusive access to anyone in search of narratives. A narrative that offers a sweeping explanation of history is attractive to people who are jolted by the rapidity of technological change and its disorienting effects on identity. According to McLuhan, "When man is overwhelmed by information, he resorts to myth. Myth is inclusive, time-saving, and fast." Myths are as old as history itself, stories that unite past, present, and future. "A mythic, or all-at-once, vision of the beginning, middle, and end of an historic cycle (the Trojan War)" is even more indispensable in an age of instability. Even the master dialectician Plato uses myth to warn about the effects of writing on the memory (see chapter 3).

The big challenge that faces anyone who seeks to understand and control technological change in a democracy is that the most powerful interests employ their own myths. Although we have seen McLuhan doubt the wisdom of the leaders who control the media industries, he never doubts their power to influence the masses. In the same essay in which he celebrates the mythical possibility of every consumer becoming a producer of media, he also warns that the advertising industry constructs its own myths by striving "to comprise in a single image the total social action or process that is imagined as desirable." Myth (along with formal causality) performs the task, as McLuhan explains elsewhere, "of perceiving and stating causes and effects at the same time." As much as possible, advertisers imagine a desirable effect on their consumers before it happens. In other words, the media industry can employ myth and formal causality as well as anyone.

The hope that McLuhan sometimes entertains is that human beings in the electric or digital age can apply formal causality on their own, free of domination by powers that desire centralized control of the flow of information. In practical terms, this task would require the slowing down of technological innovation to anticipate the effects before they are irreversible. Although McLuhan admits that this "environmental programing" may cause panic, he believes that it "could actually be conducted quite constructively and humanistically." None of this would be easy. As the big state "becomes more cohesively involved in a world of instant information," McLuhan and Parker assert, "opposition would seem to become increasingly necessary but also intolerable." Worst of all, the dominance of the space bias within the high-technology industries is so entrenched that any interference with rushing a product to market would provoke tremendous opposition as well. Yet a society that insists on this control would be a true democracy. "The need of our time," McLuhan and Parker declare, "is for a means of measuring sensory thresholds and a means of discovering what changes occur in these thresholds as a result of the advent of any particular technology. . . . It would seem only reasonable to extend such controls to all the sensory thresholds of our being. We have no reason to be grateful to those who haphazardly juggle the thresholds in the name of innovation."

The populist myth of a vigilant democratic citizenry is one way to encourage the necessary application of formal causality to the creators who "haphazardly" manufacture new media. "WE the people," as McLuhan once put it, can demonstrate that we are the sole content of the institutions that we create, bearing the responsibility of anticipating "the EFFECTS of means upon our ends BEFORE creating their causes." This attempt to "put on" the voters will not succeed, of course, unless the numb prisoners of the electric cave grow weary of their chains.

Besides appeals to democratic virtue, it may be necessary to employ more drastic means to awaken the *vox populi*. The symbolism of the apocalypse may have to fulfill this task. Once again, only bad news can sell good news.

10

SURVIVING THE APOCALYPSE

In 2011, the centennial of McLuhan's birth, the journalist Alan Jacobs published an article entitled "Why Bother with Marshall McLuhan?" Jacobs's ultimate answer to this question focused on the predictive value of McLuhan's ideas and reflections. "To read McLuhan," he said, "is to gain at least an inkling of what it might be like to look around the next corner of history." During McLuhan's heyday as an intellectual celebrity in the 1960s, Jonathan Miller, the author of a book that was viscerally critical of McLuhan, offered this ambivalent praise: "Everything that McLuhan says opens new doors. I think he often opens doors to chaos, but enough of the doors that he opens are exciting and productive to make him worth studying." A great deal of the critical commentary devoted to McLuhan's legacy is similarly preoccupied with the accuracy (or inaccuracy) of his numerous predictions. The famous management consultant Peter Drucker made this blunt assessment: "Not one of McLuhan's specific predictions has come true and not one of them is likely to come true."

Given McLuhan's penchant for predicting the effects of new media, in accord with his application of formal causality, it is unsurprising that different interpreters have focused on this prophetic quality within his oeuvre. Yet it is far from obvious that McLuhan himself would have enjoyed being classified as a futurist guru. This status is analogous to that of a cultish figure whose every pronouncement is interpreted as the unvarnished truth. McLuhan flatly rejected this posture on the grounds that it would interfere with the flexibility and freedom needed to explore new or undiscovered realities. McLuhan did not want followers who dogmatically parroted every changeable insight that he offered at a given moment. As he explained to Gerald Stearn, "You can be quite sure that if there are going to be McLuhanites, I am not going to be one of them.... If I just keep writing with great energy, no McLuhanite will ever be able to digest it all." In an interview with Tom Wolfe in 1970, he offered this cautionary observation about the severe limitations of prediction or prophecy: "I've always been very careful never to predict anything that had not already happened. The future is not what it used to be. It is here.... The present includes the past and the future."

This last reference to the coexistence of past, present, and future refers, we have seen, to a recurrent theme in McLuhan's reflections on the pattern of simultaneity. Any prediction or prophecy should study the past as much as the present and future. This analysis of history is not the same as the rear-view mirror mentality, which judges the present through the criteria of a previous era or century. Rather, this study is constantly searching for patterns from the past that help us anticipate the future of new media before their effects are irreversible.

Given the pattern of ignorance that, according to McLuhan, has accompanied the creation of any new medium, skepticism about the capacity of humanity to apply formal causality is very tempting. As a Christian, McLuhan refuses to succumb to the sin of despair over the possibility of awakening his fellow human beings to the dangers emanating from the uncontrolled and thoughtless usage of untried media. The possibility of surviving the maelstrom always exists. If people make the effort to apply the laws of media to a new medium, survival may not be a utopian dream. What McLuhan and his son Eric claim about the laws of media could apply to many of his ideas: they "are empirical, and form a practical means of perceiving the action and effects of ordinary human tools and services."

Although the dispassionate study of media is essential, it is not sufficient in an age in which control of the media is concentrated in the hands of a few corporations. Notwithstanding McLuhan's refusal to substitute moral judgments for sober analysis of technological change, he is willing to make these judgments if they have the effect of awakening popular consciousness. As he writes in *Counterblast*, the media "can be entrusted only to new artists because they are art forms." The focus on *new* artists is deliberate, one that recurs in his later works. Without them, human beings will continue to be servo-mechanisms that worship idols created by their own hands. Unfortunately, in sharp opposition to the artist, what McLuhan once described as "mesmerized practical men who are efficiently arranging for the obsequies of our world's mind and body alike" not only do not understand the media they create and use, to the detriment of the human beings in their care; they advance the eager "embrace of man when deloused of his humanity by technics." Given this environment, rational arguments alone may not be enough to jolt a numbed populace out of its complacency about the media. Even science fiction writers have not been notably successful in persuading people to address the dystopian potential of new technologies.

Apocalypse Now

Unfortunately, new artists rarely have the power of the "mesmerized" elites in charge of government and corporations. Although all three groups want to create new ways of relating to the world, the power of creation generally lies with big business (and its ally the warfare-welfare state, discussed in chapter 7). To pin one's hopes on the lone individual who can take on a system of domination is an epiphenomenon of the old bourgeois print age, an ideal that is probably obsolete. To be sure, McLuhan's religious beliefs occasionally inspired him to muse about the emergence of this solitary heroic figure. Given the growing division between the haves and the have-nots in the divided global village, McLuhan warns, "the new technologic man, hypnotized by his own electronic navel, must become his brother's keeper, in spite of himself." How will this moral awakening happen? "The role of the shepherd, a continuing archetype in biblical literature, invariably entails a spiritual quest." If the shepherd does not emerge, there is always the prospect of the "wolf prowling ravenously about the flock," also acting as God's "agent for self-examination."

Although McLuhan never claims to be this shepherd, he sincerely wants to liberate his fellow human beings from their self-imposed enslavement. (As a Christian, he may have felt that a perfect deity would not inevitably trap his creation in a Platonic cave forever.) Yet he is also aware that the global village is too diverse to welcome any "imposed pattern" from a powerful interest, including nation-states. His playful use of probes, puns, and put-ons has nothing in common with creating a new blueprint for the future, given the fact that the future usually reflects the biases of the present in any case. As a Christian, McLuhan has even more reason to be skeptical toward grand designs to impose an ambitious ethical vision on human beings who do not want this top-down planning. In his dissertation, he notes how the idea of a "common good" that unites all of humanity has always been subject to rational disputation. While pagan authors equated the common good with the health of the city-state, Christians identified it with the City of God.

The reader may wonder why a religious myth, particularly a biblical myth, is so indispensable to the task of awakening people to the most destructive effects of media. McLuhan's answer is that this type of narrative is more effective in communicating a dire message about the media than any other. The truth or falsehood of a myth is not the main issue for McLuhan. What matters is the *effect* of the story on its audience. Christianity illustrates this dynamic. McLuhan describes the Christian "myth" as a narrative that "is not fiction but something more than ordinarily real." Its powerful symbolism is intelligible only with reference to the impact that it has on the readers of the Bible. In fact, these readers are the *content* of the Bible. As McLuhan puts it, "The words are not the message: the message is the effect on us, and that is conversion." For this reason, McLuhan took aim at the demythologizing effects of Vatican II in the 1960s. In a 1969 letter to Pierre Trudeau, McLuhan noted, "Even the good news of the gospel can only be sold by hellfire. Vatican II made a very big mistake in this matter as in other matters."

Despite the caution that he often manifests toward the role that his faith plays in shaping his thought, McLuhan looks to Christian symbolism as the foundation for one of his most dramatic prophecies. In his interview with *Playboy* in 1969, the dueling possibilities of divine redemption and demonic destruction were real to him. "The extensions of man's consciousness induced by the electric media could conceivably usher in the millennium," he said, "but it also holds the potential for realizing the Anti-Christ—Yeats' rough beast, its hour come round at last, slouching toward Bethlehem to be born." In pithy words that conclude an essay on the end of hierarchy in the Catholic Church, McLuhan remarks, "We are on the verge of the apocalypse. In fact, we are living in it."

There are different ways of understanding McLuhan's provocative reference to the apocalypse, which has more than one meaning. "Apocalypse" comes from the Greek word *apokálupsis*, which means a "revealing" that awakens the consciousness of humanity. In a 1977 interview with Edward Wakin, McLuhan welcomed the apocalypse in this sense. "I have never been an optimist or a pessimist," he said. "Our only hope is apocalypse." The hope to which he alluded in this interview was probably his long-held desire that the effects of the electric age would awaken human beings to their awesome responsibility to understand the objects they create. (McLuhan's reference to a "garbage apocalypse" illustrates this strategy.) As he predicts in *Understanding Media*, it may be possible to develop an "immunity" to new media as long as we, like the artist, make an effort to anticipate their effects before they are irreversible. Because electric media operate at the speed of light, the "revealing" that occurs in acoustic space is identical to a greater awareness of the "potencies" (formal causes) that these media manifest.

Apocalypse has another meaning: the cosmic conflict between good and evil leading to the destruction of the world. McLuhan makes use of this version as well. In a 1977 conversation with Pierre Babin, he provocatively refers to the electric age as "the time of the Antichrist." The simultaneous access to information that all human beings enjoy is also "Lucifer's moment. He is the greatest electrical engineer." (Lucifer means "light-bringer.") McLuhan goes so far as to predict that many human beings may end up confusing good with evil, reminiscent of the "false messiahs and false prophets" to which the book of Matthew (24:24) refers. Christianity, he maintains, reveals the "timeless beyond time and 'under the aspect of eternity.'" Unfortunately, the Anti-Christ can employ this language as well. The "eternity" to which McLuhan refers is the understanding of existence as simultaneous, including past, present, and future. Once again, this is an example of his usage of paradox. The past is just as present as the future, a truth that is alien to the linear and visual thinking of progressivism. With the visual sense, one periodizes history according to the different stages of past, present, and future. With the acoustic sense, one can more easily grasp how past, present, and future involve us all at once. Christianity is able to reveal this paradox because simultaneity helps believers understand God "as an eternal Being," one "with centres everywhere and boundaries nowhere" a spirit (namely, Jesus Christ) who participates in divine and human existence all at once.

In contrast, the secular progressivist mind focuses on the potential or "inevitable" future at the expense of the past. Progressivists are ill prepared to deal with media that revive an understanding of time as simultaneous, as McLuhan contends. Our "total history," he observes, "is now potentially present in a kind of simultaneous transparency." Moreover, we "have been rapt in 'the artifice of eternity' by the placing of our own nervous system around the entire globe." This condition of simultaneity may facilitate the rise of an Anti-Christ figure with the opportunity to project his power on a global scale. Unlike angels, who can be in only one place at a time, as McLuhan once noted (see chapter 6), the Anti-Christ can be everywhere at all times. For this reason, McLuhan warns, "technically speaking, the age in which we live is certainly favorable to an Antichrist. Just think: each person can instantly be tuned to a 'new Christ' and mistake him for the real Christ. At such times it becomes crucial to hear properly and to tune yourself to the right frequency." This all-too-human temptation to act like a god who can transform every human being into a servo-mechanism around the world captures the meaning of what the Anti-Christ is to McLuhan. In secular terms, the Anti-Christ could be a powerful figure in business or politics who promises to fulfill the Christian myth of global unity and charity for all by demanding unlimited access to the private data of millions of human beings while the latter lease their eyes and ears to this private interest (see chapter 5).

It is not McLuhan's purpose to encourage despair or hopelessness. His religious faith forbids these sentiments. There is always reason to hope in the face of apocalypse. As already noted, he never describes himself as an optimist or a pessimist. The current obsession with "doomscrolling," or the compulsive fascination with negative news stories, is not something that McLuhan would welcome, although he would urge us to understand how digital media encourage it. He would probably interpret it as an effect of the nonstop news cycle whose progenitors understand all too well that bad news sells good news. The most powerful individuals in the media field today occasionally issue apocalyptic predictions about the technologies they have unleashed but apparently do not control. They fear that the AI revolution is unstoppable and may even lead to the extinction of human existence at the hands of these programs that will presumably one day surpass human intelligence. Elon Musk has warned that AI may inevitably develop "super intelligence" of a magnitude that could destroy humanity. This new intellect would have the same power as a god, to recall McLuhan, with centers everywhere and boundaries nowhere.

This message of inevitability makes it easy to forget that human beings have created these media. By understanding a new medium, McLuhan insists, we can dictate a "new environment." This is, of course, easier said than done. Given the overwhelming effects of electric media, McLuhan observes, "we are losing all confidence in our right to assign guilt." Guilt presupposes responsibility, which the wizards of high-tech downplay lest they be held accountable for their creations. No matter how tempting it is to conflate technological change with a deterministic force that human agency cannot resist, McLuhan, who is often falsely accused of being a technological determinist himself, urges us to remember that there "is no inevitability where there is a willingness to pay attention." Put in paradoxical terms, we always construct our own destinies that trap us; they are not imposed on us. As McLuhan and Barrington Nevitt quip in *Take Today*, "DO-IT-YOURSELF FATE. Everyman as Finn Awake." (Of course, Joyce's *Finnegans Wake* is a pun on this declaration.) Implicit in this paradox is the egalitarian hope that everyone can awaken from the effects of technology if they make the effort.

Paradox has always been central to Christianity. The paradox of the Incarnation—what McLuhan calls the "revealed divine event"—is that it helps us to understand why human beings create what they create. This event is a paradox precisely because two apparent opposites—namely, God and humanity—come together in one person. Other religions, McLuhan claims, "were rendered obsolete at the moment of the Incarnation," even though their differences can illuminate "some aspect of Christian community." In *From Cliché to Archetype*, McLuhan and his coauthor, Wilfred Watson, devote an entire chapter to the meaning of paradox. Of all the world religions, Christianity, in their view, understands paradox best. In fact, they write, "Christianity has been paradoxical from its inception." They illustrate this truth by referring to Acts 26, where Paul defends himself before King Agrippa and the Roman procurator Festus. Paul initially identifies himself as a learned man, a *doctus orator*, by stretching out his hand, a gesture that demonstrates his command of rhetoric. This act and Paul's detailed portrait of his spiritual journey prompt Festus to shout, "Your great learning is turning you mad" (Acts 26:24). According to McLuhan and Watson,

Festus's remark is an example of paradox because it points to the coexistence of wisdom and insanity, in contrast to the typical ancient notion that erudition is a "main source of wisdom and sanity." If McLuhan is right, Christianity understands this paradox more profoundly than any other tradition because it reveals that great wisdom and insanity do not cancel each other out. Applied to technological change, this paradox brings out the sobering truth that human knowledge of newly created media can coexist with ignorance of their powerful effects, particularly if the creators of these media are convinced that they incarnate God-like power themselves. It takes the story of the Incarnation to reveal the paradox that knowledge of God's power to create will not necessarily inspire righteous and humble actions. This knowledge is just as likely to inspire demonic imitation at the hands of an Anti-Christ.

One does not have to be religious to invoke apocalyptic rhetoric, as the debate over climate change reveals. Yet even the most sophisticated secular minds may not fully understand their own paradoxical dependence on the biblical understanding of creation. This creation includes the awesome power of manufacturing environments that dwarf the power of nature itself. In *From Cliché to Archetype*, McLuhan and Watson conclude their chapter on paradox by pointing to Darwinian theory as paradoxical in supposing that "species can evolve but still persist in a world where all is change—it is a theory at once radically revolutionary and radically conservative." This paradox, which McLuhan also calls simultaneity, is impossible to reconcile with the idea of progress, which influenced Charles Darwin. The linear approach to history that is embedded within the theory of evolution presents time as forward moving, not simultaneously coexisting with past and present. In reducing all human activity to interaction with an adverse natural environment ("survival of the fittest"), evolutionary biology fails, paradoxically, to understand its own origins within the past. For McLuhan, history is not a natural phenomenon: it is a human creation that goes far beyond the desire for mere survival. The rise of technologies that transform nature itself proves this point. As McLuhan puts it, "The evolutionary habitats of the biologists since Darwin were the old nature which has now been transcended by satellite and radar." To recall his distinction between matching and making, we do not match or reflect nature and history. Rather, we create these as new environments. Darwinian theory itself is an expression of human history, not natural history, even if Darwin was not aware of this paradox. As a man of the nineteenth century, he never realized "that it would be possible to program the environment itself as evolutionary." The evolutionist's indifference to this human power over the environment leaves him unprepared for the apocalypse, the culmination of humanity's attempt to create new realities for better or worse.

The Christian (or Judeo-Christian) consciousness is most acutely aware of the necessity of understanding humanity's paradoxical relation to creation, both divine and human. By upholding the authority of God's creation above all human innovation, a Christian is most capable of resisting the worldly temptations posed by technologies. "It is not brains or intelligence that is needed to cope with the problems which Plato and Aristotle and all of their successors to the present have failed to confront," McLuhan writes. "What is needed is a readiness to undervalue the world altogether." As with any momentous act of creation, one must be ready for both good and bad effects, in accord with formal causality. Throughout this process, the thoughtful Christian will not share current anxieties over AI's alleged displacement of human intelligence. God's creation always surpasses any human innovation. AI is like any idol, whose creators erroneously assume that it rivals the power of God. This idol can never wield more power than human beings give to it. Although AI is the extension of imperfect humanity, human beings are the sole extension of God, created in his image and likeness (minus his wisdom).

Of course, undervaluing human innovation can have unintended effects, good and bad. In *From Cliché to Archetype*, McLuhan and Watson trace this otherworldly attitude toward the world back to the Old Testament, which "repudiated all technologies as pagan deities, from the Tower of Babel to the Golden Calf." This momentous rejection had paradoxical effects. On the one hand, it encouraged technological change. "Paradoxically," according to McLuhan and Watson, "it was this indifference to the traditional that permitted novelty and innovation to thrive unhindered by religious observations." On the other hand, this indifference to technology also left Christians unprepared to deal with the massive technological transformation of nature during the electric age. McLuhan and Watson write, "Christian indifference to the pagan rituals of stability and renewal, as well as Christian contempt for the world as a wreck or middenheap," are attitudes that are not helpful in an age where new technologies make possible "a reprograming of the totality of existence on the planet." In short, the worship of God above all the things of the world can potentially inflate the power of these things, leading to the apocalypse. Still, the Christian tradition, as McLuhan interprets it, helps us identify manifestations of the apocalypse.

Natural Law and the Church amid the Postliterate Apocalypse

The electric age has attempted to abolish the Christian tradition of natural law, a sure sign of the apocalypse. In brief, the philosophy of natural law is rooted in the medieval unity of the Book of Nature and the Book of Scripture. The philosophy of natural law that Aquinas famously defended is the cornerstone of this unity. In private correspondence, McLuhan described his study of media as "Thomistic to the core. It has the further advantage of being able to explain Aquinas and Aristotle in modern terms." Early on in his scholarship, McLuhan saw his task as one that longtime interpreters of Aquinas had failed to accomplish. In a 1946 letter to S. J. Walter Ong, he complained that "no Thomist has ever faced the question of training in sensibility, the education of the passions, the fluid interplay of thought and feeling" that could "re-create the total loss of human community in contemporary life." This failure among his followers was not attributable to Aquinas himself, who profoundly understood that human beings can understand the Book of Nature if they use their God-given senses properly. In *Take Today*, McLuhan's aphorism "Should Old Aquinas Be Forgotten?" includes a brief explanation as to why the answer to this question should be a resounding no. McLuhan and Nevitt credit Aquinas with understanding that consciousness, the "art of making *sense*," occurs when all the senses produce a "unified sensory experience." As McLuhan asserts in his 1952 essay "Joyce, Aquinas, and the Poetic Process," the senses and the cognitive powers of the human intellect are "properly analogous," working together to understand the natural order. McLuhan quotes Aquinas on how the senses "delight" in the "duly proportioned" and beautiful things of creation because they are "like them." In Aquinas's words, "The sense too is a sort of reason, as is every cognitive power." Although, as we have seen, McLuhan never denies that non-Christian thinkers can illuminate certain features of Christian revelation, he clearly favors the Thomistic explanation of how the senses work in harmony with the mind.

Yet belief in natural law is unfashionable in the age of discarnate identity, which separates the body (nature) from the soul (divinity). Most human beings choose one of two extremes: materialism (preoccupation with the body) or discarnatism (the gnostic escape from the body). As McLuhan explained in a 1977 letter to Pierre Trudeau, "The peculiar character of discarnate man stems from his non-relation to 'Natural' law. The mere fact of being disembodied, as we are in dreams, dissolves the relation to Nature and to 'Natural' law." To make matters worse, few authorities, even within the church, are interested in what McLuhan once described as the attempt "to recover the knowledge of that language which once man held by nature." (McLuhan and his son Eric even planned to write a book tentatively titled *The Christian in the Electronic Age*, which would have discussed the state of the church in the electric age.)

Unfortunately, the traditional institutions charged with this task are not prepared. McLuhan faulted the leadership of his own church for failing to prepare for a postliterate age. From its inception, the Catholic Church was steeped in the classical tradition of literacy. Clerics studied the great works of Greco-Roman philosophy and literature. Yet the Biblical Era did not begin with literacy. As Paul Eidelberg explains, the "breath of life" that God bestowed on Adam (Gen. 2:7), the first man, was speech. Accordingly, the word of God was spoken and heard. The strength of speech lies in its capacity (formal cause) to convey both thought and emotion, a feat that the written word does not perform easily. Even so, the written word has greater endurance than the spoken word. As Eidelberg notes, "The written word, being concrete, has a permanence denied to the spoken word. Although the Oral Torah (like every detail of the Written Torah) was as faithfully preserved from generation to generation, still, as a result of Exile and Dispersion, it had to be incorporated into the Mishna and then into the Talmud."

The coexistence of oral and written tradition never makes for an easy relationship. As the value of literacy became hegemonic in power, orality was devalued. (The same dynamic occurs with the emergence of any new medium: electric media devalue print.) As McLuhan explains, "In a highly literate culture, the dialogue form becomes repugnant." Attempts to synthesize these media have not worked well. As long as print civilization wielded the greatest influence, the private and silent nature of reading became the dominant expression of literacy. For this reason, reading aloud is seen as a "pointless" exercise in an advanced literate culture. The history of Christianity furnishes examples of this bias in action. According to McLuhan, "The bible belt is oral territory and therefore despised by the literati."

Even before the Gutenberg era, the clerical hierarchy that monopolized the interpretation of the Bible reluctantly arrived at the fateful conclusion that one could not propagate or incarnate the truth of scripture unless people could read it. In the process, they would learn to read and exist as individuals, not members of a tribe. "The early church fathers," McLuhan explained in a 1978 dialogue with Bruce R. Powers, "discovered one very disconcerting fact: tribal man is not very educable. Convince him to one point of view one day and he goes back to his old ways the next. The pre-literate has a short memory." This depth of understanding of a new medium has rarely been apparent in the history of the church. In fact, McLuhan once remarked, the church has never understood how its fate is tied to literacy. As he pointed out in a 1977 interview, the Council of Trent that convened in the sixteenth century had no understanding of "the effects of print on the spiritual schism and psychic distress of the religious and political life of that time." This somnambulistic attitude toward technological change, he added, persists well into the electric age. Taking aim at Vatican II in the 1960s, McLuhan faulted the participants for paying "no attention to the causes of their problems in their new policies and prescriptions." What does the modern church fail to grasp about electric or digital media?

According to McLuhan, the basic fact that the church has not understood is that the postliterate citizenry of the global village, including self-identified Christians, no longer read with depth or seriousness. As a result, they are unwilling to defer to a hierarchy based on the valuation of literacy, including biblical literacy. Thus, a stark challenge faces the church: "We must get rid of the hierarchy if we want participation. But we don't have to wish for it. It's happening." As I write this, there is intense debate in the church over "synodality," or the attempt to invite more participation by the laity while the priesthood is being encouraged to listen more deeply to the laity's concerns. Although the defenders of synodality have denied that they want to replace the hierarchy with the laity as "the People of God," the McLuhanesque question that they need to ponder is this: Does this "People" still read and interpret the Book of Scripture (along with Nature)?

At the surface level, electric or digital media are a boon to the church's mission of spreading the Gospel. McLuhan admitted that "now we have suddenly a way of propagating information and knowledge without literacy." Still, whereas the ancient Christian felt isolated by the world, the "modern Christian feels outdistanced by the speed." Theology at the speed of light, in which "there is no peace," is bound to change doctrinal content, a vindication of "the medium is the message." McLuhan further predicted that the church would become theatrical or the player of a role in this age: "When things speed up hierarchy disappears and global theatre sets in." When Pope Francis invited over one hundred comedians to the Vatican in June 2024, he was acknowledging, if not celebrating, this power of theater to which the Holy See is not immune. As the host to these comics, the pope was declaring that the church is on the side of laughter.

While the pope becomes a "role player," his authority as a teacher does not necessarily vanish. This role may even accelerate the process of learning. As McLuhan put it, "The Chair of Peter can jet around the world; it doesn't have to stay in Rome." Still, what will this teacher teach about the most important thing of all—salvation? Will the People of the Book in the global village have any tolerance for traditional teaching? McLuhan had his doubts that the church wanted "to shake up our present population. To do that you'd have to preach nothing but hellfire. In my life, I have never heard one such sermon from a Catholic pulpit."

Although McLuhan often suspected that Vatican II's liberalization of Catholic doctrine reflected an uncritical embrace of Protestant influences, the more pressing problem lay, once again, with media that do not require a literate laity. In fact, the decline of literacy has also spread to the hierarchy, who are oblivious to the historical connection between the church and literate civilization. McLuhan complained that the "degree of literacy" was very low in the seminaries, bringing the level of culture in the church down to a *Reader's Digest* level. This last statement suggests that what McLuhan means by the decline of literacy is not that parishioners have stopped reading *in toto*. Rather, they do not read with depth or with awareness of the new technological age. They seem to have forgotten that the life of the Christian is to be unworldly, as we have seen. The role of the church is to teach what this attitude means. Even though McLuhan was convinced that "as literacy weakens, people lose their religious affiliations," he welcomed the prospect that the "potential for teaching and learning in the Church was never greater than in the electric world."

Nevertheless, far more human beings want to be creative second Adams rather than aesthetic first Adams. In Vico's terms, human beings are inclined to forget that not all truths are created by humanity; some are eternal, independent of our making. Worst of all, the weakening of literacy among the inhabitants of the global village impedes the careful interpretation needed to recover "knowledge" of this language. These are the preconditions for the rise of the Anti-Christ, who celebrates the triumph of the second Adam over the first Adam. Once again, knowledge of the God-like power to create does not inspire humility or wisdom.

A religion that embraces the paradox of eternity and creation (ideally Christianity, for McLuhan) is the only way of countering the discarnatism that an Anti-Christ may falsely promote as the truth. As McLuhan bluntly remarked in a conversation with the Venezuelan journalist Margarita D'Amico in 1976, "When you lose your natural body, you must have a supernatural solution. Religion is the only solution when you lose your body, when you are nobody . . . if Christianity insists on a human body that is incarnate, it is the right religion for discarnate man who has lost his body."

In other words, it takes a true religion to fight false religions. McLuhan easily dismisses the atheistic expectation that modern scientific and technological progress render religion obsolete. As long as people use the technologies that extend themselves, he says, they will treat them "as gods or minor religions." (McLuhan would not be surprised that several women's studies programs in North American universities are offering courses in witchcraft.) He even predicted that "the age we are moving into will probably seem the most religious ever." Still, what is the likelihood of recovering an awareness of natural law amid the apocalypse?

McLuhan's sobering answer to this question is that humanity will probably have to learn the hard way. Philosophical defenses of natural law within a postliterate age will not be sufficient to effect change. Instead, human beings will have to suffer the effects of the dualisms that electric media foster. McLuhan is convinced that the new age of electric media has increasingly detached humanity from nature, not just from one's natural body. In the process, the certainty that nature once provided seemingly yields to substitutes that do not fill the void. Instead they widen the old dualism between the sensual and the intellectual. "When we lose nature as a direct experience we lose a balance wheel, the touchstone of natural law," he and Powers write. "With or without drugs, the mind tends to float free into the dangerous zone of abstractions." Whatever "religion" may emerge from this context will merely reflect this dualism. "Since the basis of natural law is unavailable to the TV generation, its only recourse is to supernatural law as a means of coherence and meaning. The Beatles seek the gurus, and their groupies drift into Hare Krishna." Since McLuhan wrote this in the 1960s, the number of religious cults has mushroomed in the digital age. By "supernatural law" McLuhan probably had in mind the age-old desire to escape from the body, which Gnosticism teaches (see chapter 6). None of this means that most users of electric media will rediscover natural law to expose and overcome the dualism between nature, the soul, and the mind. Lack of awareness is one constant that never completely vanishes. McLuhan and Powers quipped that this new religious age was "the age of Aquarium," full of fish unaware of their environment, once again.

Puns aside, McLuhan is deadly serious about the cost of rejecting natural law, which unifies the body and the soul. Those who live by this dualism do not only lack an identity; they also feel little loyalty to any cause or tradition. As he and his son Eric explain in *Laws of Media*, "As electric media proliferate, whole societies at a time become discarnate, detached from mere bodily or physical 'reality' and relieved of any allegiance to or sense of responsibility to or for it." If they are no longer loyal to nature, they will not be loyal to anything else. The result of this disorienting, fluid reality will be violence. "Since, however, discarnate man has no relation to natural law (or to Western lineality)," the McLuhans write, "his impulse is towards anarchy and lawlessness." As McLuhan and Powers wrote elsewhere, the effects of discarnatism "could be dangerously inflating and schizophrenic." One sign of this "anarchy and lawlessness" is to detach morality from the objective truths contained within natural law. As McLuhan warned Trudeau, "In the TV age especially, it is notable that the young feel few ties to external and private morality." He was not predicting the end of morality per se. An age that finished off privacy would cast a moralizing spotlight on anyone who deviated from the mores of the global village. Electric media, however, end up redefining the content of morality, discouraging the old bourgeois ethic of individual responsibility in favor of the latest tribal or group ethic.

As we have seen, McLuhan is certain that the use of any technology can be pushed to an extreme, whatever the conscious intention of the users or creators. The current tendency to outsource decision-making to artificial general intelligence systems has provoked anxiety over the danger of applying this practice to systems that control or manage weapons of mass destruction. Several nations already use these "lethal autonomous weapons systems" (LAWS), which, unlike traditional drones, have algorithms that enable them to select targets on their own. These LAWS grimly illustrate McLuhan's four laws of media. In tetradic terms, they simultaneously *enhance* destructive power that can be projected all over the world, they *reverse* (or flip) the role of their creators into mere technicians who maintain these systems, and they *retrieve* the "fast draw" of the archetypal sheriff in an American western by destroying a target with instantaneous precision. Most disturbingly, they *obsolesce* soldiers (especially pilots), who in a bygone age would do the dirty work necessary in war.

Because these systems have no use for human agency, they potentially complete the triumph of discarnatism: human beings are no longer responsible for the decisions that these machines make. LAWS are more dangerous than a bomber pilot who, in an example raised by McLuhan, can more easily drop napalm on a civilian population than obey an order to pour a can of gasoline over a child. The "use of weaponry at a distance" discourages the pilot from considering the effects of his actions. LAWS do not even have to go through the pseudoethical motions of rationalizing the infliction of human suffering from a safely distant vantage point. Most disturbingly, those technicians who allow LAWS to make these decisions have embraced the illusion of utter separation, not just distance, from the effects of these systems.

LAWS threaten to complete the ultimate detachment of technology from the physical (and spiritual) reality of human existence. Unsurprisingly, there has been a steady rise in apocalyptic warnings about the prospect of artificial intelligence triggering a nuclear war. António Guterres, the secretary-general of the United Nations, has warned that humanity is on a "knife's edge" because of the uncontrolled advancement of this technology. The thoughtless surrender of human autonomy to LAWS is not just another example of humanity ignoring a consequence until the technology is deeply advanced, formal causality disregarded once again. It also gravely illustrates how far the creators of this technology have fallen away from obeying the basic precepts of natural law, which include the desire for survival and the rejection of what McLuhan calls the impulse toward "anarchy and lawlessness."

Hope amid Apocalypse

As a pious Catholic, McLuhan believed that God created a universe that is both ordered and good. In the introduction to *Understanding Media*, he acknowledges how his belief or faith in the intelligibility of all things inspired him to write this book. He writes, "There is a deep faith to be found in this new attitude—a faith that concerns the ultimate harmony of all being." This faith "explores the contours of our own extended beings in our technologies, seeking the principle of intelligibility in each of them." The reward that results from understanding "these forms" is that humanity "will bring them into orderly service." Despite popular fears of the effects of AI, McLuhan may have hoped that this technology would potentially inspire human beings to retrieve the natural law synthesis of body and soul, which is more trustworthy than the numerous deepfake discarnate identities constructed by this software. In his subtle way, McLuhan sometimes implies that a new understanding of technology inspired by religious faith is required to make sense of this harmony. It is always possible to comprehend what we incarnate. "Our words," he reflects, "are analogies of the miracle by which we incarnate and utter the world."

In the absence of a religious consciousness, we will experience nothing but disorder and chaos. We will be the hapless victims of these forces. As he remarked at the end of his *Playboy* interview, even though "the world-pool of electronic information movement will toss us all about like corks on a stormy sea," understanding this movement could perpetuate our survival. Recalling the metaphor of the maelstrom to which he refers in *The Mechanical Bride*, McLuhan assured his interviewer that "if we keep our cool during the descent into the maelstrom, studying the process as it happens to us and what we can do about it, we can come through."

How does religion help us "keep our cool" amid rapid technological change? In his 1954 lecture entitled "Catholic Humanism and Modern Letters," McLuhan drew a strong connection between the Christian faith and a true understanding of the world. He averred that "our faith in the Incarnation has an immediate relevance to our art, science, and philosophy." The choice between faith and reason is a false one for thoughtful Christians, whose belief in the Incarnation helps them comprehend the "poetry of God." This poetry represents the benevolent order of the universe, which is discoverable through analogy. By believing that all things are fulfilled in Christ, we can trust "our powers of perception" and "look more securely and steadfastly on natural knowledge which at one and the same time has become easier and also less important to us."

The Christian faith, in other words, inspires believers to trust in the inherent goodness of God's created order. Yet McLuhan also prudently warned that Christians can be swept up by the technological maelstrom as much as anyone else can. These "misguided Christians kneel" before a world that is a "strictly Luciferan product" as well as a "highly plausible mock-up of the mystical body." In a 1969 letter to Fr. Robert J. Leuver, McLuhan cautions that the Christian "feels the downward mania of the earth and its treasures, and is just as inclined to conform his sensibilities to man-made environments as anyone else." Yet he adds the hopeful observation that "only the Christian can afford to laugh at" changes that inspire other human beings to "wipe out one another in order to impose them as ideals." Amid the diversity of the global village, the Christian faith manifests "detachment and amusement at human gullibility and self-deception."

This detachment is not the same as the posture of pure detachment about which McLuhan often warns. Rather, it is the sobering recognition that only belief in an order that transcends the flux of media can actually enable this separation or distance.

Despite this hope, the stakes are high. As McLuhan dramatically notes near the end of this letter, the "'Prince of this World' is a great P.R. man, a great salesman of new hardware and software, a great electrical engineer, and a great master of the media. It is His master stroke to be not only environmental but invisible, for the environment is invincibly persuasive when ignored." The additional reason for hope that McLuhan offers amid the persistent danger of ignoring an invisible environment is that human beings are responsible for the decisions they make. Taking control of the environment, not just the figure, would be an expression of conscious freedom. Ignoring the actual and potential effects of new media manifests freedom only in an unconscious sense. Neither choice is an effect of nature or fate. Unlike most periods of technological change that allowed "the individual and society to absorb and cushion their impact to some degree," McLuhan contends, human beings can witness and anticipate these effects in real time today, even though the temptation to live in a "self-induced subliminal trance" is just as probable.

CONCLUSION

McLuhan never tires of emphasizing the fact that we make the media. They are not phenomena that exist far beyond the control of human beings. Yet the main obstacle to understanding media is human nature. Our failure to understand media lies not in our stars but in ourselves. We are not naturally inclined to fully comprehend the effects of what we create at the time that we create it. We almost never ask why we ought to create the technologies that we do. This pattern in ages past was not necessarily reason for alarm, given the fact that the effects of media such as the written word and print took root in a gradual fashion across several centuries. With the advent of the electric and digital ages, the speed of technological change has accelerated so dramatically that it has become possible to understand the effects of new media in real time. It has also become more imperative to do so, given the revolutionary impact of these media on every aspect of life, ranging from politics to economics to religion.

Although McLuhan warned that there is no such thing as pure detachment from a reality that we create, a certain degree of distance from nature is necessary. Without this sort of detachment, the study of media would not be possible. The immersion of preliterate civilizations into an all-encompassing cosmic order discouraged the recognition that civilization itself is a product of human making, not the result of matching or aligning our existence with this order. The creation of history is a testament to human agency, not biological determinism. Without this creation, our second nature could never have displaced (although it never extinguished) our first nature. The values of literacy, freedom, and individualism that writing and print made possible represented a turning away from the tribalist, cosmic orders of antiquity. Paradoxically, one can trust one's senses or "natural knowledge" only if one has already distinguished between what is natural and what is created. Even the laws of media are human creations that would not be conceivable without some degree of separation from the media themselves.

Because we make media, we toy with the possibility of creating a new nature, almost by magic. Nevertheless, nature imposes real limits on the degree to which we can understand and reinvent reality. The most radical attempts by the big state or big business to impose patterns that seek to reconstruct human nature are doomed to fail. Our first nature, full of primal instincts and desires, will always interfere with our efforts to study the media in any rational (that is, literate) sense. The Book of Nature, like the Book of Scripture, must be read and studied in a literate manner. Christian love of one's fellow human beings and undervaluation of the world are hardly natural instincts. Although McLuhan is a stalwart defender of the natural law tradition, understanding this philosophy requires the unnatural faculty of literate thought as well as belief in a God who transcends nature.

The electric-digital age reminds us, as McLuhan notes, that human beings do not live well at the speed of light. The success with which electric and digital media involve, bombard, and numb our five senses and central nervous system demonstrates that they are far more aligned with our first nature than print media ever were. The desire to act like a god in discarnate space is a natural response to the terrifying absence of a stable identity in the present age. Yet it is a desire born of fear, not thought. As long as we refuse to anticipate, control, and master the effects of these creations, we will remain their natural slaves by choice. The medium will continue to be the message, the idol that is magically transformed into a maelstrom holding sway over our destinies.

Notes

INTRODUCTION

1 *"with a strange expression"* McLuhan, "*Playboy* Interview," 254.
1 *"pick up some LL.D."* McLuhan, "*Playboy* Interview," 254.
1 *"I was released"* McLuhan, "*Playboy* Interview," 254.
1 *"LL.D. a felony"* McLuhan, "*Playboy* Interview," 254.
1 *"the electric media"* McLuhan, "*Playboy* Interview," 254.
2 *"in itself is a drugless inner trip"* McLuhan, "*Playboy* Interview," 254.
2 *"subordinate"* to the medium McLuhan, "*Playboy* Interview," 247.
2 *"invisible character about it"* McLuhan, "Future of Man," 66–67.
2 *"it also becomes invisible"* McLuhan, "*Playboy* Interview," 237.
3 *"make aware"* agents McLuhan, *Understanding Media*, 48.
3 *"work us over"* McLuhan and Fiore, *Medium Is the Massage*, 26. Quentin Fiore was the graphic designer of this book.
3 *"it wasn't a fish"* McLuhan, "Marfleet Lectures," 106.
4 *"blocking of perception"* McLuhan, *Understanding Media*, 43.
5 *"let the juggernaut roll over me"* McLuhan, "Predicting Communication," 101.
5 *"where to turn off the button"* McLuhan, "Predicting Communication," 102.
5 no *"magic red button"* "Sam Altman."
5 *"junk"* McLuhan, "*Playboy* Interview," 236.
6 *"conceit"* of nations and scholars Vico, *New Science*, para. 127. McLuhan approvingly refers to this passage in McLuhan and McLuhan, *Laws of Media*, 85.
6 *"ecology of media"* McLuhan, "Living at the Speed of Light," 242.

1. A BIOGRAPHY

11 *"unknown to human beings"* Marchand, *Marshall McLuhan*, 24. I rely heavily on this biography for much of the information cited in this chapter.
12 *"the coffers of Bay Street"* McLuhan, *Counterblast*, n.p.
12 *"miseries"* of these regions Quoted in Nevitt with McLuhan, *Who Was Marshall McLuhan?*, 111.
12 *"concepts"* Marchand, *Marshall McLuhan*, 29.
13 *"unified awareness and judgment"* McLuhan, introduction to *Paradox in Chesterton*, xviii.
13 *"the work of art"* McLuhan and McLuhan, *Laws of Media*, 48.
14 *"any Catholic institution"* McLuhan and Stearn, "Even Hercules," 261.
14 *"moralistic"* judgments of mass culture McLuhan and Stearn, "Even Hercules," 263.
15 *"extremely moralistic approach"* McLuhan, "*Playboy* Interview," 265.
15 *"footnote of explanation"* McLuhan, *Gutenberg Galaxy*, 56.
16 *"but also sensibilities"* McLuhan, introduction to *Explorations in Communication*, ix.
16 *"kick them in the electrodes"* McLuhan, "*Playboy* Interview," 267.
16 *"processing and packaging of information"* Quoted in Marchand, *Marshall McLuhan*, 147.

NOTES

17 *"somnambulistic state"* McLuhan, *Understanding Media*, 229.
17 *"of all technologies"* Quoted in Marchand, *Marshall McLuhan*, 169.
18 *influences of Wyndham Lewis and the Catholic mystic Pierre Teilhard de Chardin* Lewis writes, "The earth has become one big village, with telephones laid on from one end to the other, and air transport, both speedy and safe." Lewis, *America and Cosmic Man*, 21. See also Paul Edwards, "'Good Heavens!,'" 1455. For an incisive discussion of McLuhan's debt to Teilhard's ideas, see Ripatrazone, *Digital Communion*, 28–31, 119–20.
18 *articles* Tom Wolfe, "McLuhan's New World," 23–24.
18 *"What if he is right?"* Quoted in Popova, "Tom Wolfe on Marshall McLuhan."
18 *juxtaposed with McLuhan's reflections* McLuhan and Fiore, *War and Peace*.
19 *"our kind of world"* Quoted in Marchand, *Marshall McLuhan*, 195.
19 *a "pseudo-science"* Quoted in Stahlman, "Place of Marshall McLuhan," 15.
19 *"our society provides to him"* Quigley, "Global Verbalizer."
19 *"harmful to all professions"* Roland, "Review."
19 *"branded as an arsonist"* McLuhan to Muggeridge, September 19, 1974, in *Letters of Marshall McLuhan*, 507.
20 *"pondering their problem"* McKinney, "Computers Made of Paper," 142.
20 *"history of American medicine"* Marchand, *Marshall McLuhan*, 212.
21 *"what I say"* Quoted in Marchand, *Marshall McLuhan*, 271.
21 *"the mistakes of American cities"* Quoted on the inside front cover of Nowlan and Nowlan, *Bad Trip*.
21 *the expressway's construction* Marchand, *Marshall McLuhan*, 239.
21 *"a new kind of environment"* McLuhan, "Garbage Apocalypse," 1.
21 *"every day of the week"* McLuhan to Trudeau, September 29, 1971, in Kahn, *Been Hoping*, 91.
21 *"Protestantization"* Marchand, *Marshall McLuhan*, 217.
22 *"a blossoming of liberal individualism"* McLuhan to Trudeau, March 26, 1974, in Kahn, *Been Hoping*, 108.
22 *"a form of politics"* McLuhan, *Essential McLuhan*, 274. McLuhan made this remark in 1966.

2. UNDERSTANDING AND MISUNDERSTANDING MEDIA

23 *"human thing about him"* McLuhan, "Man and Media," 289.
24 *"public"* McLuhan, *Essential McLuhan*, 272.
24 *"they were doing"* McLuhan, "Fordham University," 144.
24 *"a new process"* McLuhan, *Mechanical Bride*, v.
24 *"the chopping block"* McLuhan, "Crack in the Rear-View Mirror," 33.
24 *"social distance as well"* McLuhan, *Understanding Media*, 221.
25 *"experience is concerned"* McLuhan with Watson, *From Cliché to Archetype*, 201–2.
25 *"watchdog of the mind"* McLuhan, *Understanding Media*, 18.
25 *"what they watch"* Haidt, "Content Moderation Is a Red Herring."
25 *"They will destroy us"* McLuhan, "Man and Media," 284.
25 *understanding reality* McLuhan, *Classical Trivium*, 22.
25 *"means of reflection"* McLuhan and McLuhan, *Laws of Media*, 221. The Vico quote is from Vico, *New Science*, para. 236.
26 *new technologies and environments* McLuhan, "Man and Media," 285.
26 *"one thing at a time"* McLuhan, "Marfleet Lectures," 115.
26 *"has preceded it"* McLuhan, "*Playboy* Interview," 238. Italics in the original.
26 *"environment more visible"* McLuhan, "*Playboy* Interview," 238.

26 *"it must be lived forward"* Kierkegaard, "Sayings of Kierkegaard," 943.
26 *"mostly involuntary"* McLuhan, "Marfleet Lectures," 126.
26 *"not very much of it"* McLuhan, "Marfleet Lectures," 126.
27 *dependent on them* Srigley, "Ron Srigley on Cellphones."
27 *"strategy of evasion and survival"* McLuhan, "Man and Media," 285.
27 *"deeply willed"* Quoted in Gordon, *Marshall McLuhan*, 220.
27 *"Midas touch"* McLuhan, *Playboy* Interview," 239.
27 *"your outlook"* McLuhan, "Communication Media," 38.
28 *"we don't see"* McLuhan, "Address at Vision 65," 220.
28 *"his buddies"* Quoted in Nevitt with McLuhan, *Who Was Marshall McLuhan?*, 172.
28 *"hidden environment or 'ground'"* Quoted in Nevitt with McLuhan, *Who Was Marshall McLuhan?*, 169.
29 *"media effects"* McLuhan and McLuhan, *Laws of Media*, 85.
29 *"the wind and the tides"* McLuhan and McLuhan, *Laws of Media*, 239.
29 *"Global Electric Theatre"* McLuhan and Nevitt, "Argument," 10.
29 *"audience"* McLuhan, "Address at Vision 65," 220.
30 *"his own actions"* McLuhan and Nevitt, "Argument," 17.
30 *"ignore the* ground *(its frame, the wall, etc.)"* McLuhan, "Religion and Youth," 100. Italics in the original.
30 *"merely outside world"* McLuhan and McLuhan, *Laws of Media*, 56.
30 *"is not music"* McLuhan and Nevitt, *Take Today*, 3.
30 *"audile-tactile"* McLuhan, *Gutenberg Galaxy*, 45–46.
30 *"all the senses"* McLuhan, *Understanding Media*, 333.
30 *"than he understands"* McLuhan, *Understanding Media*, 318.
31 *"hot"* as exciting and *"cool"* as forbidding McLuhan, "Fordham University," 142.
31 *a phone conversation consumes* McLuhan, *Understanding Media*, 23, 267.
31 *"his own personal identification"* McLuhan, "*Playboy* Interview," 248.
31 *"like a lot of other people"* McLuhan, "What TV Does Best," 247.
31 *"Nixon's superiority"* McLuhan, *Understanding Media*, 299.
31 *"space-oriented"* For the differences between time and space biases, see Innis, *Empire and Communications*; and Innis, *Bias of Communication*.
32 *"determines its value"* McLuhan, *Understanding Media*, 11.
32 *"some file somewhere"* McLuhan, "Predicting Communication," 101.
32 *he wears it like clothing* Nevitt with McLuhan, *Who Was Marshall McLuhan?*, 234.
32 *effect actually materializes* Nevitt and McLuhan, *Who Was Marshall McLuhan?*, 233.
32 *"X-ray"* McLuhan, "Fordham University," 142.
33 *"coolness and calm"* McLuhan, *Understanding Media*, 336–37.
33 *"when he told the truth"* McLuhan, "*Playboy* Interview," 248.
33 *"night-world"* McLuhan with Watson, *From Cliché to Archetype*, 200.
33 *"Finn cycle"* McLuhan, *Gutenberg Galaxy*, 86.
34 *"destructive trances"* McLuhan, *Culture Is Our Business*, 64.
34 *"the sake of restoring insights"* McLuhan, "Marfleet Lectures," 135.
34 *vast military apparatus* McLuhan, "Marfleet Lectures," 135.
34 *extension of themselves* McLuhan, *Understanding Media*, 41–42.
34 *"transforming himself into them"* Vico, *New Science*, para. 405.
35 *"a new technical form"* McLuhan, *Understanding Media*, 11.
35 *"Watch yourself"* McLuhan, "Man and Media," 279.
35 *"changes people"* McLuhan, "Living at the Speed of Light," 242.
35 *"program" a fate* Nevitt with McLuhan, *Who Was Marshall McLuhan?*, 234.
35 *"against media fallout"* McLuhan, "*Playboy* Interview," 263.
35 *"detached involvement"* McLuhan, "*Playboy* Interview," 267.

3. MAKING HISTORY THROUGH MEDIA

36 *"what is understood"* McLuhan and Stearn, "Even Hercules," 284.
36 *"fictional invention"* McLuhan and Stearn, "Even Hercules," 263. Italics in the original.
36 *"physically, psychically, and socially"* McLuhan and Nevitt, "Argument," 17.
37 *"world of self-deception"* McLuhan and Parker, *Through the Vanishing Point*, 16.
37 *"a world that is making us"* McLuhan and Nevitt, *Take Today*, 3–4.
37 *"simultaneously from different directions"* McLuhan, "Violence as a Quest for Identity," 273.
37 *"transmitted from the past"* Marx, *Eighteenth Brumaire*, 595.
37 *"simultaneous in time"* McLuhan, *Understanding Media*, 347. See also p. 16.
37 *"electric nowness"* McLuhan and Nevitt, "Argument," 2.
38 *"interplay at all times"* McLuhan, *Book of Probes*, 252–53.
38 *"no past that is dead"* McLuhan, "Technology and Political Change," 194.
38 *"past 2,500 years"* McLuhan, "Art as Survival," 210.
38 *"conflicting aspects of any problem"* McLuhan, *Book of Probes*, 330–31.
38 laws of media McLuhan and McLuhan, *Laws of Media*, 129.
38 a corporate reading public McLuhan and McLuhan, *Laws of Media*, 154–55.
39 the *"sacred"* and the *"profane"* Eliade, *Sacred and the Profane*.
39 *"dimensions of archaic man* plus" McLuhan, *Gutenberg Galaxy*, 78. Italics in the original.
39 *"lineal, sequential, visual"* McLuhan, *Gutenberg Galaxy*, 80.
39 *"dominated by the visual sense"* McLuhan, *Understanding Media*, 155.
40 *"empathically into it"* McLuhan, *Gutenberg Galaxy*, 80. Italics in the original.
40 *"the divine energies"* McLuhan, *Understanding Media*, 124.
40 *"is, as it were, entranced"* McLuhan, *Gutenberg Galaxy*, 29.
40 *"always present"* McLuhan and McLuhan, *Laws of Media*, 102.
40 *"auditory field"* McLuhan, *Gutenberg Galaxy*, 127.
40 *"total, unified field"* McLuhan, *Understanding Media*, 27.
40 *"singing commercial"* McLuhan, "Environment," 110.
40 "'*Can't you remember?*'" McLuhan, *Gutenberg Galaxy*, 106. Cf. McLuhan, "It is Strange," 130: "Exact verbal recall is scarcely a problem for pre-literate cultures."
41 *"perspective"* McLuhan, *Understanding Media*, 288.
41 *"all possible meanings and levels"* McLuhan, *Gutenberg Galaxy*, 127.
41 *"vanishing point"* McLuhan, *Gutenberg Galaxy*, 64.
41 *"has ever invented"* McLuhan, *Understanding Media*, 156.
41 individual identity is inconceivable Havelock, *Preface to Plato*, 142.
41 *"without affecting everyone else"* McLuhan, "McLuhan Looks at Fashion," 156.
41 *"total field of simultaneous relations"* McLuhan, *Gutenberg Galaxy*, 35.
41 *"stolid mask"* McLuhan, "McLuhan Looks at Fashion," 156.
41 *"togetherness of the tribe"* McLuhan, "McLuhan Looks at Fashion," 156.
42 *"yet each present"* McLuhan, "McLuhan Looks at Fashion," 151.
42 *"everything all the time"* McLuhan, *Gutenberg Galaxy*, 37.
42 *"tribal and individualist man"* McLuhan, *Understanding Media*, 39.
42 *"tribal collective authority"* McLuhan, *Understanding Media*, 39.
42 *"an eye for an ear"* McLuhan, *Gutenberg Galaxy*, 31.
42 *"interior monologue"* McLuhan, "It is Strange," 130.
42 *"common sense"* McLuhan, *Understanding Media*, 108.
43 *"individualized and civilized"* second nature McLuhan and McLuhan, *Laws of Media*, 116.
43 *"terrifying and altogether shattering"* McLuhan, "Marfleet Lectures," 122.

43 *"a perpetual incest"* McLuhan, "Marfleet Lectures," 122.
43 *"product of phonetic literacy"* McLuhan and Fiore, *War and Peace*, 24.
43 *"'winged words'"* McLuhan, "Space, Time, and Poetry," 58–59.
43 *"reassemble them into patterns"* McLuhan and Stearn, "Even Hercules," 275.
43 *"It lit up the dark"* McLuhan, *Book of Probes*, 80–81.
43 *"he wrote nothing"* McLuhan, *Gutenberg Galaxy*, 27.
43 *"public speaker"* McLuhan, *Understanding Media*, 307.
43 *"buzzing confusion"* Quoted in Nevitt with McLuhan, *Who Was Marshall McLuhan?*, 245.
44 *"the conceit of wisdom"* Plato, *Phaedrus*, 520 (275a-b).
44 *"an impoverishment of being"* McLuhan, *Gutenberg Galaxy*, 60.
44 *"come out of an oral rather than a literary culture"* McLuhan and Stearn, "Even Hercules," 284.
44 *"purify the tribal encyclopedia"* McLuhan, "Marfleet Lectures," 125.
44 *"in his time or later"* McLuhan, *Gutenberg Galaxy*, 29.
44 *"the world of 'Nature'"* McLuhan and Nevitt, *Take Today*, 7.
44 *"man-made technologies"* McLuhan and Nevitt, *Take Today*, 7.
44 never wrote any works of philosophy According to his less famous student Xenophon, however, Socrates enjoyed reading great books with his friends: "And I teach them all the good I can, and recommend them to others from whom I think they will get some moral benefit. And the treasures that the wise men of old have left us in their writings I open and explore with my friends. If we come to any good thing, we extract it, and we set much store on being useful to one another." Xenophon, *Memorabilia*, 1.6.14.
45 *"straightaway nourishes itself"* Plato, "Epistle VII," 237 (341c-d).
45 *"psyche and society"* McLuhan and Nevitt, *Take Today*, 7.
45 *"art of the scribe lay ahead"* McLuhan, "Do Books Matter?," 215.
45 *"the cosmic forces"* McLuhan with Watson, *From Cliché to Archetype*, 149.
45 all words are metaphors McLuhan and Powers, *Global Village*, 30.
45 simile focuses on imitating a reality For a comprehensive interpretation of the differences between simile and metaphor, see Polka, *Truth and Interpretation*, 52–69.
45 *"descriptive rather than structural or perceptual"* McLuhan and Powers, *Global Village*, 30. See also McLuhan and McLuhan, *Laws of Media*, 230.
46 *"all human artifacts and hypotheses"* McLuhan and Powers, *Global Village*, 29.
46 *"and it makes it be* thus" McLuhan and McLuhan, *Media and Formal Cause*, 113. Italics in the original.
47 *"the objects of the natural world"* McLuhan and McLuhan, *Laws of Media*, 120.
47 *"the extension of man's own being"* McLuhan, "Garbage Apocalypse," 3.
47 "techne *from its meditations"* McLuhan to Claude Bissell, March 23, 1971, in *Letters of Marshall McLuhan*, 429. Italics in the original.
47 *"no formal cause at all"* McLuhan and McLuhan, *Media and Formal Cause*, 123.
47 a medium potentially creates McLuhan and McLuhan, *Media and Formal Cause*, 126.
47 attention that it deserved McLuhan, "Do Books Matter?," 212.
48 *"desirable in human terms"* McLuhan and Powers, *Global Village*, 78.

4. REAR-VIEW MIRROR POLITICS

49 *"yesterday's answers to today's questions"* McLuhan and Fiore, *Medium Is the Massage*, 22.
49 *"the preceding environment"* McLuhan and Parker, *Through the Vanishing Point*, xxiii.

49 *"total disorientation at all times"* McLuhan and Parker, *Through the Vanishing Point*, xxiii.
49 *"navigational guide to the new one"* McLuhan and Parker, *Through the Vanishing Point*, xxiii.
49 *"an interval of resonance"* McLuhan and Powers, *Global Village*, 149.
49 *invisible to its citizenry* McLuhan and Powers, *Global Village*, 149.
50 *"an interpreter of the American destiny"* McLuhan and Powers, *Global Village*, 150.
50 *"desperate efforts to live"* McLuhan, "Marfleet Lectures," 128.
50 *"centralized and literate political entity"* McLuhan, "*Playboy* Interview," 257.
50 *"it is un-American"* McLuhan and Nevitt, *Take Today*, 271.
50 *"specialist rational order"* McLuhan and Nevitt, *Take Today*, 272.
50 *"'socially conscious' people into conservatives"* McLuhan, *Understanding Media*, 34.
51 *"Novelty causes Antiquity"* McLuhan and McLuhan, *Media and Formal Cause*, 29–30.
51 *"loss of identity"* McLuhan, "Violence as a Quest for Identity," 269.
51 *"the hearts and minds of a minority of citizens"* Ellmers, "'Conservatism' Is No Longer Enough."
51 *"bewildered by this change"* McLuhan, "Electric Consciousness," 84–85.
52 *"utmost concern to readers"* McLuhan, *Understanding Media*, 318.
52 *"There are only groups"* McLuhan, "'Our Only Hope,'" 63.
52 *"the old ground rules of culture"* McLuhan, "Future of Man," 73.
52 *"at the present time"* McLuhan, "Future of Man," 74.
52 *"anyone who has written"* McLuhan, "Culture without Literacy," 124.
52 *"the force and energy of action"* Hume, "Liberty of the Press," 604.
52 *"cooling off period"* Wills, *Explaining America*, 197.
53 *"general liberty and independence"* Federalist No. 2, in *Federalist*, 9.
53 *"product of the eighteenth century"* Minkov and Namazi, "'Religion and the Commonweal,'" 108.
53 *"but not for irreligion"* Minkov and Namazi, "'Religion and the Commonweal,'" 108. Italics in the original. Strauss went on to note that freedom from religion was a nineteenth-century ideal.
53 *"all real values are private, personal, individual"* McLuhan, *Essential McLuhan*, 286.
54 *"scabrous paradox"* McLuhan, *Gutenberg Galaxy*, 238.
54 *"unique personal existence"* McLuhan, *Gutenberg Galaxy*, 314.
54 *"each with his own point of view"* McLuhan and McLuhan, *Media and Formal Cause*, 22.
54 *"profoundly involved in one another"* McLuhan and McLuhan, *Media and Formal Cause*, 23.
54 *"natural sucker for propaganda"* McLuhan, "Violence as a Quest for Identity," 271. In *Global Village*, McLuhan and Powers quote approvingly from Jacques Ellul's *Propaganda: The Formation of Men's Attitudes* (1965): "Propaganda cannot succeed where people have no trace of Western culture" (60).
54 *"vest it with requisite powers"* Federalist No. 2, in *Federalist*, 8.
54 *"written visual fixity of the American Constitution"* McLuhan, *Gutenberg Galaxy*, 250–51.
54 *"truths which are right everywhere and always"* Reilly, *America on Trial*, 323. Italics in the original.
55 *historicism* McLuhan and Stearn, "Even Hercules," 268.
55 *"react upon one another at the same time"* McLuhan, *Understanding Media*, 25–26.
55 *"imaginative universals"* Vico, *New Science*, para. 209.
55 *"turn from History to Nature"* Ceaser, "Foundational Concepts," 22.

55 "the thought heard around the world" Ceaser, "Foundational Concepts," 22.
55 "foundation of a full nation" Ceaser, "Foundational Concepts," 22.
55 "permanent and unchanging character of things" Ceaser, "Foundational Concepts," 58.
55 each bias can shape one's understanding of history See Comstock, "Theory of Sensory Form," 181.
56 "greatest practical statesmen who ever lived" Ahmari, "Learning from a Complex Tradition."
56 "ever-more radical 'experiments in living'" Deneen, "Despotism of Progress." See also his *Why Liberalism Failed*, 144–48; and *Regime Change*, 48–53. The reference to "experiments in living" is from Mill, *On Liberty*, 89.
56 "have free rein to experiment" McLuhan, "Playboy Interview," 253.
57 "precrime trial" Friedersdorf, "Canada's Extremist Attack."
57 "as a whole" Kendall with Carey, "'Intensity Problem,'" 500–501. Italics in the original.
57 "the process of deliberations" Kendall with Carey, "'Intensity Problem,'" 501.
57 "a radio set-up" McLuhan, "TV as a Debating Medium," 257.
58 "hottest type of medium you could imagine" McLuhan, "TV as a Debating Medium," 257.
58 "he becomes homogeneous" McLuhan, *Gutenberg Galaxy*, 242.
58 "conformity and non-conformity" McLuhan, *Gutenberg Galaxy*, 269.
58 love of one's nation McLuhan, *Gutenberg Galaxy*, 242.
58 "to the least literate minds" McLuhan, *Understanding Media*, 257.
58 mechanized conformity McLuhan, *Gutenberg Galaxy*, 238.
58 "read the same books" McLuhan, *Mechanical Bride*, 26.
58 "even before the Civil War" McLuhan, *Understanding Media*, 257.
58 "total social involvement" McLuhan, *Understanding Media*, 47.
58 "its own world of demand" McLuhan, *Understanding Media*, 67–68.
59 "role of absolute conformity" McLuhan, "Playboy Interview," 259.
59 "inner deviation" McLuhan, *Gutenberg Galaxy*, 24.
59 "the associative and the corporate" McLuhan, *Understanding Media*, 39–40.
59 "one-way pattern" McLuhan, *Understanding Media*, 35.
59 "radiating out to remote margins" McLuhan, *Understanding Media*, 273.
59 "between writer-speaker and the listener" McLuhan, *Understanding Media*, 299.
60 "the Orson Welles treatment for real" McLuhan, *Understanding Media*, 300. Italics in the original.
60 "right atmosphere for his radio chats" McLuhan, *Understanding Media*, 299.
60 "Roosevelt, Churchill, and Stalin at Yalta" McLuhan and Powers, *Global Village*, 118.
60 "Jack Kennedy in the television era" McLuhan, "Playboy Interview," 247.
60 "they all mastered their media" McLuhan, "Playboy Interview," 247.
60 "personal and monarchical" McLuhan, *Understanding Media*, 14.
60 before the polls even close McLuhan, "Playboy Interview," 261.
61 "the so-called political scene" McLuhan, *Essential McLuhan*, 274.
61 the November election Kurtz and Parnes, "Trump Can't Shake Off Taylor Swift."
61 "has gone unnoticed" McLuhan, *Understanding Media*, 304.
61 "reeling into a multiplicity" McLuhan, "Playboy Interview," 257–58.
61 "or neither will survive" McLuhan, "Playboy Interview," 258.
61 disdains the masses Wheatland, "Founding Fathers."
62 "mass man" McLuhan, "Violence as a Quest for Identity," 268.
62 "'doing one's thing'" McLuhan with Watson, *From Cliché to Archetype*, 12.
62 "for parts nor pastures" McLuhan with Watson, *From Cliché to Archetype*, 182.

5. MOTHER GOOSE AND PETER PAN EXECUTIVES

63 *"the mode of an eloquent wisdom"* McLuhan, "Edgar Poe's Tradition," 26. McLuhan once placed Lincoln in an intellectual pantheon that included Henry David Thoreau and Albert Einstein. See Gordon, *Marshall McLuhan*, 150.
63 *"economic justice for the working and middle classes"* Slotkin, *Great Disorder*, 405. For Lincoln's invocation of biblical narrative and morality as the inspirational basis for social reform, see Havers, *Lincoln and the Politics of Christian Love*.
63 *"not with it but ahead of it"* McLuhan, *Understanding Media*, 199.

5. MOTHER GOOSE AND PETER PAN EXECUTIVES

64 *"monopolized by people from the previous age"* McLuhan, *Culture Is Our Business*, 104.
65 *Guide to Chaos* Powe, *Marshall McLuhan and Northrop Frye*, 35.
65 *"the ways of utility and market"* McLuhan, *Mechanical Bride*, vii.
65 *"the night world"* McLuhan, *Mechanical Bride*, 97.
65 *"effects with causes"* McLuhan, "Myth and Mass Media," 340–41.
65 *"Mother Goose and Peter Pan executives"* McLuhan, "Media Log," in *Counterblast*, n.p. He repeated this admonition in the conclusion to his 1963 lecture "The Agenbite of Outwit."
66 *"the users of motorcars"* McLuhan, *Understanding Media*, 195.
66 *"any medium but its own"* McLuhan, *Understanding Media*, 195.
66 *one's attention* McLuhan, *Understanding Media*, 267.
66 *the phone replaced prostitution* McLuhan, *Understanding Media*, 266.
66 *a shill for capitalist interests* I discuss the leftist reception of McLuhan from the 1960s to the present day in Havers, "Right-Wing Postmodernism," 511–15.
66 *"Commodity, the bias of the world"* McLuhan, *Gutenberg Galaxy*, 185.
66 *"as readily as a big business"* McLuhan to Davey, March 8, 1971, in Kahn, *Been Hoping*, 87.
66 *"as much as do the means of production"* McLuhan, *Understanding Media*, 49.
67 *being influenced in turn* McLuhan and Nevitt, *Take Today*, 63.
67 *biases of Northern capitalism* McLuhan, "Southern Quality."
67 *"the public became the patron"* McLuhan, *Gutenberg Galaxy*, 311.
67 *children's usage of technology* Akhtar and Ward, "Bill Gates and Steve Jobs."
67 *"others and the world around them"* "Media and Technology Philosophy."
67 *"changing people just as it changes things"* McLuhan, "Future of Sex," 130.
68 *"artificial perception and arbitrary values"* McLuhan, *Understanding Media*, 199.
68 *"expressing His will to the people"* McLuhan, *Mechanical Bride*, 140.
68 *preconditions for modern capitalism* McLuhan, *Gutenberg Galaxy*, 189, 307; McLuhan, *Understanding Media*, 136–37.
68 *"Every man has his price"* McLuhan, "Pastures and Impostures," 80.
68 *"marketed for money"* McLuhan and Nevitt, "Monday-Night Seminar," 53.
68 *other human artifacts* Benchetrit, "Apple Gets Crushing Backlash."
68 *uniform and repeatable phenomena* McLuhan, *Understanding Media*, 139.
69 *"principle of absolute conformity"* McLuhan, *Book of Probes*, 134–35.
69 *"bourgeoisie in the nineteenth century"* McLuhan, *Understanding Media*, 150.
69 *"all read the same thing"* Quoted in Innis, *Bias of Communication*, 84. Italics in the original.
69 *"middle-class people"* McLuhan, *Understanding Media*, 222.
69 *"new kind of man"* McLuhan, *Gutenberg Galaxy*, 198–99.
70 *"Yet the whole mass a paradise"* Mandeville, *Fable of the Bees*, 31.
70 *"psychological split of the time"* McLuhan, "Footprints," 627.

NOTES

70 *"time-binding medium"* McLuhan, "Culture without Literacy," 119.
70 *"all the institutions of society"* McLuhan, *Understanding Media*, 247.
70 *"the literate and mechanical kind"* McLuhan, *Understanding Media*, 248.
71 *"control of space"* McLuhan, "Culture without Literacy," 120. Italics added.
71 *"your solitary quest"* McLuhan, "Organization Man."
71 *"at play or leisure"* McLuhan, *Book of Probes*, 322–23.
71 *"the whole of mankind"* McLuhan, *Understanding Media*, 254.
71 *"You just have to immerse"* McLuhan, "Living at the Speed of Light," 234.
71 Without the bad news McLuhan to Prime Minister Pierre Trudeau, January 24, 1969, in Kahn, *Been Hoping*, 65.
72 *"great things"* Machiavelli, *Prince*, 63.
72 *"from manipulation to participation"* McLuhan and Nevitt, *Take Today*, 272.
72 *"not fragmentary or partial"* McLuhan, *Understanding Media*, 255.
72 *"the instant catalysts"* McLuhan and Nevitt, *Take Today*, 295.
72 loved, not feared See Machiavelli, *Prince*, chap. 17.
72 *"being well known"* McLuhan, "The Electronic Age," 195.
72 they found no such evidence Schiffer and Newton, "Musk Fires a Top Twitter Engineer."
73 *"speedy integration"* Phelan, "Tesla Robot ATTACKS an Engineer."
73 *"this powerful and this poorly understood"* Quoted in O'Brien, "Former OpenAI Employees."
73 *"between private and corporate"* McLuhan with Watson, *From Cliché to Archetype*, 200.
73 *"'dream awake'"* McLuhan with Watson, *From Cliché to Archetype*, 200.
73 *"eliminating the private sphere"* Lucas, "Jordan Peterson."
73 *"a farmer-craftsman economy"* McLuhan, *Mechanical Bride*, 134.
74 "They talk Jefferson and follow Hamilton" McLuhan, *Mechanical Bride*, 134.
74 *"a chaos of unrelated data"* McLuhan, "End of the Work Ethic," 195.
74 *"needed hourly attention"* McLuhan with Watson, *From Cliché to Archetype*, 200–201.
74 *"who can replace him instantly"* McLuhan and Nevitt, *Take Today*, 283. Italics in the original.
74 they *"dream awake"* McLuhan with Watson, *From Cliché to Archetype*, 200.
75 "Madison Avenue PR" McLuhan with Watson, *From Cliché to Archetype*, 139.
75 *"watching the other guy"* McLuhan, "Violence as a Quest for Identity," 268.
75 *"hunters of information"* Quoted in Nevitt with McLuhan, *Who Was Marshall McLuhan?*, 110.
75 *"the less we exist"* McLuhan with Watson, *From Cliché to Archetype*, 13.
75 *"contentious content"* Hurley, "Supreme Court Tosses Out Claim."
75 Privacy is not only invaded McLuhan, "Violence as a Quest for Identity," 268.
75 *"invisible bureaucracies on the domestic front"* McLuhan and Nevitt, *Take Today*, 179.
76 *"making us imbeciles"* Quoted in Schlott, "China Is Hurting Our Kids."
76 *"private manipulation"* McLuhan, *Understanding Media*, 68.
76 *"a place to stand"* McLuhan and Nevitt, *Take Today*, 234.
77 *"all-at-once culture"* McLuhan, "*Playboy* Interview," 261.
77 *"any university even he could dream up"* McLuhan, *Understanding Media*, 49.
77 *"being thought of at all"* McLuhan, *Understanding Media*, 49.
77 *"in order to influence curriculum"* McLuhan with Hutchon and McLuhan, *City as Classroom*, 111.
77 "What the public wants" McLuhan, *Understanding Media*, 68.
78 "Galvanic Response Bracelets" Cody, *Educator and the Oligarch*, 110.
78 *"a connection to the internet"* Cody, *Educator and the Oligarch*, 139.

NOTES

78 *voice of the late John Lennon* Butterfield, "'New' Beatles Song."
78 *assessing the happiness of a worker* Karadeglija, "Workplace Surveillance Has 'Skyrocketed.'"
78 *"servo-mechanisms"* McLuhan and McLuhan, *Laws of Media*, 65, 98.
79 *"as a monopoly"* McLuhan, *Understanding Media*, 68.
79 *the "misuse" of this technology* Mollman, "ChatGPT Must Be Regulated."
79 *"gone into widespread distribution"* MacDonald, "AI Could Have Catastrophic Consequences."
79 *"massive extrasensory perception"* McLuhan, *Understanding Media*, 130.
79 *"makes things up"* Stokel-Walker, "Generative AI Is Coming."
80 *"would then be unlocked"* Quoted in Allen, "Deal with the Digital Devil," 11.
80 *"collective harmony and peace"* McLuhan, "*Playboy* Interview," 262.
80 *"know everything"* Quoted in Srigley, "Ron Srigley on Cellphones."
80 *"simulate consciousness"* McLuhan, *Essential McLuhan*, 295.
80 *ChatGPT cannot solve logical puzzles* Biever, "Easy Intelligence Tests."
80 *"critical faculties"* McLuhan, "Psychopathology," 159.
80 *"match humans in this regard"* Stackpole, "Content Moderation Is Terrible."
80 *"cultural assumptions"* McLuhan, *Gutenberg Galaxy*, 208.
80 *"its racial bias"* Piers, "ChatGPT Is Racially Biased."
81 *"guaranteed income"* McLuhan, "Guaranteed Income," 196–97.
81 *"universal high income"* Mancini, "Musk Predicts a 'Universal High Income.'"
81 *"here in North America"* McLuhan, "Catholic Humanism," 163.

6. NEW MEDIA ARE NATURE

82 *"they are nature"* McLuhan, *Essential McLuhan*, 272.
83 *"the origin of the sounds they hear"* McLuhan and Fiore, *War and Peace*, 175.
83 *"the case with man"* McLuhan and Fiore, *War and Peace*, 175.
83 *"countervailed by imaginative response"* McLuhan, "Roles, Masks, and Performances," 522.
83 *"defend themselves against these effects"* McLuhan, "End of the Work Ethic," 203.
83 *"metamorphosing man"* McLuhan, "*Playboy* Interview," 268.
83 *"his total history"* McLuhan and Fiore, *War and Peace*, 177.
84 *"wars fought with hardware weapons"* McLuhan and McLuhan, *Laws of Media*, 97.
84 *suicide went viral on TikTok* Zheng and Kaye, "Content Moderation," 80–81.
84 *"a laboratory for experiments"* McLuhan, *Book of Probes*, 111.
84 *"could swiftly change"* McLuhan, "Future of Sex," 135.
84 *"They're made by man"* McLuhan, "On Nature and Media."
84 *"one's own nature"* McLuhan, "Open-Mind Surgery," 149. Italics added.
84 *"eschewing overt violence"* McLuhan and Powers, *Global Village*, 94.
85 *"no more nature"* McLuhan, "Culture without Literacy," 123.
85 *"no more external nature"* McLuhan, "Culture without Literacy," 123.
85 *"presatellite (Sputnik) man"* McLuhan and Nevitt, *Take Today*, 295.
85 *"without any further prompting"* McLuhan, "End of the Work Ethic," 197.
85 *"the situation in which we live"* McLuhan, "Man and Media," 293.
86 *"religion and the inner trip"* McLuhan, *Culture Is Our Business*, 162.
86 *"ever dreamed of being"* McLuhan, "Garbage Apocalypse," 17.
86 *"meet and mingle"* McLuhan, "Space, Time, and Poetry," 59.
86 *"been erased"* McLuhan, "Space, Time, and Poetry," 59.
86 *"just at the end of any era"* McLuhan, "Future of Sex," 135.
86 *feminism reverses into maleness* McLuhan and McLuhan, *Laws of Media*, 210.

NOTES 173

87 *"the tension of the interchange"* McLuhan and Powers, *Global Village*, 4. Italics added.
87 *"abrasive interplay"* McLuhan and Powers, *Global Village*, 4.
87 Eric Voegelin's definition of Gnosticism See Voegelin, *Science, Politics, and Gnosticism*. For an informative discussion of McLuhan's sympathy with Voegelin's philosophy, see Stahlman, "Place of Marshall McLuhan," 11.
87 *"cults and secret societies"* Quoted in McEwen, "Voegelin-McLuhan Correspondence." See also Powe, *Marshall McLuhan and Northrop Frye*, 153–57.
87 *"neo-Platonism and gnosticism"* McLuhan, "Nihilism Exposed," 99.
87 *"a cheap art work"* McLuhan, "Nihilism Exposed," 99.
87 *"entertainment has become the art of government"* McLuhan, "Nihilism Exposed," 99.
87 *"'Let us rejoin the One'"* McLuhan, "Nihilism Exposed," 99.
87 *"wild body"* McLuhan and McLuhan, *Laws of Media*, 116.
88 *"remakes himself with his extensions"* McLuhan and McLuhan, *Laws of Media*, 223.
88 *"ever less involvement"* McLuhan, *Essential McLuhan*, 283.
88 *"an individualized and civilized"* McLuhan and McLuhan, *Laws of Media*, 116.
88 *"run to obey"* Machiavelli, *Discourses on Livy*, 114.
88 *"modes of mental hysteria"* McLuhan, "American Advertising," 134. Italics added.
88 *"totalitarian remaking of human nature"* McLuhan, "Catholic Humanism," 160.
89 *"emotional consciousness of archaic man"* McLuhan, "Space, Time, and Poetry," 59–60.
89 *"their servo-mechanism"* McLuhan and McLuhan, *Laws of Media*, 98. Italics in the original.
89 *"each one of our artifacts"* McLuhan and McLuhan, *Laws of Media*, 117.
89 *"the vagaries of second nature"* McLuhan and McLuhan, *Laws of Media*, 119.
89 *"natural man"* McLuhan and Powers, *Global Village*, 8.
90 The need to get *"noticed"* McLuhan, "Violence as a Quest for Identity," 266.
90 *"are duds"* McLuhan, "End of the Work Ethic," 198.
90 *"drop out"* and *"tune in"* McLuhan and Powers, *Global Village*, 143.
90 *"drop out"* of the economy McLuhan and Nevitt, *Take Today*, 280.
91 *"closed-circuit at home"* McLuhan offered this comment on the CBC show *Take 30*, April 1, 1965. Quoted in Ripatrazone, *Digital Communion*, xiv.
91 racial justice and equity Lipman, "Pandemic Revealed."
91 *"contained in the political sense of limited association"* McLuhan, *Understanding Media*, 5. Italics in the original.
91 *"super soldiers"* Nawaz, "Air National Guardsman Arrested."
91 *"involved in the action"* McLuhan, *Understanding Media*, 5.
91 *"fantasy has no such commitment"* McLuhan and Powers, *Global Village*, 97.
92 *"they are discarnate beings"* McLuhan and Nevitt, "Monday-Night Seminar," 44.
92 *"interfacing or encounters are very weak"* McLuhan and Nevitt, "Monday-Night Seminar," 45. See also McLuhan, "Violence as a Quest for Identity," 268.
92 *"sheer abstraction at the other"* McLuhan, "Nihilism Exposed," 98.
92 *"divine ideas that create reality"* Edwards, "'Good Heavens!,'" 1458.
92 *"the medium and the message are one and the same"* McLuhan, "Religion and Youth," 103. McLuhan also remarks, "Christ, after all, is the ultimate extension of man." McLuhan, "Playboy Interview," 262.
93 *"besetting sin of academic hypothesis"* McLuhan and Powers, *Global Village*, 12.
93 *"one place at a time"* McLuhan, "End of the Work Ethic," 201.
93 *"worthwhile to examine the fact"* McLuhan, "Keys to the Electronic Revolution," 50.
93 *"with centres everywhere and boundaries nowhere"* Quoted in Nevitt with McLuhan, *Who Was Marshall McLuhan?*, 279.

NOTES

93 *"biological longevity and digital immortality"* Allen, "Deal with the Digital Devil," 13–14.
93 *"social consciousness"* McLuhan, *Understanding Media*, 47.
93 *"what private guilt can be anymore"* McLuhan and Fiore, *Medium Is the Massage*, 61.
94 *"far more guilty than he did"* McLuhan, "TV News as a New Mythic Form," 165.
94 *"superimposed co-existence"* McLuhan, *Gutenberg Galaxy*, 37.
94 *"equivalences in the rest of the country"* Cooper and Navarro-Génie, *COVID-19*, 117.
94 *"at the speed of light"* McLuhan and Powers, *Global Village*, 97.

7. THE DIVIDED GLOBAL VILLAGE

95 *"the global village"* McLuhan, *Understanding Media*, 93.
95 *"media or technologies we probe with"* McLuhan with Watson, *From Cliché to Archetype*, 150.
95 *"center-margin structure"* McLuhan, *Understanding Media*, 93.
95 *"unified cosmic Happening"* McLuhan, "Crack in the Rear-View Mirror," 32.
95 *"a single city"* McLuhan, "Later Innis," 45.
95 *"no passengers but all are crew"* McLuhan, "End of the Work Ethic," 193.
95 *"harmony"* McLuhan, "*Playboy* Interview," 257.
95 *"peoples, arts, and thoughts"* McLuhan, "McLuhan Looks at Fashion," 147.
95 *"gory little schoolhouse at that"* McLuhan and Fiore, *War and Peace*, 125.
96 *"impatient with each other"* McLuhan, "Violence as a Quest for Identity," 265.
96 *"very abrasive situations"* McLuhan, "Violence as a Quest for Identity," 265.
96 Terrorists and hijackers McLuhan, "Violence as a Quest for Identity," 266.
96 *"No blood, no news"* Quoted in Said and Jones, "Gaza Chief's Brutal Calculation."
96 *"at the speed of light"* McLuhan, "Violence as a Quest for Identity," 266.
97 *"psychic and social consequences"* McLuhan, "*Playboy* Interview," 268.
97 few *"rebels"* McLuhan, "*Playboy* Interview," 260.
97 *"the most acceptable words and notions"* McLuhan, "Culture without Literacy," 118.
97 *"thousands of families in the same city"* McLuhan and Stearn, "Even Hercules," 272.
97 set of traditions McLuhan, *Gutenberg Galaxy*, 250.
97 *"totally involved kinship groups"* McLuhan, "Introduction to H. A. Innis," 78.
97 *"fission, not fusion, in depth"* McLuhan and Stearn, "Even Hercules," 272.
97 *"African cultural and social roots"* McLuhan, "*Playboy* Interview," 256.
98 *"dehumanization of the Negro"* McLuhan, "*Playboy* Interview," 256.
98 *"shared attributes and interests"* Lancaster, "Identity Politics."
98 *"respect for oneself as different"* Kruks, *Retrieving Experience*, 85.
98 *"white supremacy"* Rufo, "DEI Corrupts America's Universities."
98 *"original state and language of the race"* McLuhan, *Understanding Media*, 155.
98 *"sub-primitive man"* McLuhan, "Five Sovereign Fingers Taxed the Breath," in *Counterblast*, n.p.
98 "Orson Welles treatment for real" McLuhan, *Understanding Media*, 300. Italics in the original.
98 centralized and bureaucratic government Innis, *Bias of Communication*, 82.
98 *"very little consequence"* McLuhan, *Understanding Media*, 300.
99 *"class conflict resumes tribal warfare"* McLuhan and Nevitt, *Take Today*, 182.
99 hits the wall of tribalism See Havers, "History as Progress."
99 *"was killed by Hitler"* McLuhan and Nevitt, *Take Today*, 277. Italics in the original.
100 *"against imposed patterns"* McLuhan, *Understanding Media*, 5.
100 *"by such violence"* McLuhan and Powers, *Global Village*, 159.
100 liberal-minded North and the fundamentalist South Noll, *Civil War*.

100 *"made America exceptional"* Slotkin, *Great Disorder*, 128.
100 *"undeveloped arable land"* Slotkin, *Great Disorder*, 128.
100 *"wonderful myth"* McLuhan, "Marfleet Lectures," 136.
101 *"made their fathers great"* Slotkin, *Great Disorder*, 128-29.
101 *"we have a mandate for war"* McLuhan and Fiore, *War and Peace*, 97.
101 *"unanswered questions of poverty and surplus"* Kennedy, "Acceptance of Democratic Nomination."
101 *"the American frontier for centuries"* McLuhan, "Marfleet Lectures," 121.
101 the *"new frontiersmen"* New Frontiersmen.
101 *"without noticing what they were doing"* McLuhan, "Marfleet Lectures," 121.
102 *"American home itself"* McLuhan and Fiore, *War and Peace*, 134.
102 *"All sons become ours on TV"* McLuhan, *Culture Is Our Business*, 52.
102 *"untakable"* McLuhan, "Open-Mind Surgery," 156.
102 cope with its effects McLuhan, "Marfleet Lectures," 114.
102 wars of westward expansion McLuhan, "Marfleet Lectures," 121.
102 *"with vast cost to ourselves"* McLuhan, "Marfleet Lectures," 132-33.
102 *"colossal fiction"* McLuhan, "TV News as a New Mythic Form," 170.
102 *"mythic form"* McLuhan, "TV News as a New Mythic Form," 170.
102 *"their backward technology"* McLuhan, "Marfleet Lectures," 131-32.
102 *"private and tribal"* McLuhan, "Marfleet Lectures," 131.
103 *"take full advantage of it"* McLuhan, "Marfleet Lectures," 128.
103 *"better positioned to lead the world than America"* Biden, "Remarks by Joe Biden."
103 *"tension"* McLuhan and Powers, *Global Village*, 4.
104 discovering an objective reality McLuhan and Parker, *Through the Vanishing Point*, 20.
104 the mind cannot detach itself McLuhan and McLuhan, *Laws of Media*, 60–62.
104 *"come upon us"* McLuhan and Nevitt, *Take Today*, 172.
104 *"transmission of various cultural institutions"* Thiel, "Straussian Moment," 210.
104 *"pushes people into escalating rivalry"* Thiel, "Straussian Moment," 210.
104 *"While ye have the night for morn"* Quoted in McLuhan, *Understanding Media*, 35. McLuhan slightly altered the original wording of this passage, which reads, "The west shall shake the east awake. Walk while ye have the night for morn, lightbreakfastbringer, morroweth every past shall full fost asleep. Amain." Joyce, *Finnegans Wake*, 473.
104 *"consciousness of the Unconscious"* McLuhan, *Understanding Media*, 35.
105 *"giving us all the inner trip"* McLuhan, "Fordham University," 144. See also McLuhan, "'Our Only Hope,'" 60.
105 it will have become Orientalized McLuhan, "Open-Mind Surgery," 151.
105 *"become a way of life"* McLuhan and Nevitt, *Take Today*, 171.
105 *"nineteenth-century world of consumer services and packages"* McLuhan and Nevitt, *Take Today*, 292.
105 the *"forms"* of tribal loyalty to the regime McLuhan and Nevitt, *Take Today*, 292.
106 with other financial services Tate, "Coming Soon."
106 *"punishes them in various ways"* Quoted in Gottfried, "Digital Currency Ruse," 6.
106 *"Government, culture and business are now one"* McLuhan, *Culture Is Our Business*, 16.
106 *"both systems simultaneously"* McLuhan and Powers, *Global Village*, x.
106 *"interchange and simultaneous metamorphosis"* McLuhan and Nevitt, *Take Today*, 292.
107 *"proximity to massive power"* McLuhan, "Canada," 228.
107 *"an inclusive consciousness"* McLuhan, "Canada," 247–48.

107 *"it's just the beginning"* McLuhan, "'Achieving Relevance,'" 139.
108 *"naturally from below"* McLuhan to Trudeau, December 6, 1978, in Kahn, *Been Hoping*, 140.
108 *"keep them intact without merging"* McLuhan, "Violence as a Quest for Identity," 275.
108 *the Canadian identity* Mansur, *Muddle of Multiculturalism*, 1.
108 *first "postnational" country* Foran, "Canada Experiment."
109 *"filling the coffers of Bay Street"* McLuhan, *Counterblast*, n.p.
109 *"their miseries are invented there"* Quoted in Nevitt with McLuhan, *Who Was Marshall McLuhan?*, 111.
109 *"multiple borderlines"* McLuhan, "Canada," 245.
109 *"neighborly dialogue on the ground"* McLuhan, "Canada," 247.
109 *"clutch at" a bygone age* McLuhan and Fiore, *War and Peace*, 126.
109 *its content became Canadian* Marchand, *Marshall McLuhan*, 39.
109 *"show up in search results"* Pugh, "New Streaming Bill."

8. THE RETRIEVAL OF THE BOOK
110 *"reawakened critical faculties"* McLuhan, "Psychopathology," 159.
110 *"agony"* McLuhan, "Psychopathology," 159.
110 *"unnecessary for communication"* Macdonald, "He Has Looted All Culture," 204.
110 *"the habits of cannibals"* McLuhan and Stearn, "Even Hercules," 282.
110 *"on the side of print"* McLuhan, letter to the editor, *Globe and Mail*, June 17, 1970, in *Letters of Marshall McLuhan*, 410.
111 *"an act of discovery"* McLuhan and Stearn, "Even Hercules," 282.
111 *"positive virtues of print"* McLuhan, *Gutenberg Galaxy*, 294.
111 *"a corporate probe of society"* McLuhan, "Crack in the Rear-View Mirror," 32.
111 *"the probe is not very efficient"* McLuhan and Stearn, "Even Hercules," 277.
111 *"1 in 4 American adults buys a print newspaper"* Waletzko, "Print Media Is Back."
111 *impoverished academics and university libraries* Agar, "Reaches of Big Academia."
111 *"tactile" experience* McLuhan, *Understanding Media*, 325.
112 *"the power of man to act without reaction"* McLuhan, "*Playboy* Interview," 267.
112 *"reconsider" the entire intellectual tradition* McLuhan, *Classical Trivium*, 8.
112 *"men could come to know"* McLuhan and McLuhan, *Laws of Media*, 221. The quote is from Vico, *New Science*, para. 331. As Vico contends elsewhere, what is true (*verum*) is also what is made (*factum*). It "is possible to conclude with certainty that the criterion and rule of the true is to have made it." Vico, *Selected Writings*, 55.
112 *"YES AND NO"* Nevitt with McLuhan, *Who Was Marshall McLuhan?*, 245, 268.
112 *"YES OR NO"* Nevitt with McLuhan, *Who Was Marshall McLuhan?*, 245.
113 *"diminishing each other"* Freud, *New Introductory Lectures*, 73.
113 *"dualism"* McLuhan and Parker, *Through the Vanishing Point*, 20.
113 *"by the new means"* McLuhan, "Crack in the Rear-view Mirror," 33.
114 *"feudal dungeon"* McLuhan, "Five Sovereign Fingers Taxed the Breath," in *Counterblast*, n.p.
114 *"sopping up packaged data"* McLuhan, "Cybernetics and Human Culture," 53.
114 *"grasping interrelationships"* McLuhan, "Cybernetics and Human Culture," 53.
114 *"total field" study* McLuhan with Watson, *From Cliché to Archetype*, 170.
114 *"threaten our entire way of life"* McLuhan, "Crack in the Rear-view Mirror," 33.
114 *"perception in all the arts"* McLuhan, review of Erich Auerbach, *Mimesis*, 109.
114 *"less obvious in Europe"* McLuhan, "Media Fit the Battle of Jericho," 301.
115 *"an anti-environment with the next"* McLuhan, "Environment," 119.

115	*"ancient quarrel"* McLuhan, "Ancient Quarrel," 223–25.
115	*"counterpoison"* Strauss, *Liberalism Ancient and Modern*, 5.
115	*young readers searching for the truth* Trepanier, "AI Could Save Liberal Education."
115	*"diversity of thinking"* Quoted in Berger, "Rise of the English Major."
115	*"technical tasks"* Quoted in Berger, "Rise of the English Major."
116	*"imprimatur of Great on them"* Nisbet, *Present Age*, 131.
116	*"in which he [the educator] lives"* McLuhan, *Mechanical Bride*, 43.
116	*"immediate use"* McLuhan, *Mechanical Bride*, 43.
116	*"thought and language for study"* McLuhan, "Media Fit the Battle of Jericho," 300.
116	*"in the electric age"* McLuhan, "Do Books Matter?," 213.
116	*"we'll have to smash all of them!"* Quoted in Nevitt with McLuhan, *Who Was Marshall McLuhan?*, 84. Cf. McLuhan and Stearn, "Even Hercules": "Most media, though, are pure poison—TV, for example, has all the effects of LSD. I don't think we should allow this to happen" (286).
116	*"the great minds* via *great books"* McLuhan, *Mechanical Bride*, 44. Italics in the original.
116	*"art, philosophy, or society"* McLuhan, *Mechanical Bride*, 45.
117	*"in doctrine and emphasis"* McLuhan, *Classical Trivium*, 65.
117	*"sheer abstraction at the other"* McLuhan, "Nihilism Exposed," 98.
117	*severance of rhetoric and wisdom* McLuhan, "Ancient Quarrel," 227.
117	*"an old quarrel between philosophy and poetry" Republic of Plato*, 290 (607b).
117	*"itself only a phantom" Republic of Plato*, 281 (598b).
117	*"They don't lay hold of the truth" Republic of Plato*, 283 (600e).
117	*"a kind of play and not serious" Republic of Plato*, 285 (602b).
118	*a mere imitation of eternity* McLuhan, *Classical Trivium*, 18.
118	*"most significant and esoteric teaching"* McLuhan, *Classical Trivium*, 17. As Vico notes, Homer's poetry was "the source of all Greek philosophies." See Vico, *New Science*, para. 901.
118	*"far from 'natural'"* McLuhan and Nevitt, *Take Today*, 7.
118	*"effects of man-made technology"* McLuhan and McLuhan, *Laws of Media*, 120.
118	*even dethrone it* McLuhan with Watson, *From Cliché to Archetype*, 149–50.
118	*the making of reality* McLuhan and McLuhan, *Laws of Media*, 68.
118	*an intolerance of paradox* McLuhan and McLuhan, *Laws of Media*, 74.
119	*"at the expense of the other"* McLuhan and McLuhan, *Laws of Media*, 74.
119	*"our communication patterns"* Logan with McLuhan, *Future of the Library*, 156.
119	*"like robots"* McLuhan and Parker, *Through the Vanishing Point*, 239.
119	*"a supreme release from conflict"* McLuhan and McLuhan, *Laws of Media*, 79.
119	*"timid and tentative"* McLuhan, *Gutenberg Galaxy*, 62.
119	*"his own figure as his ground"* McLuhan and Powers, *Global Village*, 99.
119	*preliterate and postliterate civilizations alike* McLuhan and McLuhan, *Laws of Media*, 79.
120	*"may well both be true"* McGilchrist, *Master and His Emissary*, 330.
120	*"between subject and object"* McLuhan, *Gutenberg Galaxy*, 315.
120	*"the right world of synthesis"* Logan with McLuhan, *Future of the Library*, 156.
120	*"doctrinal sectarian passions"* McLuhan to Edward T. Hall, July 23, 1969, in *Letters of Marshall McLuhan*, 384.
120	*"awareness of process"* McLuhan to Edward T. Hall, July 23, 1969, in *Letters of Marshall McLuhan*, 384.
121	*"phonetic or Western culture"* McLuhan and Powers, *Global Village*, 60.
121	*"minus literacy"* McLuhan, "Violence as a Quest for Identity," 271.
121	*"a world he never made"* McLuhan and Fiore, *War and Peace*, 59.

178 NOTES

121 *between divine and human agency* McLuhan and McLuhan, *Media and Formal Cause*, 124.
121 *in his dialogue The Cratylus* McLuhan, *Gutenberg Galaxy*, 32. See also McLuhan, *Classical Trivium*, 15–16. The passage in this dialogue that McLuhan has in mind is at 438c, where Cratylus observes, "I believe, Socrates, the true account of the matter to be that a power more than human gave things their first names, and that the names which are thus given are necessarily their true names." See *Collected Dialogues of Plato*, 472.
121 *"old cliché"* McLuhan, "Future of the Book," 181.
121 *"the first Adam had not known"* McLuhan and Fiore, *War and Peace*, 59.
121 *"the mandatory role of being creative"* McLuhan, "De-Romanization," 55.
121 *"quite superhuman manipulation"* McLuhan and Fiore, *War and Peace*, 59.
121 *"its potency was enormously enhanced"* McLuhan, "De-Romanization," 55.
121 *"this language of nature"* McLuhan, *Classical Trivium*, 16.
121 *"once man held by nature"* McLuhan, *Classical Trivium*, 16.
122 *the Book of Nature* McLuhan, *Classical Trivium*, 7.
122 *"of the fall of the first man"* Autobiography of Giambattista Vico, 122.
122 *"formal cause of the Incarnation"* McLuhan, "Letter to Fr. John Culkin."
122 *"Greco-Roman idea of civilization"* McLuhan, "Living at the Speed of Light," 228.
122 *"the Greek mythmaker"* McLuhan, *Understanding Media*, 45.
122 *"conforms men to them"* McLuhan, *Understanding Media*, 45–46. Italics in the original.
123 *against a pagan ground* McLuhan and Nevitt, *Take Today*, 285.
123 *"the need for change in man"* McLuhan, "Liturgy and Media," 128.
123 *"extensions of God"* McLuhan, "Liturgy and Media," 129.
123 *"the clouding of the mind"* McLuhan, "Liturgy and Media," 129.
123 *"fate and* hubris" McLuhan, "Liturgy and Media," 129. Italics in the original.
123 *"to confuse his mind"* McLuhan with Watson, *From Cliché to Archetype*, 14.
123 *"lack of 'awareness'"* Quoted in Gordon, *Marshall McLuhan*, 220.
123 *"wreck or middenheap"* McLuhan with Watson, *From Cliché to Archetype*, 121.
124 *"properly analogous"* McLuhan, "Joyce, Aquinas," 5.
124 *"the Novum Organum of Francis Bacon"* McLuhan, "Francis Bacon," 94.
124 *"toboggan slide"* McLuhan, "G. K. Chesterton," 6.
124 *"excuse for procrastination"* McLuhan, "G. K. Chesterton," 6.
124 *understood as a "percept"* McLuhan and Fiore, *War and Peace*, 81–82; McLuhan with Watson, *From Cliché to Archetype*, 166; McLuhan and Parker, *Through the Vanishing Point*, 254.

9. THE ELECTRIC CAVE

126 *"backward-looking misanthropy"* McLuhan and Stearn, "Even Hercules," 279.
126 *"the present actuality"* McLuhan, *Understanding Media*, 70.
127 *"reveal it and compensate for it"* McLuhan and Parker, *Through the Vanishing Point*, 238.
127 *"instead of readjusting it"* McLuhan and Parker, *Through the Vanishing Point*, 241.
127 *"rather than as consumers"* McLuhan and Parker, *Through the Vanishing Point*, 247.
127 *"a strategy of evasion and survival"* McLuhan, "Man and Media," 285.
128 *"shadows and selective ignorance"* O'Neill, *Plato's Cave*, 3.
128 *"into the light of the sun"* Republic of Plato, 194 (515e–516a).
129 *"wouldn't they kill him?"* Republic of Plato, 195–96 (517a).
129 *"natural response or natural instinct"* McLuhan, "Man and Media," 285.

129 *"the order of nature"* McLuhan, *Classical Trivium*, 21.
129 *"provided by Madison Avenue"* McLuhan, *Culture Is Our Business*, 240.
129 *"corporate, not private, origin"* McLuhan, *Culture Is Our Business*, 48. Italics in the original.
130 *"a means of proving reality"* McLuhan, "Catholic Humanism," 165. See also Havers, "Global Electric Republic," 188–89.
130 *"carrying us instantly anywhere"* McLuhan, "Catholic Humanism," 169.
130 *"things don't move quite as fast"* Quoted in Jargon, "TikTok Brain Explained."
130 *"as Marshall McLuhan said"* Von Heyking, "Liberal Education," 63.
130 *"their own means of liberation"* Von Heyking, "Liberal Education," 61.
130 *"To the blind all things are sudden"* McLuhan, *Culture Is Our Business*, 162.
131 *"reverse the flow"* McLuhan, "Catholic Humanism," 169.
131 both past and future McLuhan, "Man and Media," 281, 293.
131 *"weak identity"* McLuhan, "Violence as a Quest for Identity," 271.
131 *"for being unable to do so"* Von Heyking, "Liberal Education," 60. On the "natural ignorance" inside Plato's cave, see Strauss, "Review of Julius Ebbinghaus," 215.
131 *"our central nervous system"* McLuhan, *Understanding Media*, 68.
131 the *"primitive"* McLuhan, *Gutenberg Galaxy*, 35.
131 *"the formal cause of his philosophy"* McLuhan, "Letter to Fr. John Culkin."
132 *"the first archetypal storehouse"* McLuhan with Watson, *From Cliché to Archetype*, 119–20.
132 *"into his cave"* McLuhan with Watson, *From Cliché to Archetype*, 128.
132 *"light through"* and *"light on"* McLuhan, *Gutenberg Galaxy*, 280. See also 120–23 and 128.
132 *"a tyrant such as Priscus Tarquin"* McLuhan, "Psychopathology," 159. Priscus Tarquin was the fifth king of ancient Rome.
132 *"corporate"* hero McLuhan and Parker, *Through the Vanishing Point*, 260–61.
132 *"banana-skin pirouette and collapse"* McLuhan, *Understanding Media*, 68. Italics in the original.
133 *"specialist exchanges of an 'in-group'"* McLuhan, "Roles, Masks, and Performances," 517.
133 a participant in a dialogue See also Gasché, *Plato's Stranger*.
133 *"human and divine"* Plato, *Laws*, 1316.
133 *"a stranger in the back seat"* McLuhan, "Roles, Masks, and Performances," 517.
133 *"in my conversations"* McLuhan and Stearn, "Even Hercules," 286.
133 *"critical awareness by nonartists"* McLuhan, "Playboy Interview," 238.
133 *"the put-on has also been a turn-on"* McLuhan, "Roles, Masks, and Performances," 531.
133 *"on a world scale"* McLuhan, *Understanding Media*, 307.
133 McLuhan seeks to transform it Cf. Bloom, "Interpretive Essay": "The Enlightenment teaches that the cave can be transformed; Socrates teaches that it must be transcended and that this transcendence can be accomplished only by a few" (403).
134 *"influencers"* who wrote those comments Rogers, "Secret Digital Behaviors."
134 *"learning through reading"* Strauss, "Review of Julius Ebbinghaus," 215.
134 *"massive extrasensory perception"* McLuhan, *Understanding Media*, 130.
134 *"self-direction and self-reflection"* Von Heyking, "Liberal Education," 71.
135 most important ideas of modernity I discuss McLuhan's recurrent interest in Machiavelli in Havers, "Machiavellian Use of Religious Violence."
135 *"all the situations of the culture"* McLuhan with Watson, *From Cliché to Archetype*, 46.
135 *"the outcome of a thing"* Machiavelli, *Prince*, 71.
135 *"its own distorted forces"* McLuhan, *Classical Trivium*, 195.

NOTES

135 *"passionate and blind violence of men"* McLuhan, *Classical Trivium*, 195.
135 *"from high theology to high finance"* McLuhan, "Ancient Quarrel," 231.
136 *"eloquence is useless"* McLuhan, *Classical Trivium*, 196.
136 *"divorcing technique from social purpose"* McLuhan, *Mechanical Bride*, 87.
136 *"the art and grammar of power"* McLuhan, "Catholic Humanism," 159.
136 *"erects his system for obtaining power"* McLuhan, "Catholic Humanism," 159.
136 *"fashioning cities and states"* McLuhan, "Catholic Humanism," 160.
136 *"with a clear conscience"* McLuhan, "Catholic Humanism," 160.
137 *"a new circle of the Inferno"* McLuhan, "Catholic Humanism," 160.
137 *"conflicting interests"* McLuhan, *Gutenberg Galaxy*, 237, 268.
137 *"power technique"* McLuhan, *Gutenberg Galaxy*, 198.
138 *"violent scission of nature and grace"* McLuhan, *Classical Trivium*, 195.
138 *"until our own day"* McLuhan, "American Advertising," 134.
138 *"the dim dreams of collective consciousness"* McLuhan, *Mechanical Bride*, vii.
138 *"electronic eavesdropping"* Quoted in Nevitt with McLuhan, *Who Was Marshall McLuhan?*, 169.
138 *"the hidden environment or 'ground'"* Quoted in Nevitt with McLuhan, *Who Was Marshall McLuhan?*, 169.
138 *"that's done by rumors, not by coverage"* McLuhan, *Book of Probes*, 206.
139 *"is almost certainly corrupt"* McLuhan, "Marfleet Lectures," 132.
139 *"as soon as possible"* McLuhan, "Marfleet Lectures," 132.
139 *"democratic public opinion and slogans"* Von Heyking, "Liberal Education," 64.
139 Donald Trump "Trump Jokes about Sexual Assault."
139 *"Psychological decentralization"* McLuhan, "Psychopathology," 159.
140 *"make anyone do anything"* "What Happened."
140 *"is finished"* McLuhan, "*Playboy* Interview," 260–61.
140 *"the comaker of the work"* McLuhan and Nevitt, "Argument," 15.
140 platforms on YouTube Justice, "YouTube Deplatforms Pro-Life Group."
140 *"considered important enough"* Bucher, "Want to Be on the Top?," 1171.
141 *"that we are seeing"* Bhaimiya, "Gen Z Lack Workplace Skills."
141 *"take very seriously"* McLuhan and Stearn, "Even Hercules," 261.
141 *"members of the body of Christ"* McLuhan and Stearn, "Even Hercules," 261.
141 *"inherited from the alphabet"* McLuhan, "Keys to the Electronic Revolution," 52.
142 *"according to visual criteria"* McLuhan, "Keys to the Electronic Revolution," 48.
142 associate with acoustic space McLuhan and Powers, *Global Village*, 100.
142 "Moralistic therapeutic deism" Smith and Denton, *Soul Searching*.
142 *"algorithmic spirituality"* Quay, "Algorithmic Spirituality."
142 *"Identity now changes faster than rules"* McLuhan and Nevitt, *Take Today*, 271.
143 educating the uneducated Von Heyking, "Liberal Education," 75.
143 *"all-time, out of time"* McLuhan, "Electric Consciousness," 88.
143 "*Myth is inclusive, time-saving, and fast*" McLuhan and Stearn, "Even Hercules," 273.
143 *"end of an historic cycle (the Trojan War)"* McLuhan and Parker, *Through the Vanishing Point*, 203.
143 *"that is imagined as desirable"* McLuhan, "Myth and Mass Media," 340.
143 *"at the same time"* McLuhan, "The Electronic Age," 179.
144 *"constructively and humanistically"* McLuhan, "*Playboy* Interview," 261.
144 *"increasingly necessary but also intolerable"* McLuhan and Parker, *Through the Vanishing Point*, 244.
144 *"in the name of innovation"* McLuhan and Parker, *Through the Vanishing Point*, 253.
144 *"*BEFORE* creating their causes"* Quoted in Nevitt with McLuhan, *Who Was Marshall McLuhan?*, 261.

10. SURVIVING THE APOCALYPSE

145 *"the next corner of history"* Jacobs, "Why Bother," 135.
145 *"make him worth studying"* Miller, interviewed in Stearn, *McLuhan: Hot & Cool*, 235.
145 *"likely to come true"* Quoted in Nevitt with McLuhan, *Who Was Marshall McLuhan?*, 123.
146 *"ever be able to digest it all"* McLuhan and Stearn, "Even Hercules," 291.
146 *"the past and the future"* McLuhan, "TV News as a New Mythic Form," 172.
146 *"ordinary human tools and services"* McLuhan and McLuhan, *Laws of Media*, 98.
146 *"they are art forms"* McLuhan, "Media Log," in *Counterblast*, n.p.
146 idols created by their own hands McLuhan and McLuhan, *Laws of Media*, 98.
146 *"deloused of his humanity by technics"* McLuhan, "Psychopathology," 159.
147 *"agent for self-examination"* McLuhan and Powers, *Global Village*, 100.
147 with the City of God McLuhan, *Classical Trivium*, 73–74.
148 *"more than ordinarily real"* McLuhan, "Electric Consciousness," 86.
148 *"that is conversion"* McLuhan, "Religion and Youth," 104.
148 *"as in other matters"* McLuhan to Trudeau, January 24, 1969, in Kahn, *Been Hoping*, 65.
148 *"slouching toward Bethlehem to be born"* McLuhan, "*Playboy* Interview," 268.
148 *"we are living in it"* McLuhan, "De-Romanization," 56.
148 *"Our only hope is apocalypse"* McLuhan, "'Our Only Hope,'" 59.
148 *"immunity"* McLuhan, *Understanding Media*, 64.
148 *"potencies"* McLuhan and McLuhan, *Laws of Media*, 64.
148 *"the greatest electrical engineer"* McLuhan, "Tomorrow's Church," 209.
149 *"'under the aspect of eternity'"* Quoted in Nevitt with McLuhan, *Who Was Marshall McLuhan?*, 95.
149 *"boundaries nowhere"* Quoted in Nevitt with McLuhan, *Who Was Marshall McLuhan?*, 279.
149 *"simultaneous transparency"* McLuhan and Fiore, *War and Peace*, 177.
149 *"around the entire globe"* McLuhan and Fiore, *War and Peace*, 177.
149 *"tune yourself to the right frequency"* McLuhan, "Tomorrow's Church," 209.
150 bad news sells good news See Markham, "Pattern Recognition"; Sharma, Lee, and Johnson, "Dark at the End of the Tunnel."
150 *"super intelligence"* Garcia, "Musk Believes 'Super Intelligence' Is Inevitable."
150 *"new environment"* McLuhan, "*Playboy* Interview," 265.
150 *"our right to assign guilt"* McLuhan, *Understanding Media*, 16.
150 *"willingness to pay attention"* McLuhan and McLuhan, *Laws of Media*, 128.
150 *"Everyman as Finn Awake"* McLuhan and Nevitt, *Take Today*, 295.
150 *"revealed divine event"* McLuhan, "Electric Consciousness," 87.
150 *"some aspect of Christian community"* McLuhan, "Electric Consciousness," 87.
150 *"paradoxical from its inception"* McLuhan with Watson, *From Cliché to Archetype*, 159.
151 *"main source of wisdom and sanity"* McLuhan with Watson, *From Cliché to Archetype*, 160.
151 *"radically revolutionary and radically conservative"* McLuhan with Watson, *From Cliché to Archetype*, 166.
151 *"transcended by satellite and radar"* McLuhan and Fiore, *War and Peace*, 190.
151 *"environment itself as evolutionary"* McLuhan, "Open-Mind Surgery," 152.
152 *"undervalue the world altogether"* McLuhan, "'Peculiar War to Fight,'" 91–92.
152 *"from the Tower of Babel to the Golden Calf"* McLuhan with Watson, *From Cliché to Archetype*, 120.

152 *"unhindered by religious observations"* McLuhan with Watson, *From Cliché to Archetype*, 121.
152 *"totality of existence on the planet"* McLuhan with Watson, *From Cliché to Archetype*, 121.
153 *"Aquinas and Aristotle in modern terms"* McLuhan to J. M. Davey, March 8, 1971, in *Letters of Marshall McLuhan*, 427.
153 *"human community in contemporary life"* McLuhan to Ong, May 18, 1946, in *Letters of Marshall McLuhan*, 187.
153 *"unified sensory experience"* McLuhan and Nevitt, *Take Today*, 96. Italics in the original.
153 *"properly analogous"* McLuhan, "Joyce, Aquinas," 5.
153 *"as is every cognitive power"* Quoted in McLuhan, "Joyce, Aquinas," 5. This passage is in Aquinas, *Summa Theologica*, 1.5.4. See *Introduction to St. Thomas Aquinas*, 40.
153 *"to Nature and to 'Natural' law"* McLuhan to Trudeau, May 11, 1977, in Kahn, *Been Hoping*, 134.
153 *"once man held by nature"* McLuhan, *Classical Trivium*, 16.
153 the state of the church in the electric age McLuhan, "Christian in the Electronic Age."
154 *"and then into the Talmud"* Eidelberg, *Jerusalem vs. Athens*, 280.
154 *"the dialogue form becomes repugnant"* McLuhan and Stearn, "Even Hercules," 284.
154 a *"pointless"* exercise McLuhan, *Gutenberg Galaxy*, 143.
154 *"despised by the literati"* McLuhan, *Book of Probes*, 340–41.
154 "The pre-literate has a short memory" McLuhan and Powers, *Global Village*, 137.
154 its fate is tied to literacy McLuhan, "'Our Only Hope,'" 63.
154 *"the religious and political life of that time"* McLuhan, "'Our Only Hope,'" 58.
154 *"their new policies and prescriptions"* McLuhan, "'Our Only Hope,'" 58.
155 *"It's happening"* McLuhan, "De-Romanization," 55.
155 *"knowledge without literacy"* McLuhan, "'Our Only Hope,'" 60.
155 *"outdistanced by speed"* McLuhan and Nevitt, *Take Today*, 286.
155 *"there is no peace"* McLuhan, "'Our Only Hope,'" 64.
155 *"global theatre sets in"* McLuhan, "'Our Only Hope,'" 61.
155 the church is on the side of laughter Allen, "Comedians Meet the Pope."
155 *"it doesn't have to stay in Rome"* McLuhan, "'Our Only Hope,'" 64.
155 *"from a Catholic pulpit"* McLuhan, "'Our Only Hope,'" 62.
155 uncritical embrace of Protestant influences McLuhan, "'Our Only Hope,'" 62.
155 *"degree of literacy"* McLuhan, "'Our Only Hope,'" 63–64.
155 the life of the Christian is to be unworldly McLuhan, "'Our Only Hope,'" 65.
156 *"never greater than in the electric world"* McLuhan, "Violence as a Quest for Identity," 271.
156 independent of our making *Autobiography of Giambattista Vico*, 127.
156 *"discarnate man who has lost his body"* Quoted in Nevitt with McLuhan, *Who Was Marshall McLuhan?*, 236.
156 *"as gods or minor religions"* McLuhan, *Understanding Media*, 46.
156 *"the most religious ever"* McLuhan, "Electric Consciousness," 88.
156 *"dangerous zone of abstractions"* McLuhan and Powers, *Global Village*, 95.
157 *"their groupies drift into Hare Krishna"* McLuhan and Powers, *Global Village*, 102.
157 *"the age of Aquarium"* McLuhan and Powers, *Global Village*, 102.
157 *"responsibility to or for it"* McLuhan and McLuhan, *Laws of Media*, 96–97.
157 *"towards anarchy and lawlessness"* McLuhan and McLuhan, *Laws of Media*, 72.
157 *"dangerously inflating and schizophrenic"* McLuhan and Powers, *Global Village*, 97.
157 *"external and private morality"* McLuhan to Trudeau, May 11, 1977, in Kahn, *Been Hoping*, 134.

NOTES

158 *destroying a target with instantaneous precision* McLuhan and his son Eric made this point about retrieving the gunslinger in a tetrad about the computer. See McLuhan and McLuhan, *Laws of Media*, 188.
158 *"use of weaponry at a distance"* McLuhan, "Man and Media," 286.
158 *"knife's edge"* Borger, "Humanity on 'Knife's Edge.'"
158 *"will bring them into orderly service"* McLuhan, *Understanding Media*, 5–6.
159 *"we incarnate and utter the world"* McLuhan, "Catholic Humanism," 169.
159 *"we can come through"* McLuhan, "*Playboy* Interview," 268.
159 *"and also less important to us"* McLuhan, "Catholic Humanism," 169.
159 *"mock-up of the mystical body"* McLuhan, "'Logos Reaching across Barriers,'" 69.
159 *"human gullibility and self-deception"* McLuhan, "'Peculiar War to Fight,'" 92.
160 *"invincibly persuasive when ignored"* McLuhan, "'Peculiar War to Fight,'" 93.
160 *"to some degree"* McLuhan, "*Playboy* Interview," 238.
160 *"self-induced subliminal trance"* McLuhan, "*Playboy* Interview," 239.

Bibliography

WORKS BY MARSHALL McLUHAN

McLuhan, Marshall. "'Achieving Relevance': Letters to Mole and Sheed." In *The Medium and the Light: Reflections on Religion*, edited by Eric McLuhan and Jacek Szlarek, 136–40. Toronto: Stoddart, 1999.

McLuhan, Marshall. "Address at Vision 65." In *Essential McLuhan*, edited by Eric McLuhan and Frank Zingrone, 219–32. Toronto: House of Anansi, 1995.

McLuhan, Marshall. "The Agenbite of Outwit." *McLuhan Studies* 2 (1996). https://mcluhan-studies.artsci.utoronto.ca/v1_iss2/1_2art6.htm.

McLuhan, Marshall. "American Advertising." *Horizon*, October 1947, 132–41.

McLuhan, Marshall. "An Ancient Quarrel in Modern America." In *The Interior Landscape: The Literary Criticism of Marshall McLuhan*, edited by Eugene McNamara, 223–34. New York: McGraw-Hill, 1969.

McLuhan, Marshall. "Art as Survival in the Electric Age." In *Understanding Me: Lectures and Interviews*, edited by Stephanie McLuhan and David Staines, 206–24. Cambridge, MA: MIT Press, 2005.

McLuhan, Marshall. *The Book of Probes*. Edited by David Carson, Eric McLuhan, William Kuhns, and Mo Cohen. Richmond, CA: Gingko, 2003.

McLuhan, Marshall. "Canada: The Borderline Case." In *The Canadian Imagination: Dimensions of a Literary Culture*, edited by David Staines, 226–48. Cambridge, MA: Harvard University Press, 1977.

McLuhan, Marshall. "Catholic Humanism and Modern Letters." In *The Medium and the Light: Reflections on Religion*, edited by Eric McLuhan and Jacek Szlarek, 153–74. Toronto: Stoddart, 1999.

McLuhan, Marshall. "The Christian in the Electronic Age." In *The Medium and the Light: Reflections on Religion*, edited by Eric McLuhan and Jacek Szlarek, 175–77. Toronto: Stoddart, 1999.

McLuhan, Marshall. *The Classical Trivium: The Place of Thomas Nashe in the Learning of His Time*. Corte Madera, CA: Gingko, 2006.

McLuhan, Marshall. "Communication Media: Makers of the Modern World." In *The Medium and the Light: Reflections on Religion*, edited by Eric McLuhan and Jacek Szlarek, 33–44. Toronto: Stoddart, 1999.

McLuhan, Marshall. *Counterblast*. Berkeley, CA: Gingko, 2011. Originally published in 1954.

McLuhan, Marshall. "The Crack in the Rear-View Mirror." *McGill Journal of Education/Revue des sciences de l'éducation de McGill* 1, no. 001 (1966): 31–34.

McLuhan, Marshall. *Culture Is Our Business*. Eugene, OR: Wipf and Stock, 2015. Originally published in 1970.

McLuhan, Marshall. "Culture without Literacy." *Explorations* 1 (December 1953): 117–27.

McLuhan, Marshall. "Cybernetics and Human Culture." In *Understanding Me: Lectures and Interviews*, edited by Stephanie McLuhan and David Staines, 44–55. Cambridge, MA: MIT Press, 2005.

McLuhan, Marshall. "The De-Romanization of the American Catholic Church." In *The Medium and the Light: Reflections on Religion*, edited by Eric McLuhan and Jacek Szlarek, 54–56. Toronto: Stoddart, 1999.

McLuhan, Marshall. "Do Books Matter?" In *On the Nature of Media: Essays in Understanding Media, 1952–1978*, edited by Richard Cavell, 209–20. Berkeley, CA: Gingko, 2016.

McLuhan, Marshall. "Edgar Poe's Tradition." *Sewanee Review* 52, no. 1 (Winter 1944): 24–33.

McLuhan, Marshall. "Electric Consciousness and the Church." In *The Medium and the Light: Reflections on Religion*, edited by Eric McLuhan and Jacek Szlarek, 79–88. Toronto: Stoddart, 1999.

McLuhan, Marshall. "The Electronic Age—The Age of Implosion." In *Mass Media in Canada*, edited by John A. Irving, 179–205. Toronto: McGraw-Hill Ryerson, 1969.

McLuhan, Marshall. "The End of the Work Ethic." In *Understanding Me: Lectures and Interviews*, edited by Stephanie McLuhan and David Staines, 187–205. Cambridge, MA: MIT Press, 2005.

McLuhan, Marshall. "Environment: The Future of an Erosion." In *On the Nature of Media: Essays in Understanding Media, 1952–1978*, edited by Richard Cavell, 109–24. Berkeley, CA: Gingko, 2016.

McLuhan, Marshall. *Essential McLuhan*. Edited by Eric McLuhan and Frank Zingrone. Toronto: House of Anansi, 1995.

McLuhan, Marshall. "Footprints in the Sands of Crime." *Sewanee Review* 54, no. 4 (October–December 1946): 617–34.

McLuhan, Marshall. "Fordham University: First Lecture." In *Understanding Me: Lectures and Interviews*, edited by Stephanie McLuhan and David Staines, 139–46. Cambridge, MA: MIT Press, 2005.

McLuhan, Marshall. "Francis Bacon: Ancient or Modern?" *Renaissance and Reformation* 10, no. 2 (1974): 93–98.

McLuhan, Marshall. "The Future of Man in the Electric Age." In *Understanding Me: Lectures and Interviews*, edited by Stephanie McLuhan and David Staines, 56–75. Cambridge, MA: MIT Press, 2005.

McLuhan, Marshall. "The Future of Sex." In *On the Nature of Media: Essays in Understanding Media, 1952–1978*, edited by Richard Cavell, 129–42. Berkeley, CA: Gingko, 2016.

McLuhan, Marshall. "The Future of the Book." In *Understanding Me: Lectures and Interviews*, edited by Stephanie McLuhan and David Staines, 173–86. Cambridge, MA: MIT Press, 2005.

McLuhan, Marshall. "G. K. Chesterton: A Practical Mystic." In *The Medium and the Light: Reflections on Religion*, edited by Eric McLuhan and Jacek Szlarek, 3–13. Toronto: Stoddart, 1999.

McLuhan, Marshall. "A Garbage Apocalypse." in *Art et perception: Compte rendu du 2e Congrès Extraordinaire*, 1–18. Ottawa: Association Internationale des Critiques d'Art, August 1970.

McLuhan, Marshall. "Guaranteed Income in the Electric Age." In *The Guaranteed Income: Next Step in Socioeconomic Evolution?*, edited by Robert Theobald, 185–97. Garden City, NY: Anchor Books, 1967.

McLuhan, Marshall. *The Gutenberg Galaxy: The Making of Typographic Man*. Toronto: University of Toronto Press, 2011. Originally published in 1962.

McLuhan, Marshall. Introduction to *Explorations in Communication*, edited by Edmund Carpenter and Marshall McLuhan, ix–xii. Boston: Beacon, 1960.

McLuhan, Marshall. "Introduction to H. A. Innis, *The Bias of Communication*." In *On the Nature of Media: Essays in Understanding Media, 1952-1978*, edited by Richard Cavell, 71-81. Berkeley: Gingko, 2016.
McLuhan, Marshall. Introduction to *Paradox in Chesterton*, by Hugh Kenner, xi-xxii. New York: Sheed and Ward, 1947.
McLuhan, Marshall. "It is Strange that the Popular Press as an Art Form has often attracted the Enthusiastic Attention of Poets and Aesthetes while rousing the Gloomiest Apprehensions in the Academic Mind." In *McLuhan: Hot & Cool; A Primer for the Understanding of & a Critical Symposium with a Rebuttal by McLuhan*, edited by Gerald Emanuel Stearn, 128-42. New York: Signet Books, 1967.
McLuhan, Marshall. "Joyce, Aquinas, and the Poetic Process." *Renascence* 4, no. 1 (Autumn 1951-52): 3-11.
McLuhan, Marshall. "Keys to the Electronic Revolution: First Conversation with Pierre Babin." In *The Medium and the Light: Reflections on Religion*, edited by Eric McLuhan and Jacek Szlarek, 45-53. Toronto: Stoddart, 1999.
McLuhan, Marshall. "The Later Innis." In *On the Nature of Media: Essays in Understanding Media, 1952-1978*, edited by Richard Cavell, 39-47. Berkeley: Gingko, 2016.
McLuhan, Marshall. "Letter to Fr. John Culkin." In *The Medium and the Light: Reflections on Religion*, edited by Eric McLuhan and Jacek Szlarek, 74. Toronto: Stoddart, 1999.
McLuhan, Marshall. *Letters of Marshall McLuhan*. Edited by Matie Molinaro, Corinne McLuhan, and William Toye. Oxford: Oxford University Press, 1987.
McLuhan, Marshall. "Liturgy and Media: Do Americans Go to Church to Be Alone?" In *The Medium and the Light: Reflections on Religion*, edited by Eric McLuhan and Jacek Szlarek, 117-35. Toronto: Stoddart, 1999.
McLuhan, Marshall. "Living at the Speed of Light." In *Understanding Me: Lectures and Interviews*, edited by Stephanie McLuhan and David Staines, 225-43. Cambridge, MA: MIT Press, 2005.
McLuhan, Marshall. "'The Logos Reaching across Barriers': Letters to Ong, Mole, Maritain, and Culkin." In *The Medium and the Light: Reflections on Religion*, edited by Eric McLuhan and Jacek Szlarek, 66-74. Toronto: Stoddart, 1999.
McLuhan, Marshall. "Man and Media." In *Understanding Me: Lectures and Interviews*, edited by Stephanie McLuhan and David Staines, 277-98. Cambridge, MA: MIT Press, 2005.
McLuhan, Marshall. "The Marfleet Lectures." In *Understanding Me: Lectures and Interviews*, edited by Stephanie McLuhan and David Staines, 103-38. Cambridge, MA: MIT Press, 2005.
McLuhan, Marshall. "McLuhan Looks at Fashion." In *On the Nature of Media: Essays in Understanding Media, 1952-1978*, edited by Richard Cavell, 147-62. Berkeley: Gingko, 2016.
McLuhan, Marshall. *The Mechanical Bride: Folklore of Industrial Man*. Corte Madera, CA: Gingko, 2002. Originally published in 1951.
McLuhan, Marshall. "The Media Fit the Battle of Jericho." In *Essential McLuhan*, edited by Eric McLuhan and Frank Zingrone, 298-302. Toronto: House of Anansi, 1995.
McLuhan, Marshall. "Myth and Mass Media." *Daedalus* 88, no. 2 (Spring 1959): 339-48.
McLuhan, Marshall. "Nihilism Exposed." *Renascence* 8, no. 2 (Winter 1955): 97-99.

McLuhan, Marshall. "On Nature and Media: A Dialogue of Effects." Library of Consciousness, July 17, 1978. https://www.organism.earth/library/document/nature-and-media.
McLuhan, Marshall. "Open-Mind Surgery." In *Understanding Me: Lectures and Interviews*, edited by Stephanie McLuhan and David Staines, 147–57. Cambridge, MA: MIT Press, 2005.
McLuhan, Marshall. "The Organization Man." *Explorations* 8 (October 1957): n.p.
McLuhan, Marshall. "'Our Only Hope Is Apocalypse.'" In *The Medium and the Light: Reflections on Religion*, edited by Eric McLuhan and Jacek Szlarek, 57–65. Toronto: Stoddart, 1999.
McLuhan, Marshall. "Pastures and Impostures of Managers Past." In *Essential McLuhan*, edited by Eric McLuhan and Frank Zingrone, 76–86. Toronto: House of Anansi, 1995.
McLuhan, Marshall. "'A Peculiar War to Fight': Letter to Robert J. Leuver, C.M.F." In *The Medium and the Light: Reflections on Religion*, edited by Eric McLuhan and Jacek Szlarek, 89–104. Toronto: Stoddart, 1999.
McLuhan, Marshall. "*Playboy* Interview: A Candid Conversation with the High Priest of Popcult and Metaphysician of Media." In *Essential McLuhan*, edited by Eric McLuhan and Frank Zingrone, 233–69. Toronto: House of Anansi, 1995.
McLuhan, Marshall. "Predicting Communication via the Internet." In *Understanding Me: Lectures and Interviews*, edited by Stephanie McLuhan and David Staines, 98–102. Cambridge, MA: MIT Press, 2005.
McLuhan, Marshall. "The Psychopathology of 'Time' and "Life.'" In *The Scene before You: A New Approach to American Culture*, edited by Chandler Brossard, 147–60. New York: Rinehart, 1955.
McLuhan, Marshall. "Religion and Youth: Second Conversation with Pierre Babin." In *The Medium and the Light: Reflections on Religion*, edited by Eric McLuhan and Jacek Szlarek, 94–104. Toronto: Stoddart, 1999.
McLuhan, Marshall. Review of Erich Auerbach, *Mimesis: The Representation of Reality in Western Literature*. *Renascence* 10, no. 2 (1957): 107–9.
McLuhan, Marshall. "Roles, Masks, and Performances." *New Literary History* 2, no. 3 (Spring 1971): 517–31.
McLuhan, Marshall. "The Southern Quality." In *The Interior Landscape: The Literary Criticism of Marshall McLuhan*, edited by Eugene McNamara, 185–209. New York: McGraw-Hill, 1969.
McLuhan, Marshall. "Space, Time, and Poetry." *Explorations* 4 (February 1955): 56–62.
McLuhan, Marshall. "Technology and Political Change." *International Journal* 7, no. 3 (Summer 1952): 189–95.
McLuhan, Marshall. "Tomorrow's Church: Fourth Conversation with Pierre Babin." In *The Medium and the Light: Reflections on Religion*, edited by Eric McLuhan and Jacek Szlarek, 203–9. Toronto: Stoddart, 1999.
McLuhan, Marshall. "TV as a Debating Medium." In *Understanding Me: Lectures and Interviews*, edited by Stephanie McLuhan and David Staines, 256–63. Cambridge, MA: MIT Press, 2005.
McLuhan, Marshall. "TV News as a New Mythic Form." In *Understanding Me: Lectures and Interviews*, edited by Stephanie McLuhan and David Staines, 158–72. Cambridge, MA: MIT Press, 2005.
McLuhan, Marshall. *Understanding Media: The Extensions of Man*. Cambridge, MA: MIT Press, 1994. Originally published in 1964.
McLuhan, Marshall. "Violence as a Quest for Identity." In *Understanding Me: Lectures and Interviews*, edited by Stephanie McLuhan and David Staines, 264–76. Cambridge, MA: MIT Press, 2005.

McLuhan, Marshall. "What TV Does Best." In *Understanding Me: Lectures and Interviews*, edited by Stephanie McLuhan and David Staines, 244–55. Cambridge, MA: MIT Press, 2005.

Works Coauthored by Marshall McLuhan

Logan, Robert K., with Marshall McLuhan. *The Future of the Library: From Electric Media to Digital Media*. New York: Peter Lang, 2016.

McLuhan, Marshall, and Quentin Fiore. *The Medium Is the Massage: An Inventory of Effects*. Produced by Jerome Agel. Richmond, CA: Gingko, 2001. Originally published in 1967.

McLuhan, Marshall, and Quentin Fiore. *War and Peace in the Global Village*. Produced by Jerome Agel. Richmond, CA: Gingko, 2023. Originally published in 1968.

McLuhan, Marshall, with Kathryn Hutchon and Eric McLuhan. *City as Classroom: Understanding Language and Media*. Agincourt, ON: Book Society of Canada, 1977.

McLuhan, Marshall, and Eric McLuhan. *Laws of Media: The New Science*. Toronto: University of Toronto Press, 1988.

McLuhan, Marshall, and Eric McLuhan. *Media and Formal Cause*. Houston: NeoPoiesis, 2011.

McLuhan, Marshall, and Barrington Nevitt. "The Argument: Causality in the Electric World." *Technology and Culture* 14, no. 1 (January 1973): 1–18.

McLuhan, Marshall, and Barrington Nevitt. "A Monday-Night Seminar." In *Who Was Marshall McLuhan? Exploring a Mosaic of Impressions*, by Barrington Nevitt with Maurice McLuhan, 41–68. Toronto: Stoddart, 1994.

McLuhan, Marshall, and Barrington Nevitt. *Take Today: The Executive as Dropout*. New York: Harcourt Brace Jovanovich, 1972.

McLuhan, Marshall, and Harley Parker. *Through the Vanishing Point: Space and Poetry in Painting*. New York: Harper and Row, 1968.

McLuhan, Marshall, and Bruce R. Powers. *The Global Village: Transformations in World Life and Media in the 21st Century*. Oxford: Oxford University Press, 1992.

McLuhan, Marshall, and Gerald Emanuel Stearn. "Even Hercules Had to Clean the Augean Stables but Once!" In *McLuhan: Hot & Cool; A Primer for the Understanding of & a Critical Symposium with a Rebuttal by McLuhan*, edited by Gerald Emanuel Stearn, 260–92. New York: Signet Books, 1967.

McLuhan, Marshall, with Wilfred Watson. *From Cliché to Archetype*. New York: Viking, 1970.

WORKS ON MARSHALL McLUHAN

Cavell, Richard. *McLuhan in Space: A Cultural Geography*. Toronto: University of Toronto Press, 2003.

Comstock, W. Richard. "Marshall McLuhan's Theory of Sensory Form: A Theological Reflection." *Soundings* 51, no. 2 (Summer 1968): 166–83.

Culkin, S. J., John M. "A Schoolman's Guide to Marshall McLuhan." *Saturday Review*, March 18, 1967.

Danesi, Marcel. *Marshall McLuhan: The Unwitting Semiotician*. Nanjing: Nanjing Normal University Press, 2018.

Duffy, Dennis. *Marshall McLuhan*. Toronto: McLellan and Stewart, 1969.

Edwards, Paul. "'Good Heavens! That's Where I Got It!' McLuhan Reads Wyndham Lewis." *Textual Practice* 35, no. 9 (2021): 1453–71.

Genosko, Gary, ed. *Marshall McLuhan: Critical Evaluations in Cultural Theory.* New York: Routledge, 2005.

Gordon, W. Terrence. *Marshall McLuhan: Escape into Understanding—a Biography.* New York: Basic Books, 1997.

Grosswiler, Paul. *Method Is the Message: Rethinking McLuhan through Critical Theory.* Montreal: Black Rose, 1998.

Havers, Grant. "The Global Electric Republic: Teaching the Timeless in the Digital Age." In *Foundations of Education: A Christian Vision,* edited by Matthew Etherington, 181–91. Eugene, OR: Wipf and Stock, 2014.

Havers, Grant. "History as Progress or Reversal? The Mythical Prognostications of Kojève and McLuhan." In *Canadian Conservative Political Thought,* edited by Lee Trepanier and Richard Avramenko, 205–19. New York: Routledge, 2023.

Havers, Grant. "Marshall McLuhan and the Machiavellian Use of Religious Violence." In *Faith, War, and Violence,* vol. 39 of *Religion and Public Life,* edited by Gabriel R. Ricci, 179–203. New Brunswick, NJ: Transaction, 2014.

Havers, Grant. "Marshall McLuhan, George Grant, and the Ancient-Modern-Protestant Quarrel in Canada." In *Liberal Education, Civic Education, and the Canadian Regime,* edited by David Livingstone, 140–68. Montreal: McGill-Queen's University Press, 2015.

Havers, Grant. "Remembering Marshall McLuhan: The Oracle of Mass Media." *Chronicles* 46 (October 2022): 20–23.

Havers, Grant. "The Right-Wing Postmodernism of Marshall McLuhan." *Media, Culture & Society* 25 (2011): 511–25.

Jacobs, Alan. "Why Bother with Marshall McLuhan?" *New Atlantis,* Spring 2011.

Kahn, Elaine. *Been Hoping We Might Meet Again: The Letters of Pierre Elliott Trudeau and Marshall McLuhan.* Toronto: Novalis, 2019.

Kroker, Arthur. *Technology and the Canadian Mind: Innis/McLuhan/Grant.* Montreal: New World Perspectives, 1984.

Macdonald, Dwight. "He Has Looted All Culture, from Cave Painting to *Mad* Magazine, for Fragments to Shore Up against the Ruin of His System." In *McLuhan: Hot & Cool; A Primer for the Understanding of & a Critical Symposium with a Rebuttal by McLuhan,* edited by Gerald Emanuel Stearn, 203–10. New York: Signet Books, 1967.

Marchand, Philip. *Marshall McLuhan: The Medium and the Messenger.* Cambridge, MA: MIT Press, 1998.

Marchessault, Janine. *Marshall McLuhan: Cosmic Media.* London: Sage, 2005.

McEwen, Cameron. "The Voegelin-McLuhan Correspondence." *VoegelinView,* October 21, 2021. https://voegelinview.com/mcluhans-secret-societies-problem/.

McKinney, Cait. "Computers Made of Paper, Genders Made of Cards." In *Re-understanding Media: Feminist Extensions of Marshall McLuhan,* edited by Sarah Sharma and Rianka Singh, 142–62. Durham, NC: Duke University Press, 2022.

Miller, Jonathan. *McLuhan.* London: Fontana, 1971.

Morrissey, Christopher S. "Marshall McLuhan: Canadian Political Philosophy for the Digital Age." In *Canadian Conservative Political Thought,* edited by Lee Trepanier and Richard Avramenko, 189–204. New York: Routledge, 2023.

Nevitt, Barrington, with Maurice McLuhan. *Who Was Marshall McLuhan? Exploring a Mosaic of Impressions.* Edited by Frank Zingrone, Wayne Constantineau, and Eric McLuhan. Toronto: Stoddart, 1994.

Nowlan, David, and Nadine Nowlan. *The Bad Trip: The Untold Story of the Spadina Expressway.* Toronto: House of Anansi, 1970.

Powe, B. W. *Marshall McLuhan and Northrop Frye: Apocalypse and Alchemy*. Toronto: University of Toronto Press, 2014.
Rae, Alice. "McLuhan's Unconscious." PhD diss., School of History and Politics, University of Adelaide, May 2008.
Ripatrazone, Nick. *Digital Communion: Marshall McLuhan's Spiritual Vision for a Virtual Age*. Minneapolis: Fortress, 2022.
Sharma, Sarah, ed. *Re-understanding Media: Feminist Extensions of Marshall McLuhan*. Durham, NC: Duke University Press, 2022.
Stahlman, Mark D. "The Place of Marshall McLuhan in the Learning of His Times." *Renascence* 64, no. 1 (Fall 2011): 5–17.
Stamps, Judith. *Unthinking Modernity: Innis, McLuhan, and the Frankfurt School*. Montreal: McGill-Queen's University Press, 1995.
Stearn, Gerald Emanuel, ed. *McLuhan: Hot & Cool; A Primer for the Understanding of & a Critical Symposium with a Rebuttal by McLuhan*. New York: Signet Books, 1967.
Theall, Donald. *The Virtual McLuhan*. Montreal: McGill-Queen's University Press, 2001.
Trujillo Liñán, Laura. *Formal Cause in Marshall McLuhan's Thinking: An Aristotelian Perspective*. New York: Institute of General Semantics, 2022.
Willmott, Glenn. *McLuhan, or Modernism in Reverse*. Toronto: University of Toronto Press, 1996.
Wolfe, Tom. "McLuhan's New World." *Wilson Quarterly* 28, no. 2 (Spring 2004): 18–25.

OTHER WORKS CITED

Agar, Nicholas. "Beyond the Reaches of Big Academia, There Could [Be] a Bright Future for the Humanities in Pamphleteering." *Religion & Ethics*, April 15, 2024. https://www.abc.net.au/religion/nicholas-agar-humanities-phamphlets-big-academic-publishing/103729186.
Ahmari, Sohrab. "Learning from a Complex Tradition." *American Conservative*, February 14, 2023. https://www.theamericanconservative.com/learning-from-a-complex-tradition.
Akhtar Allana, and Marguerite Ward. "Bill Gates and Steve Jobs Raised Their Kids with Limited Tech—and It Should Have Been a Red Flag about Our Own Smartphone Use." *Business Insider*, May 15, 2020. https://www.businessinsider.com/screen-time-limits-bill-gates-steve-jobs-red-flag-2017-10.
Allen, Elise Ann. "More than a Hundred Comedians Meet the Pope." *Catholic Herald*, June 15, 2024. https://catholicherald.co.uk/more-than-a-hundred-comedians-meet-the-pope.
Allen, Joe. "A Deal with the Digital Devil." *Chronicles* 47, no. 6 (June/July 2023): 10–14.
Aquinas, St. Thomas. *Introduction to St. Thomas Aquinas*. Edited with an introduction by Anton C. Pegis. New York: Modern Library, 1948.
Aristotle. *Metaphysics*. Translated by Richard Hope. Ann Arbor: University of Michigan Press, 1985.
Benchetrit, Jenna. "Apple Gets Crushing Backlash to Its 'Gross' iPad from Celebrities and Artists." *CBC News*, March 9, 2024. https://www.cbc.ca/news/business/apple-ad-backlash-hydraulic-press-1.7198704.
Berger, Chloe. "The Rise of the English Major: BlackRock COO Wants to Recruit Liberal Arts Consultants That 'Have Nothing to Do with Finance or Technology.'" *Fortune*, May 17, 2024. https://fortune.com/2024/05/17/blackrock-coo-robert-goldstein-english-history-liberal-arts-hiring/.

Bhaimiya, Sawdah. "Gen Z Lack Workplace Skills like Debating and Seeing Different Points of View Because They Spend Too Much Time on Social Media, TV Boss Says." *Business Insider*, September 22, 2023. https://www.businessinsider.com/gen-z-lacking-workplace-skills-social-media-channel-4-boss-2023-9.

Biden, Joe. "Remarks by Joe Biden on the Third Anniversary of the January 6 Attack and Defending the Sacred Cause of American Democracy/Blue Bell, PA." January 5, 2024. https://www.whitehouse.gov/briefing-room/speeches-remarks/2024/01/05/remarks-by-president-biden-on-the-third-anniversary-of-the-january-6th-attack-and-defending-the-sacred-cause-of-american-democracy-blue-bell-pa/.

Biever, Celeste. "The Easy Intelligence Tests That AI Chatbots Fail." *Nature* 619 (July 27, 2023): 686–89.

Bloom, Allan. "Interpretive Essay." In *The Republic of Plato*, 307–436. New York: Basic Books, 1968.

Borger, Julian. "Guterres Warns Humanity on 'Knife's Edge' as AI Raises Nuclear War Threat." *The Guardian*, June 7, 2024. https://www.theguardian.com/world/article/2024/jun/07/ai-nuclear-war-threat-un-secretary-general.

Bucher, Taina. "Want to Be on the Top? Algorithmic Power and the Threat of Invisibility on Facebook." *New Media & Society* 14, no. 7 (2012): 1164–80.

Burnham, James. *The Managerial Revolution: What Is Happening in the World*. New York: John Day, 1941.

Butterfield, Michelle. "A 'New' Beatles Song Is Coming, with a Little Help from AI." *Global News*, June 13, 2023. https://globalnews.ca/news/9765489/new-beatles-song-artificial-intelligence/.

Ceaser, James W. "Foundational Concepts and American Political Development." In *Nature and History in American Political Development*, edited by James W. Ceaser, 3–89. Cambridge, MA: Harvard University Press, 2008.

Cody, Anthony. *The Educator and the Oligarch: A Teacher Challenges the Gates Foundation*. New York: Garn, 2014.

Cooper, Barry, and Marco Navarro-Génie. *COVID-19: The Politics of a Pandemic Moral Panic*. Winnipeg: Frontier Centre for Public Policy, 2021.

Deneen, Patrick J. "JS Mill and the Despotism of Progress." *UnHerd*, May 1, 2023. https://unherd.com/2023/05/js-mill-and-the-despotism-of-progress/.

Deneen, Patrick J. *Regime Change: Toward a Postliberal Future*. New York: Sentinel, 2023.

Deneen, Patrick J. *Why Liberalism Failed*. New Haven, CT: Yale University Press, 2019.

Eidelberg, Paul. *Jerusalem vs. Athens: In Quest of a General Theory of Existence*. Lanham, MD: University Press of America, 1983.

Eliade, Mircea. *The Sacred and the Profane: The Nature of Religion*. Translated by W. R. Trask. New York: Harcourt Brace, 1959.

Ellmers, Glenn. "'Conservatism' Is No Longer Enough." *American Mind*, March 24, 2021. https://americanmind.org/salvo/why-the-claremont-institute-is-not-conservative-and-you-shouldnt-be-either/.

The Federalist. New York: Modern Library, 1964.

Foran, Charles. "The Canada Experiment: Is This the World's First 'Postnational' Country?" *The Guardian*, January 4, 2017. https://www.theguardian.com/world/2017/jan/04/the-canada-experiment-is-this-the-worlds-first-postnational-country.

Freud, Sigmund. *New Introductory Lectures on Psycho-Analysis*. Translated by James Strachey. New York: W. W. Norton, 1965.

Friedersdorf, Conor. "Canada's Extremist Attack on Free Speech." *The Atlantic*, June 6, 2024.
Garcia, Refugio. "Elon Musk Believes 'Super Intelligence' Is Inevitable and Could End Humanity." *Observer*, March 26, 2024. https://observer.com/2024/03/elon-musk-discuss-artificial-general-intelligence/.
Gasché, Rodolphe. *Plato's Stranger: An Essay*. Albany: SUNY Press, 2022.
Gottfried, Paul. "The Administrative State's Digital Currency Ruse." *Chronicles* 47, no. 11 (November 2023): 6–8.
Haidt, Jonathan. "Marshall McLuhan on Why Content Moderation Is a Red Herring." *AfterBabel*, February 22, 2024. https://www.afterbabel.com/p/content-moderation-red-herring.
Havelock, Eric A. *Preface to Plato*. Cambridge, MA: Harvard University Press, 1963.
Havers, Grant. *Lincoln and the Politics of Christian Love*. Columbia: University of Missouri Press, 2009.
Holy Bible. Revised Standard Version. San Francisco: Ignatius, 2006.
Hume, David. "Of the Liberty of the Press." In *Essays Moral, Political, and Literary*, edited by Eugene F. Miller, 604–5. Indianapolis: Liberty Classics, 1985.
Hurley, Lawrence. "Supreme Court Tosses Out Claim Biden Administration Coerced Social Media Companies to Remove Content." NBC News, June 26, 2024. https://www.nbcnews.com/politics/supreme-court/supreme-court-tosses-claim-biden-administration-coerced-social-media-c-rcna151356.
Innis, Harold A. *The Bias of Communication*. 2nd ed. Toronto: University of Toronto Press, 2008. Original edition published in 1951.
Innis, Harold A. *Empire and Communications*. Toronto: University of Toronto Press, 1950.
Jargon, Julie. "TikTok Brain Explained: Why Some Kids Seem Hooked on Social Video Feeds." *Wall Street Journal*, April 2, 2022. https://www.wsj.com/articles/tiktok-brain-explained-why-some-kids-seem-hooked-on-social-video-feeds-11648866192.
Joyce, James. *Finnegans Wake*. New York: Penguin, 1988.
Justice, Tristan. "Google-Owned YouTube Deplatforms Pro-Life Group LifeSiteNews." *The Federalist*, February 10, 2021. https://thefederalist.com/2021/02/10/google-owned-youtube-deplatforms-pro-life-group-lifesitenews/.
Karadeglija, Anja. "With AI, Workplace Surveillance Has 'Skyrocketed': But Are Canadian Laws Keeping Up?" *Canadian Press*, March 9, 2024: https://globalnews.ca/news/10347042/artificial-intelligence-workplace-surveillance/.
Kendall, Willmoore, with George W. Carey. "The 'Intensity Problem' and Democratic Theory." In *Willmoore Kendall contra Mundum*, edited by Nellie D. Kendall, 469–506. New Rochelle, NY: Arlington House, 1971.
Kennedy, John F. "Acceptance of Democratic Nomination for President." John F. Kennedy Presidential Library and Museum, July 15, 1960. https://www.jfklibrary.org/learn/about-jfk/historic-speeches/acceptance-of-democratic-nomination-for-president.
Kierkegaard, Søren. "The Sayings of Kierkegaard." In *Classics of Philosophy*, edited by Louis P. Pojman and Lewis Vaughn, 942–44. New York: Oxford University Press, 2011.
Kruks, Sonja. *Retrieving Experience: Subjectivity and Recognition in Feminist Politics*. Ithaca, NY: Cornell University Press, 2001.
Kurtz, Judy, and Amie Parnes. "Trump Can't Shake Off Taylor Swift Talk in Courting Young Voters." *The Hill*, June 22, 2024. https://thehill.com/homenews/campaign/4734062-trump-taylor-swift-endorsement/.

Lancaster, Roger. "Identity Politics Can Only Get Us So Far." *Jacobin*, August 3, 2017. https://www.jacobinmag.com/2017/08/identity-politics-gay-rights-neoliberalism-stonewall-feminism-race.

Lewis, Wyndham. *America and Cosmic Man*. Garden City, NY: Doubleday, 1949.

Lipman, Joanne. "The Pandemic Revealed How Much We Hate Our Jobs. Now We Have a Chance to Reinvent Work." *Time*, May 27, 2021. https://time.com/6051955/work-after-covid-19/.

Lucas, Fred. "Jordan Peterson: Government-Corporate Collusion 'Threatens Everyone's Freedom Equally.'" *Daily Signal*, March 7, 2024. https://www.dailysignal.com/2024/03/07/jordan-peterson-warns-congress-we-are-in-danger-of-eliminating-the-private-sphere.

MacDonald, Brennan. "AI Could Have Catastrophic Consequences—Is Canada Ready?" CBC News, March 17, 2024. https://www.cbc.ca/news/politics/advanced-artificial-intelligence-ri.k-extinction-humans-1.7144372.

Machiavelli, Niccolò. *Discourses on Livy*. Translated by Harvey C. Mansfield and Nathan Tarcov. Chicago: University of Chicago Press, 1996.

Machiavelli, Niccolò. *The Prince*. Translated by Harvey C. Mansfield. Chicago: University of Chicago Press, 1998.

Mancini, Jeannine. "Elon Musk Predicts a 'Universal High Income' as Jobs Are Phased Out and Employment Becomes Obsolete—It'll Be 'Somewhat of an Equalizer.'" *Yahoo Finance*, March 18, 2024. https://finance.yahoo.com/news/elon-musk-predicts-universal-high-160015532.html.

Mandeville, Bernard. *The Fable of the Bees, or Private Vices, Publick Benefits*. Edited by Lewis Primer. New York: Capricorn Books, 1962.

Mansur, Salim. *The Muddle of Multiculturalism: A Liberal Critique*. Halifax, NS: Atlantic Institute for Market Studies, 2010.

Markham, Annette N. "Pattern Recognition: Using Rocks, Wind, Water, and Doom Scrolling in a Slow Apocalypse (to Learn More about Methods for Changing the World)." *Qualitative Inquiry* 27, no. 7 (2021): 914–27.

Marx, Karl. *The Eighteenth Brumaire of Louis Bonaparte*. In *The Marx-Engels Reader*, edited by Robert C. Tucker, 594–617. New York: W. W. Norton, 1978.

McGilchrist, Iain. *The Master and His Emissary: The Divided Brain and the Making of the Modern World*. New Haven, CT: Yale University Press, 2009.

"Media and Technology Philosophy." Waldorf School of the Peninsula. Accessed July 12, 2024. https://waldorfpeninsula.org/curriculum/media-technology-philosophy/.

Mill, John Stuart. *On Liberty*. In *On Liberty, and Other Essays*, 5–128. Oxford: Oxford University Press, 1991.

Minkov, Svetozar, and Rasoul Namazi. "'Religion and the Commonweal': An Unpublished Lecture by Leo Strauss." *American Political Thought* 10 (Winter 2021): 86–120.

Mollman, Steve. "ChatGPT Must Be Regulated and A.I. 'Can Be Used by Bad Actors,' Warns OpenAI's CTO." *Fortune*, February 25, 2023. https://fortune.com/2023/02/05/artificial-intelligence-must-be-regulated-chatgpt-openai-cto-mira-murati/.

Nawaz, Anna. "Air National Guardsman Arrested, Accused of Leaking Classified Documents Online." PBS NewsHour, April 13, 2023. https://www.pbs.org/newshour/show/air-national-guardsman-arrested-accused-of-leaking-classified-documents-online.

The New Frontiersmen: Profiles of the Men around Kennedy. Washington, DC: Public Affairs Press, 1961.

Nisbet, Robert. *The Present Age: Progress and Anarchy in Modern America.* Indianapolis: Liberty Fund, 1988.

Noll, Mark A. *The Civil War as a Theological Crisis.* Chapel Hill: University of North Carolina Press, 2006.

O'Brien, Matt. "Former OpenAI Employees Lead Push to Protect Whistleblowers Flagging Artificial Intelligence Risks." Associated Press, June 4, 2024. https://apnews.com/article/openai-whistleblowers-chatgpt-15a02ca9c0b5170d99bfc0172c35b6ba.

O'Neill, John. *Plato's Cave: Television and Its Discontents.* Cresskill, NJ: Hampton, 2004.

Phelan, Matthew. "Tesla Robot ATTACKS an Engineer at Company's Texas Factory during Violent Malfunction—Leaving 'Trail of Blood' and Forcing Workers to Hit Emergency Shutdown." *Daily Mail*, December 26, 2023. https://www.dailymail.co.uk/sciencetech/article-12869629/Tesla-robot-ATTACKS-engineer-companys-Texas-factory-violent-malfunction-leaving-trail-blood-forcing-workers-hit-emergency-shutdown-button.html.

Piers, Craig. "Even ChatGPT Says ChatGPT Is Racially Biased." *Scientific American*, February 9, 2024. https://www.scientificamerican.com/article/even-chatgpt-says-chatgpt-is-racially-biased/.

Plato. *Cratylus.* In *The Collected Dialogues of Plato, including the Letters*, edited by Edith Hamilton and Huntington Cairns, 421–74. Princeton, NJ: Princeton University Press, 1982.

Plato. "Epistle VII." In *Epistles*, translated by Glenn R. Morrow, 215–50. New York: Bobbs-Merrill, 1962.

Plato. *The Laws.* In *The Collected Dialogues of Plato, including the Letters*, edited by Edith Hamilton and Huntington Cairns, 1225–513. Princeton, NJ: Princeton University Press, 1982.

Plato. *Phaedrus.* In *The Collected Dialogues of Plato, including the Letters*, edited by Edith Hamilton and Huntington Cairns, 475–525. Princeton, NJ: Princeton University Press, 1982.

Plato. *The Republic of Plato.* Translated by Allan Bloom. New York: Basic Books, 1968.

Poe, Edgar Allan. "A Descent into the Maelstrom." In *The Complete Tales and Poems of Edgar Allan Poe*, 57–67. Secaucus, NJ: Castle, 1985.

Polka, Brayton. *Truth and Interpretation: An Essay in Thinking.* New York: St. Martin's, 1990.

Popova, Maria. "Tom Wolfe on Marshall McLuhan for His 100th Would-Be Birthday." *The Marginalian*, June 21, 2011. https://www.themarginalian.org/2011/07/21/tom-wolfe-on-marshall-mcluhan/.

Postman, Neil. *The Disappearance of Childhood.* New York: Vintage, 1982.

Pugh, Joseph. "A New Streaming Bill Is Close to Becoming Law in Canada." CBC News, March 3, 2023. https://www.cbc.ca/news/entertainment/bill-c-11-explained-1.6759878.

Quay, Grayson. "Algorithmic Spirituality." *First Things*, June 7, 2024. https://www.firstthings.com/web-exclusives/2024/06/algorithmic-spirituality.

Quigley, Carroll. "McLuhan as a Global Verbalizer." *Sunday Star* (Washington, DC), September 15, 1968.

Reilly, Robert R. *America on Trial: A Defense of the Founding.* San Francisco: Ignatius, 2020.

Rogers, Adam. "The Secret Digital Behaviors of Gen Z." *Business Insider*, June 25, 2024. https://www.businessinsider.com/gen-z-most-trusted-news-source-online-comment-sections-google-2024-6.

Roland, Charles G. "Review of 'Through the Vanishing Point: Space in Poetry and Painting.'" *JAMA* 207, no. 12 (March 24, 1969): 2287.

Rufo, Christopher F. "How DEI Corrupts America's Universities." *City Journal*, June 23, 2024. https://www.city-journal.org/article/how-dei-corrupts-americas-universities.

Said, Summer, and Rory Jones. "Gaza Chief's Brutal Calculation: Civilian Bloodshed Will Help Hamas." *Wall Street Journal*, June 10, 2024. https://www.wsj.com/world/middle-east/gaza-chiefs-brutal-calculation-civilian-bloodshed-will-help-hamas-626720e7.

"Sam Altman: There's No 'Magic Red Button' to Stop AI." *OpenAI Developer Forum*, January 18, 2024. https://community.openai.com/t/sam-altman-there-s-no-magic-red-button-to-stop-ai/592718.

Schiffer, Zoë, and Casey Newton. "Elon Musk Fires a Top Twitter Engineer over His Declining View Count." *Platformer*, February 9, 2023. https://www.platformer.news/elon-musk-fires-a-top-twitter-engineer/.

Schlott, Rikki. "China Is Hurting Our Kids with TikTok but Protecting Its Own Youth with Douyin." *New York Post*, February 26, 2023. https://nypost.com/2023/02/25/china-is-hurting-us-kids-with-tiktok-but-protecting-its-own/.

Sharma, Bhakti, Susanna S. Lee, and Benjamin K. Johnson, "The Dark at the End of the Tunnel: Doomscrolling on Social Media Newsfeeds." *Technology, Mind, and Behavior* 3, no. 1 (Spring 2022): 1–13.

Slotkin, Richard. *A Great Disorder: National Myth and the Battle for America*. Cambridge, MA: Belknap Press of Harvard University Press, 2024.

Smith, Christian, and Melinda Lundquist Denton. *Soul Searching: The Religious and Spiritual Lives of American Teenagers*. Oxford: Oxford University Press, 2005.

Srigley, Ron. "Ron Srigley on Cellphones: Why Were They Ever Allowed in Schools?" *Telegraph-Journal* (Moncton, New Brunswick), March 2, 2024. https://tj.news/new-brunswick/srigley-why-were-cellphones-ever-allowed-in-schools.

Stackpole, Thomas. "Content Moderation Is Terrible by Design." *Harvard Business Review*, November 9, 2022.

Stokel-Walker, Chris. "Generative AI Is Coming for the Lawyers." *Wired*, February 21, 2023. https://www.wired.co.uk/article/generative-ai-is-coming-for-the-lawyers.

Strauss, Leo. *Liberalism Ancient and Modern*. Chicago: University of Chicago Press, 1995.

Strauss, Leo. "Review of Julius Ebbinghaus, *On the Progress of Metaphysics*." In *The Early Writings (1921–1932)*, translated by Michael Zank, 214–16. Albany: SUNY Press, 2002.

Tate, Kristin. "Coming Soon: America's Own Social Credit System." *The Hill*, August 3, 2021. https://thehill.com/opinion/finance/565860-coming-soon-americas-own-social-credit-system/.

Thiel, Peter. "The Straussian Moment." In *Politics and Apocalypse*, edited by Robert Hamerton-Kelly, 189–218. East Lansing: Michigan State University Press, 2007.

Trepanier, Lee. "How AI Could Save Liberal Education." *Law & Liberty*, March 17, 2023. https://lawliberty.org/how-ai-could-save-liberal-education/.

"Trump Jokes about Sexual Assault Verdict at CNN Town Hall Event." *Al Jazeera*, May 11, 2023. https://www.aljazeera.com/news/2023/5/11/trump-jokes-about-sexual-assault-verdict-repeats-election-lies.

Vico, Giambattista. *The Autobiography of Giambattista Vico*. Translated by Max Fisch and Thomas Goddard Bergin. Ithaca, NY: Cornell University Press, 1975.

Vico, Giambattista. *The New Science of Giambattista Vico*. Translated by Thomas Goddard Bergin and Max Harold Fisch. Ithaca, NY: Cornell University Press, 1984.

Vico, Giambattista. *Selected Writings*. Edited and translated by Leon Pompa. Cambridge: Cambridge University Press, 1982.

Voegelin, Eric. *Science, Politics, and Gnosticism: Two Essays*. Washington, DC: Regnery, 1997.

Von Heyking, John. "Liberal Education, Friendship, and the 'Political Art in the True Sense.'" In *Human Dignity, Education, and Political Society: A Philosophical Defense of the Liberal Arts*, edited by James Greenaway, 57–85. Lanham, MD: Lexington Books, 2020.

Waletzko, Anna. "Why Print Media Is Back and Better than Ever." *Canvas* 8, October 9, 2023. https://www.canvas8.com/blog/2023/september/why-print-media-is-back-and-better-than ever.

"What Happened When Reporter Asked AI to Destroy Her Life." CNN News Central, March 13, 2024. https://transcripts.cnn.com/show/cnc/date/2024-03-13/segment/12.

Wheatland, Casey. "Founding Fathers and Red Caesar." *American Mind*, October 20, 2023. https://americanmind.org/salvo/founding-fathers-and-red-caesar/.

Wills, Garry. *Explaining America: The Federalist*. New York: Penguin Books, 1982.

Xenophon. *Memorabilia*. In *Memorabilia. Oeconomicus. Symposium. Apology*, translated by E. C. Marchant and O. J. Todd, 2–359. Loeb Classical Library. Cambridge, MA: Harvard University Press, 1923.

Zheng, Jing, and D. Bondy Valdovinos Kaye. "From Content Moderation to *Visibility Moderation*: A Case Study of Platform Governance on TikTok." *Policy & Internet* 14 (2022): 79–95.

Index

absenteeism, 90
acoustic space, 40, 42, 73, 74, 85, 97, 142, 149. *See also* orality; tribalism; visual space
Adler, Mortimer, 115–16
advertising, 32, 64–66, 129, 143
Agrippa, King, 150
Africa, 97
Ahmari, Sohrab, 56
Allen, Joe, 93
Allen, Woody, 6, 22
alphabet (phonetic), 34, 42, 44, 103, 119, 141
Altman, Sam, 5
Amazon, 73, 76
angelism, 92–93, 149
Annie Hall, 6
Anti-Christ, 10, 148–49, 151, 156
anti-environment, 49, 82, 114–15
Apocalypse, 9, 93, 148–60. *See also* Bible
Apple, 67–68
Aquinas, Saint Thomas, 93, 124, 152–53
archaism, 126
archetype, 55. *See also* cliché
Aristotle, 7, 32, 42–47, 112, 152, 153; on causation, 46; on contradiction, 112–13, 122; dualism and, 117; on human nature, 88; *Metaphysics*, 46; on nature, 45; *Physics*, 45; on speech, 79. *See also* formal causality
art, 27, 86, 114, 123, 129, 138, 159; French symbolism, 32; vorticist, 14, 27, 127
artificial intelligence (AI), 4, 6, 34, 73, 78–81, 115, 119–20, 134, 139–40, 150, 152, 158–59
artist, 29, 89, 126–27, 146–47
Assumption College (Windsor), 14
atheism, 124, 156
auditory space, 131

Babin, Pierre, 93, 141–42, 148
Bacon, Francis, 112, 124, 131
banks, 106; data, 75
Beatles, the, 157
Belloc, Hilaire, 12
Bible: creation and, 121, 151; on the Fall, 121, 122; false prophets, 149; history and, 55; literacy and, 153–55; morality of, 141–42; Old Testament, 135; the role of the shepherd in, 147; on sin, 123; on slavery, 100; Torah, 154. *See also* Anti-Christ; Apocalypse; Christianity; Genesis; Nature, Book of; Scripture, Book of; Torah, the
bicameral mind, 9, 119. *See also* left hemisphere (brain); right hemisphere (brain); split-brain
Biden, Joe, 75, 103, 106
Black power movement, 97
BlackRock, 115
Blake, William, 123
Bloom, Allan, 179n
Bonanza, 109
books, 71; private goals and, 116; as probe, 111
bourgeois, 8, 52, 56, 58–59, 61, 97–98, 103, 147; capitalism, 68–70, 73–74, 85, 105; economics, 99; fixed identity, 58; fragmented individuals in, 77; outer trip, 105; politics, 60; preoccupation with rights, 76; visual bias of, 58. *See also* individualism; privacy; private identity
Bradbrook, Muriel C., 14
Brokaw, Tom, 57
Burnham, James, 74
ByteDance, 75

C-11, Bill (Online Streaming Act), 109
Cadmus, King, 34
Calvin, John, 137–38
Cambridge University, 141
Canada, 9, 107–9; as anti-environment, 49; bilingualism, 108; borderlines, 109; central, 109; cultural mosaic, 108; identity of, 107; Maritime provinces, 109; multiculturalism, 108; relation to United States, 49–50, 100, 107–9; western, 12, 109
cancel culture, 76–77
capitalism, 8, 17, 64–81, 124, 134; artificial intelligence and, 78; competition within, 69; education and, 77–78; nature and, 83–84; postbourgeois, 70–76, 105–6; Protestantism and, 135; surveillance state and, 105–6; tribalism and, 68, 99. *See also* bourgeois
Carey, George W., 57
Carnegie, Dale, 136

199

Carpenter, Edmund, 15
cars, 66
Carter, Jimmy, 57
Catholic Church, 93, 148, 153–56; synodality, 155. *See also* Vatican II
Ceaser, James W., 55
centre/margin, 58–60, 72, 75, 95, 104, 107, 109
Centre for Culture and Technology, 17, 22
Chaillan, Nicolas, 76
Chardin, Teilhard de, 18
charity, 141, 149. *See also* Golden Rule
ChatGPT, 78, 80, 115. *See also* artificial intelligence
Chesterton, G. K., 12, 124
childhood, 25
China, 9, 75, 106; Communist Party, 75–76, 105
Christianity, 10; on change, 123, 159; charity, 141, 149; church, 93; and City of God, 147; creation and, 120, 151–52; "death" of, 124; and democracy, 141; discarnate identity and, 156; against dualisms, 92, 156; on faith and reason, 159; formal causality and, 122; myth of, 148–49; paradox and, 150–52; propaganda, 120; on love, 162; simultaneity and, 149; on sin, 122, 146; theology, 88, 124, 155; unworldly, 155. *See also* Anti-Christ; Bible; Jesus Christ; natural law; Paul, Saint
Churchill, Winston, 60
CIA, 75
Cicero, 122
Civil War, 58, 100
cliché, 45, 55, 95, 121. *See also* archetype
climate change, 151
Clinton, Bill, 138
clocks, 69
Cody, Anthony, 78
Cold War, 105
Common Core, 77–78
communism, 101. *See also* Marxism
computers, 77–78, 80, 93, 183
concepts, 12, 124. *See also* percepts
Confucius, 133
conservatism, 5, 50–51, 54, 70
Constitution (US), 53, 54
content moderation, 25
cool media, 30–31, 57–58, 61. *See also* hot media
Cooper, Barry, 94
correspondence theory of truth, 36–37. *See also* matching
COVID-19 lockdown, 91, 94
credit card, 70
Cronkite, William, 71

cubism, 37. *See also* art
Culkin, Fr. John, 122

Dahl, Roald, 76
D'Amico, Margarita, 156
Darwin, Charles, 151
Davey, Jim, 21, 66
debate, 57
deism, moralistic therapeutic, 142
democracy, 9, 33, 73, 103, 115, 128, 139–42
Deneen, Patrick, 56–7
Denton, Melinda Lundquist, 142
Descartes, René, 79, 124
detached involvement, 35
detachment, 29, 36, 40–41, 70, 85, 104, 160–61; Christian faith and, 159–60; the ear and, 41; education and, 114; the eye and, 42; nature and, 119; politics and, 60; versus involvement, 71; left hemisphere and, 118
determinism, 124; biological, 161; economic, 124; technological, 150
Dew-Line newsletter, 20
dialectics, 112–13, 115, 117. *See also* Aristotle; logic; philosophy; Plato
discarnate identity, 8, 10, 92–94, 134, 153, 156–59, 162. *See also* electric and digital media; Gnosticism
Distant Early Warning (DEW) system, 49
distributism, 12
Diversity, Equity, and Inclusion (DEI), 98
doomscrolling, 149
Drucker, Peter, 145
dualism, 9, 10, 47, 92–93, 104, 113, 115, 117, 123–24, 129, 156–57. *See also* dialectics; Gnosticism

education, 77, 113–14
Edwards, Paul, 92
Egypt, 42
Eichmann, Adolf, 94
Eidelberg, Paul, 153–54
electric and digital media, 7, 37, 47–48, 51, 64, 70–76, 86, 89, 161; all-at-once, 26, 40, 70, 74, 89–90; attention span and, 131; central nervous system and, 2, 71, 78, 131, 162; decentralization and, 107, 109, 111, 133, 139, 143; decline of literacy and, 50, 156; democracy and, 139, 143; dialogue, 134; first nature, 88–89; inclusive politics of, 60–61; instantaneous information and, 26, 31, 74, 92, 97, 99; lack of secrecy in, 138; magic in, 86; morality and; 157; natural law and, 153, 157; privacy and, 50, 90; reading and, 111; reality and, 90; religion and, 86, 93,

142; second nature and, 89; space-oriented, 31, 53, 55, 70–76, 111, 144; speed of light, 3, 39, 48, 62, 84, 92, 94, 96, 127, 130–31, 148, 155, 162; tribalism and, 97, 157; work and, 90–91. *See also* artificial intelligence (AI); discarnate identity; global village; Gnosticism; radio; social media; television; tribalism
Eliade, Mircea, 39
Ellmers, Glenn, 51
energy, vortices of, 127
enhancement (law of media), 24, 38, 157–58
Enlightenment, the, 50, 53, 124, 179n
entelechies, 46–47
equality, 97, 98
evolution, theory of, 151
Explorations magazine, 15–16, 97

Facebook/Meta, 25, 75–76, 106, 140
fantasy, 91
Fascism, 61
fatalism, 33–35, 41, 123. *See also* paganism
Faulkner, William, 38
Federalist, The, 53, 57
Feigen, Gerald, 18
feminism, 86–87
Festus, 150–51
feudalism, 68
figure, 28, 30, 46, 59, 87, 119, 160. *See also* ground
Fiore, Quentin, 163n
First Amendment, 53
first nature, 8, 43, 87–89, 91, 94, 96, 99, 131, 137, 161–62; discarnate identity and, 92. *See also* nature; second nature
Fleming, Ian, 76
Floyd, George, 91
Ford, Gerald, 57
Ford, Henry, 24, 65
Ford Foundation, 15
Fordham University, 20, 24
formal causality, 7, 32, 39, 46–48, 65–66, 70, 78–79, 83, 86, 106, 111, 122, 127, 131, 143–44, 146, 158. *See also* Aristotle
Francis, Pope, 155
freedom of speech, 57, 72, 97, 99
Freud, Sigmund, 22, 112–13
Fulford, Robert, 5
futurism, 126

Garner, Rempel, 79
Gates, Bill, 77–78
Gay, John, 70
Gen Z, 134, 141

gender, 86–87
Genesis, 9, 131; Eden, 121; the Fall, 121–22; first Adam, 113, 121, 125, 153–54, 156; second Adam, 9, 113, 121–22, 156. *See also* Bible; Christianity
Gestalt, 30
Gibson, Henry, 18
Giovanelli, Felix, 14
global theatre, 29, 62, 72, 91
global village, 8, 18, 50, 56, 62, 70, 75, 89–90, 114, 147, 154, 156, 159: conformity in, 97; instantaneous information in, 99; involvement with, 97; lack of privacy in, 157; violence in, 95–109
Gnosticism, 8, 87, 92–93, 123, 153, 157
Golden Rule, 142. *See also* charity
Goldman Sachs, 115
Goldstein, Robert, 115
Goldwater, Barry, 52
Google, 134
Gossage, Howard, 18
Gould, Glenn, 17
grammar, 14, 16, 117–18, 122, 132
great books programs, 9, 113–16
Great Depression, 61
Greeks, ancient, 42, 43, 44, 46–47, 88, 112, 119, 121, 122, 134. *See also* Aristotle; Heraclitus; Plato; Socrates
ground, 28, 30, 46, 47, 59, 87, 92, 119, 120, 138, 160. *See also* figure
guaranteed income, 81
Gutenberg, Johannes, 68, 121, 142, 154
Guterres, António, 158

Haidt, Jonathan, 25
Hamas, 96
Hamilton, Alexander, 52, 74
hardware, 107; versus software, 99
Havelock, Eric A., 41, 47
Hawn, Goldie, 18
Hearst, William Randolph, 58
Heraclitus, 25, 112
historicism, 54–5
Hitler, Adolf, 59–60, 98–99
Hoffman, Abbie, 18
Hollywood, 61, 65, 87
Homer, 117, 177n
Hopkins, Gerard Manley, 12
hot media, 30–31, 57–58, 61. *See also* cool media
hubris, 123
Hume, David, 52
Hutchins, Robert Maynard, 115–16
Hutchon, Kathryn, 16, 77

INDEX

identity: and electric media, 84, 98, 157, 162; group, 52, 98, 100, 157; loss of, 51, 92; politics of, 98; search for, 129, 134; violence and, 84, 90, 95–96. *See also* private identity
idolatry, 122–23, 152, 162. *See also* Bible; Christianity
individualism, 5, 41–46, 51, 53, 56, 59, 61, 70, 71, 83, 98, 103, 147. *See also* bourgeois; literacy; privacy; private identity
Industrial Revolution, 11, 13, 26, 68
inner trip, 1–2, 86, 105; and outer trip, 105
Innis, Harold Adams, 15, 31, 47, 53, 55, 70, 97, 98
Instagram, 140
interchange, 87, 106
interface, 67, 84, 87, 92, 96, 103, 114
internet, misinformation on, 57
iPad, 67–68

Jacobs, Alan, 145
Jacobs, Jane, 21
Jay, John, 53
Jefferson, Thomas, 63, 73–74
Jeopardy!, 32
Jesus Christ, 92; Anti-Christ and, 149; Incarnation, 92, 121, 141, 150–51, 159; as second Adam, 121–22
Jigsaw Research, 134
Jobs, Steve, 67
Johnson, Lyndon B., 33, 101
Johnson, Paul, 19
journalism, 71
Joyce, James, 12; *Finnegans Wake*, 21, 33, 104, 150, 175n

Kendall, Willmoore, 57
Kennedy, John F., 31, 33, 60, 101
Kenner, Hugh, 87
Kermode, Frank, 52
Kierkegaard, Søren, 26
Kokotajlo, Daniel, 73
Kruks, Sonia, 98
Kurzweil, Ray, 80

Lancaster, Roger, 98
language, 38, 88, 113, 121, 123, 132. *See also* grammar
Laugh-In, 18
law of noncontradiction, 47, 112, 132. *See also* dialectics; logic; paradox
laws of media, 5, 24, 38, 146. *See also* enhancement (law of media); obsolescence (law of media); retrieval (law of media); reversal (law of media); tetrad

Leary, Timothy, 1
Leavis, F. R., 13
Lee, George, 115
left hemisphere (brain), 9, 22, 113, 118–20, 132. *See also* right hemisphere (brain)
Lennon, John, 18, 78
lethal autonomous weapons systems (LAWS), 157–58
Leuver, Fr. Robert J., 159
Lewis, Percy Wyndham, 14, 16, 18, 87, 164n
liberalism, 53, 56–57. *See also* individuality; privacy
Lincoln, Abraham, 62–63
literacy, 5, 7, 41, 43, 45, 50, 53, 56, 59, 69–71, 83, 112. *See also* individuality; print media; privacy
Logan, Robert K., 119
logic, 14, 80, 85, 112–13, 115, 117, 118, 120, 122, 131. *See also* Aristotle; dialectics; law of noncontradiction
Lucifer, 148, 159
Luther, Martin, 137

Macdonald, Dwight, 110
Machiavelli, Niccolò, 9, 72, 88, 127, 134–39
Mackay, David, 21
Madison, James, 52
Madison Avenue, 75, 129
magazines, 64, 111
magic, 8, 43, 60, 85–87, 89, 92, 94, 129, 162
Mahon, Alex, 141
making, 36–37, 45–46, 80, 90, 118–19, 132, 151, 161. *See also* matching
Mandeville, Bernard, 70, 72, 90, 135, 137
Manos, Michael, 130
Maritain, Jacques, 92
Marx, Karl, 37, 55
Marxism, 37, 61, 66, 99. *See also* communism
Massey Report, 16
matching, 36–37, 45–46, 80, 90, 118–19, 132, 151, 161. *See also* correspondence theory of truth; dualism; making
materialism, 153
McCartney, Paul, 78
McGilchrist, Iain, 120
McKinney, Cait, 20
McLuhan, Elsie, 11
McLuhan, Eric, 13, 16, 20, 25, 29, 42, 47, 77, 118, 146, 153, 183n
McLuhan, Herbert Marshall (father), 11
McLuhan, Marshall: at Cambridge, 12–13; cameo in *Annie Hall*, 6; on charisma, 31; as a conservative, 5; Catholicism, 13, 158; death of, 22; on dropouts, 114; at Fordham University, 20; on figure versus ground,

28, 30; on the "fish in the water," 3, 7, 50, 82–83, 89–90, 113–14, 157; on the "fixed" point of view, 5, 29, 54; formative years in Canada, 11–12; on the human brain, 26–27; on the instincts, 25; on the "laws" of media, 5, 24; marries Corinne Lewis, 13; on "McLuhanites," 146; on moral indignation, 24, 64–67; on politics, 49; poor health, 19–20, 22; popularity in the 1960s, 3, 16–21, 66, 132; professor at St. Michael's College, 14; pro-life and environmental activism, 21–22; on side of print, 110; on television, 116, 177n; as young teacher in North America, 13–14

McLuhan, Marshall, works of: "The Argument: Causality in the Electric World" (with Barrington Nevitt), 140; *The Book of Probes*, 38; "Canada in the Electronic Age," 19; "Catholic Humanism and Modern Letters," 159; *City as Classroom* (with Eric McLuhan and Kathryn Hutchon), 16, 77; *The Classical Trivium*, 14, 121; *Counterblast*, 12, 16, 65, 98, 109, 146; "The Crack in the Rear-View Mirror," 111; *Culture Is Our Business*, 21, 64, 129; "Footprints in the Sands of Crime," 70; *From Cliché to Archetype* (with Wilfred Watson), 21, 25, 45, 55, 132, 135, 150–52; *The Future of the Library* (with Robert K. Logan), 119; "The Future of Sex," 67, 86; "A Garbage Apocalypse," 21, 47, 148; *The Global Village* (with Bruce R. Powers), 45, 87, 93, 94; *The Gutenberg Galaxy*, 15, 17, 39, 40, 41, 58, 66–68, 97, 111, 119, 137; "Joyce, Aquinas, and the Poetic Process," 153; *Laws of Media* (with Eric McLuhan), 13, 25, 29, 40, 84, 112, 118, 119; Marfleet Lectures, 19, 101, 139; *The Mechanical Bride*, 15, 24, 58, 64–68, 73, 116, 136, 138, 159; *The Medium is the Massage*, 18, 49; "Nihilism Exposed," 92; "On Nature and Media," 84, 88; "Open-Mind Surgery," 105; *Playboy* interview, 1–2, 33, 96, 140, 148, 159; "Roles, Masks, and Performances," 133; "Space, Time, and Poetry," 88–89; *Take Today* (with Barrington Nevitt), 21, 30, 37, 44, 72, 74, 85, 99, 105, 106, 142, 150, 153; *Through the Vanishing Point* (with Harley Parker), 21, 49, 119, 126; *Understanding Media*, 17, 23, 39, 40, 41, 65–66, 93, 98, 99, 111, 126, 148, 158; *War and Peace in the Global Village*, 18, 82, 83, 101, 121

McLuhan, Maurice, 11

media: biases of, 15, 31, 55; ecology of, 6; as extensions, 23–24, 30, 71, 89, 132; as forms, 27–28, 31; as hidden environments, 2–3, 26–30, 67, 85, 35, 93, 138, 160; human ignorance of, 27; nature of, 82–94; somnambulistic state and, 17; unintended effects of, 24–25. *See also* social media

medium: as the massage, 18, 32, 127; meaning of, 2, 24; as the message, 2, 4, 18, 30–33, 46, 66, 92, 110, 130

Meredith, George, 11

metaphor, 43, 45, 124

#MeToo movement, 56

Middle Ages, 26, 45, 111, 124, 126

Mill, John Stuart, 56–57

millennials, 130

Miller, Jonathan, 145

Milton, John, 123

mimesis, 44, 103–7, 134

Mishna, 154

movies (film), 64, 75, 87, 129–30

Muggeridge, Malcolm, 17, 19

Murati, Mira, 79

music, 30, 78, 86, 118

Musk, Elon, 72, 81, 150

Mussolini, Benito, 60

myth, 34, 37, 63, 118; the American frontier and, 100; ancient Greek, 122, 128; effect of, 100; religious, 39, 147–49; retrieval of, 143–44

narcissism, 142

Narcissus, 34–35, 122–23, 132. *See also* narcosis

narcosis, 4, 34. *See also* Narcissus

Nashe, Thomas, 117, 129, 135, 137

nation-state, 97

National Association of Educational Broadcasters, 16

nationalism, 58, 97

natural law, 10, 152–59, 162

natural rights, 53, 54

nature: desacralization of, 124; history and, 83, 151; human nature and, 83, 88, 162; instinct, 129; internal versus external, 84–85. *See also* first nature; second nature

Nature, Book of, 113, 121, 123–24, 152–53, 162. *See also* Scripture, Book of

Navarro-Génie, Marco, 94

Nevitt, Barrington, 21, 29, 30, 36, 44–45, 50, 68, 72, 75, 85, 99, 105, 140, 142, 150

New Age, 95

new criticism, 12

Newman, Edwin, 57

Newman, Peter C. 12, 75, 109

news, 71, 89–90; bad news versus good news, 71, 144
newspapers, 57, 71, 111
Newton, Isaac, 124
nihilism, 87, 92
Nisbet, Robert, 116
Nixon, Richard, 31
Noll, Mark A., 100
nostalgia, 51, 53, 84

obsolescence (law of media), 38, 50, 72, 107, 158
Oedipus Rex, 43
O'Neill, John, 128
Ong, Walter, S. J., 153
Online Harms Act (Canada), 57
OpenAI, 5, 73
orality, 7, 40–43, 68–69, 85, 154. *See also* tribalism: preliterate
Oswald, Lee Harvey, 32–33
Oxley, Tom, 79–80

paganism, 122–23, 152. *See also* Aristotle; fatalism; Plato
panic terrors, 94
paradox, 10, 14, 28, 37–38, 47, 53, 54, 82, 98, 112–13, 118, 120, 122, 123, 140, 149–52, 162. *See also* law of noncontradiction
Parker, Harley, 21, 49, 113, 119, 126–27, 132, 144
pattern recognition, 27, 35, 114; feedback and feedforward, 35
Paul, Saint, 123, 150
PayPal, 106
perception, 4, 13, 30, 68, 79, 114, 120, 126, 127, 133, 134, 159
percepts, 12, 124. *See also* concepts
Peterson, Jordan, 73
philosophy: neo-Platonism, 87, 92; pre-Socratic, 86; versus poetry, 117–18. *See also* Aristotle; dialectics; Heraclitus; Plato; Vico
Plato, 22; and the Bible, 122; cave allegory, 9, 127–34, 143, 179n; *Cratylus*, 121, 178n; on democracy, 140; dialectics of, 117; on dialogue, 44, 133; on education, 77; *The Laws*, 133; on making, 45–46, 117–18, 131; on mimesis (imitation), 117–18, 129, 131, 134; on myth, 118, 128, 143; on nature, 44–46, 118, 129; on orality, 43–44; *Phaedrus*, 44; philosopher-king, 132; on poetry, 9, 113, 117, 129, 131; *Republic*, 117, 127–31; on the senses, 129; *Seventh Epistle*, 44; on the "stranger," 133; on technology, 118, 152; on writing, 6, 44–45, 119, 132

Playboy magazine, 1, 33
Poe, Edgar Allan, 27, 65
poet, the, 131
poetry, 11, 115, 117–18, 159. *See also* philosophy; Plato
populism, 9, 62, 128, 144
postliterate, 5, 85–86, 119, 140, 142. *See also* electric and digital media; preliterate; tribalism
Postman, Neil, 25
Powers, Bruce R., 45, 49, 60, 89, 91, 93, 94, 100, 106, 119, 120, 142, 156
Prasad, Eswar, 106
preliterate, 39, 83, 85–86, 119, 131, 161. *See also* postliterate; tribalism
print media, 8, 24, 30, 52, 56, 58, 68–70;; centralism of, 107; conformity and, 53–54, 58–59, 69; deliberation and, 57; homogeneity of, 58, 69, 97; as hot media, 59; individualism and, 52; morality and, 135; retrieval of, 111; time-oriented, 31, 52–53, 68–70; work and, 90. *See also* books; reading; writing
printing press, 53, 68, 142
privacy, 5, 9, 50, 53, 56, 59, 71, 75, 90, 106, 140, 157. *See also* bourgeois; individuality; literacy; private identity
private identity, 41–46, 51, 59, 62, 92–93, 129; and guilt, 93–94, 150; versus public image, 73. *See also* bourgeois; individuality; literacy; privacy
probes, 19, 20, 84, 111, 147
progress, idea of, 124, 129, 143, 149
propaganda, 54, 120
Protestantism, 21, 155; and capitalism, 135; in the electric age, 141–42; and literacy, 141; and nature, 135, 137; work ethic, 70
Psalms, 122
publishing, academic, 111
puns, 147
put-on, the, 19, 71, 74, 76, 147

Quigley, Carroll, 19

racism, 24, 62–63
radio, 30, 92, 98–99; as a hot medium, 31, 33, 57, 59–60
reading, 51–52, 118, 154. *See also* literacy
Reagan, Ronald, 22
rear-view mirror, 7, 26, 49, 124, 146; and US politics, 49–63
Reilly, Robert R., 54
religion, 39, 53, 121, 141, 156–57, 159. *See also* Bible; Christianity; myth

Renaissance, 26, 136
retrieval (law of media), 38, 101, 111, 143–44, 158
reversal (law of media), 38, 61, 74, 85, 86–87, 89, 104, 133, 140, 158
rhetoric, 11, 14, 115, 117, 122, 150
Richards, I. A., 12–13
right hemisphere (brain), 9, 22, 113, 118–20, 132. *See also* left hemisphere (brain)
robotism, 119
roles: versus jobs, 90–91
Roosevelt, Franklin Delano, 60–61
Roosevelt, Theodore, 100–101
Ruby, Jack, 32
Rumble, 140

St. Louis University, 13, 14
Santayana, George, 69
Satan, 123
science, 28–29, 86, 89, 92, 159
science fiction, 147
Schwartz, Eugene, 20
Schwartz, Tony, 20
Scripture, Book of, 113, 123–24, 152, 162. *See also* Bible; Christianity; Nature, Book of
second nature, 8, 43, 87–89, 91, 161. *See also* first nature
Segall, Laurie, 140
senses, the, 42, 76, 78–79, 83, 89, 162; "light through" versus "light on," 132; as natural knowledge, 162; natural law and, 153; ratio of, 38
servo-mechanisms, 78, 89, 122
Shakespeare, William, 66
Silicon Valley, 67
simile, 45
simultaneity, 33, 37–39, 40, 41, 43, 46, 55, 60, 69, 96, 118, 146, 149, 151. *See also* time
Sinwar, Yahya, 96
slavery, 62
Slotkin, Richard, 63, 100–101
Smith, Adam, 70
social media, 3, 4, 25, 32, 61, 62, 76, 84, 111, 130, 141. *See also* electric and digital media; TikTok
Socrates, 43, 117, 128–29, 167n, 179n
somnambulism, 17, 34, 66
southern agrarianism, 13
Spadina Expressway, 21
speech, 30–31, 40–41, 79, 97, 110, 154; versus speechlessness, 80, 134
split-brain, 22. *See also* bicameral mind; left hemisphere (brain); right hemisphere (brain)

Sputnik, 85
spying, 75
Stackpole, Thomas, 80
Stalin, Joseph, 60
statue removal, 62–63
Stearn, Gerald Emanuel, 36, 126, 133, 146
Strauss, Leo, 53, 115, 134
superimposed existence, 94
Swift, Jonathan, 70
Swift, Taylor, 61
symbolism, 43

Talmud, 154
Tarquin, Priscus, 132
Teixeira, Jack, 91
telegraph, 70, 100
telephone, 66, 72, 92, 94
television: advertising and, 32; audile-tactile, 30, 111; capitalism and, 65; as a cool medium, 30–31, 33, 57–58; discarnate identity and, 92; effect on childhood, 25, 114; effect on senses, 32; government and, 75; natural law and, 157; wars and, 102
terrorism, 90, 96
Tesla, 73
tetrad, 22, 38, 130, 157, 183n. *See also* enhancement (law of media); laws of media; obsolescence (law of media); retrieval (law of media); reversal (law of media)
Thamus, King, 44
theology, 88, 122, 124
Theuth, 44
Thiel, Peter, 104
TikTok, 75–76, 84, 111, 130, 140
time: cyclical, 41, 69; linear, 69. *See also* simultaneity
Today Show, 57
Torah, the, 154
Toronto, 28
total field study, 41, 114
transgenderism, 86
transhumanism, 79–80, 93, 134, 137
Trent, Council of, 154
tribalism, 7, 97; global village and, 96–99, 102; postliterate, 7, 56, 59–61, 77, 85–86, 89, 94, 119; preliterate, 40–42, 68–69, 83, 85–86, 119, 129, 154; right hemisphere (brain), and, 118; values of, 98; violence of, 95–96, 99
trivium, 14, 16, 122
Trojan War, 143
Trudeau, Justin, 108
Trudeau, Pierre, 17, 21, 22, 66, 108, 153, 157

Trump, Donald, 61, 103, 138, 139
Turner, Frederick Jackson, 100
Twitter (X), 61, 72, 75–76, 89

United States: book-culture, 114; Congress, 59; conservatism of, 51, 56; Constitution, 53, 59; eighteenth-century origins, 50, 52; identity crisis, 50–51; individualism, 8, 50–52; Machiavellianism in, 136; melting pot, 53, 108; myth of the frontier, 100–103; nineteenth-century, 69; North and South, 67; origins in literacy, 50, 53; politics of, 49–63; postliterate age and, 57–63; presidency, 59, 60; print media, 51; rear-view mirror, 51; republicanism, 52; Revolution, 55; slavery in, 62; tribalism in, 61
University of Chicago, 115
University of Colorado Boulder, 98
University of Manitoba, 11–12
University of Toronto, 14, 20
University of Wisconsin, 13

Vatican II, 21, 148, 154, 155
Vico, Giambattista, 6, 25, 55, 112, 156, 176n, 177n
Vietnam War, 9, 20, 101–2, 104
virtue signaling, 72
visual sense, 28, 42, 43, 50, 66, 69, 115, 124, 132, 142, 149

visual space, 42, 74. *See also* acoustic space; auditory space
Voegelin, Eric, 87
Von Heyking, John, 130, 131, 134, 139

Wakin, Edward, 148
Waldorf School of the Peninsula, 67
warfare-welfare state, 105–6
Washington, George, 103
Watergate, 138
Watson, Wilfred, 21, 25, 45, 62, 73, 74, 75, 132, 135, 150
Welles, Orson, 60, 98
West, the, 41, 54, 62, 75, 99; Christianity and, 120–21; the East and, 75, 103–7
Wills, Garry, 52
witchcraft, 156
Wolfe, Tom, 18, 22, 102, 146
World War II, 105
writing, 30, 38, 41–46, 161; and the left hemisphere, 118. *See also* print media

Xenophon, 167n

Yeats, William Butler, 132, 148
York University, 127
YouTube, 76, 140, 141

Zoom, 72
Zuckerberg, Mark, 25, 140

www.ingramcontent.com/pod-product-compliance
Lightning Source LLC
Chambersburg PA
CBHW052214240426
43670CB00037B/602